KNIGHT

Yorkshireman, Storyteller, Spy

GREG CHRISTIE

Ouen Press

Published in Great Britain in 2018
by Ouen Press

Suite One, Ingles Manor, Castle Hill Avenue
Folkestone, Kent, UK
www.ouenpress.com

ISBN: 978-0-9956299-8-1

Printed by CreateSpace, SC, USA

A CIP catalogue record of this book is available from the British Library.

Cover Design: Ouen Press, Main illustration: Self-portrait by Eric Knight, c1935

For the girl in the spotty frock.

CONTENTS

ACKNOWLEDGMENT

Before we proceed, I need to say a few words about the genesis of this project and highlight the special support I have received to bring it to fruition.

In 1992, when I was very ill and confined to bed, my wife handed me a copy of Eric Knight's comic stories *The Flying Yorkshireman*. I enjoyed them immensely, but was puzzled by a note on the fly-leaf that credited Knight with the authorship of *Lassie, Come-Home*. Having watched the TV series as a boy, I knew *Lassie* as an American character who had, surely, to be created by an American author – and yet here was the dog's creator talking to me from the pages of this book in broad Yorkshire. This is where my twenty-year research project started – with a challenge.

In order to equip myself for the task I enrolled in a writing class in North Yorkshire run by Alan Wilkinson. I mentioned to him that I had no qualifications, and that my primary school headmistress had declared me 'backward'. Alan took a look at my writing, suggested I apply to study for a degree in English, and wrote a letter of recommendation. Four years later I was working towards an M.A.

Over the years I kept Alan up to date with what I had come to term 'the Lassie project'. He listened, read the work in progress, advised, and of course encouraged me. In 2004, he wrote a letter supporting my application for a Winston Churchill Travelling Fellowship, an award that would allow me to spend three months in the USA, first at Yale in the Knight archive, later in New York state, Pennsylvania and California, where I tracked down a wide range of source material and contacts.

During all this time I became used to picking up the phone to Alan to tell him of some new, exciting thread I had teased out of Knight's life, linking this scrawny lad from Hunslet to the heart of the pre-war literary, artistic and political world, partly in Britain, more widely in the USA. The circle of friends and associates I uncovered embraced the artists Peter Hurd and Andrew Wyeth, writers such as ee cummings and Ernest Hemingway, movie people like Walt Disney and Frank Capra, Spencer Tracy and Katherine Hepburn. These people became a part of our ever more animated conversations as a new species of contact crept in, people from the world of espionage and intelligence: Ian Fleming and Denis Wheatley, O.S.S. chief Bill Donovan; and then Lord Halifax, the aristocrat in whose woods young Eric had played as a boy, later British ambassador to Washington. Finally, there was Franklin Delano Roosevelt – and his wife Eleanor, who just happened to be Eric's tennis partner at the President's Hyde Park retreat. As the story took shape I published newspaper and magazine articles, and wrote and presented a BBC radio documentary on Knight.

By 2008 I had written *'The Knight Biography'*. And then tragedy struck. First, my wife of forty years was assailed by a cruel disease and died. Then my eyesight started to fail. Not surprisingly, I lost heart. By the time I finally went blind, in 2014, I was ready to concede defeat. Alan promised that some day, when he had a little more time, he would help me edit the biography and have a go at selling it. In 2016, he was finally able to fulfil his promise. Re-reading the manuscript after a break of eight years he said he was genuinely shocked at what he found: a story that literally set his pulse racing. However, at 147,000 words, there was no question that it was a tad long. Alan waded in, cut 60,000 words, suggested some changes, and submitted it to Paula Comley at Ouen Press. She had no hesitation in taking it on.

It has been a privilege and a pleasure to be associated with Alan, who has always supported me in my writing, and particularly this work, which he tells me is 'A heroic, epic, thrilling story, whose component parts have been teased out and woven into a narrative which will enthral, entertain and inform its readers while re-drawing the map of Anglo-American writing in the mid-twentieth century.' I truly cannot thank him enough. This work simply would not have made it to press without his belief in both me and the project.

Greg Christie

PROLOGUE:

HOW THE STORY ENDS

On the morning of January 15ᵗʰ 1943, a Douglas C-54 Skymaster took to the skies above Waller Field, Trinidad. Its intended destination was North Africa, but it would hug the coastline of South America for the first few hundred miles of its journey. Trans-atlantic flying was still in its infancy at the time, and the circuitous flight-path was normal. The fewer hours spent over water, the better – especially as the ocean was now infested with enemy submarines.

The plane was 25 miles east-north-east of Paramaribo, in Dutch Guiana, when it came down in a desolate patchwork of jungle and mud-flats. An eyewitness who lived nearby, on the west bank of the Mata Pica canal, reported, 'I saw a burning plane coming down slowly. It disappeared behind some bushes on the coast, then there was an explosion.'

All 35 people on board perished, making it the worst air disaster in America's brief aviation history. Only one name made the headlines – that of an English passenger. The *New York Post* had him on page 1:

35 DEAD IN AIRPLANE CRASH
IN SOUTH AMERICA
ERIC KNIGHT VICTIM

The front page of the Washington *Evening Standard* had a picture of him under its headline:

35 DIE IN AIR CRASH EN ROUTE TO AFRICA
Army Officers, Including Maj. Eric Knight Killed

1

In Knight's homeland in industrial West Yorkshire they weren't sure how important the news was, but they found a space for it all the same. On page 2 of the *Halifax Courier and Guardian* its readers would have noted,

Trouble on a Bus from Brighouse

And, beside a report of late-night rowdyism, warranting roughly the same number of column inches, they might have spotted the news from abroad:

Halifax Mill Boy Who Wrote Filmed Novel
ERIC KNIGHT KILLED IN PLANE CRASH
Author of 'This Above All'

Shortly after these reports were published, Knight's widow received a letter of condolence dated February 4th 1943. 'My heart,' it said, 'goes out to you in this great sorrow that you are meeting with such an excellent spirit.' It was signed by Franklin D. Roosevelt, President of the United States of America – who, two months later, would award Eric the Legion of Merit.

o0o

Ask about Eric Knight today and it's unlikely you will find anyone with whom the name resonates. If you're lucky, you may get a tentative, *'Didn't he write Lassie?'*. He certainly did. *Lassie Come-Home* was published in 1942 and went on to sell 100 million copies, as well as spawning eight movie versions and 675 episodes of a TV series. He also wrote several novels, and they didn't do badly either. In 1940, Knight's friend Ernest Hemingway read *The Happy Land* (1940) and declared that Knight had written 'the British Grapes of Wrath' and in 1941, *This Above All* outsold two blockbusters in *Random Harvest* and *Gone With The Wind*. The Sage of Baltimore, H.L. Mencken, known for his caustic dismissal of anything second-rate, called Knight 'our new Mark Twain'. A critic for the London *Times* rated him 'our best social chronicler since Dickens'.

On that evidence alone, Eric Knight surely deserves to be revisited and reassessed as an author of serious fiction. But search the biographies of his close friends Hemingway, the poet e e cummings, British novelist J B Priestley or double Pulitzer Prize-winner Paul Horgan, and you'll find little mention of him. The huge success of *Lassie* offers one clue to his absence from the literary histories of the 1930s and '40s. His serious work is simply, tragically, over-shadowed by his biggest hit. And, there was another area of his life, cloaked in secrecy, which offers an alternative reason for his relative obscurity and the obfuscation surrounding his demise.

Eric Knight was, above all, a storyteller. And because he grew up listening to tales the old way – by ear – he formed a conviction that a story was a living thing, always growing and re-forming over successive re-tellings. Once you wrote it down, he believed, you killed it. Until now, Eric Knight's story has never been told. What little record we have is a thing of shreds and patches, of speculation, half-truths and collective amnesia. The fact is, his life was a tangled business, and he was complicit in leaving false trails. In one of his last letters, responding to an enquiry about getting someone to record his life, he wrote, 'No-one could write it but me because no-one knows anything about me. Ninety percent of what's been written is half-true, which is worse than a total lie because it sounds more credible.' In piecing together his story here, my aim has been to nail it down rather than to kill it, to de-code the fictions that swarm around him, and to revive the reputation of a talented, but forgotten man. At the outset, I envisaged a conventional biography, but I believe we have transcended that. In the last few years of his life, Eric entered a sphere I had little knowledge of and was not entirely competent to deal with. And so I announce myself here – as author, yes, but also as a researcher who was thrilled by what he found, but perplexed too. One thing I have learned, however, is to discern the meaning behind some of Knight's deliberately misleading statements, the truths behind his fictions and code-talk.

While the first part of this drama shows us who Eric Knight was and what he accomplished, it leads us inexorably to a second act in which there are rather more questions than answers. While the story unfolds, as a conventional biography told in the traditional way, I shall wait in the wings. When we enter the world Knight later inhabited, a world of military operations, coded messages and false trails, I will go further and attempt the role of guide and interpreter.

GREG CHRISTIE

CHAPTER ONE

There was no ignoring the stench. That followed him everywhere. Nor could he rid himself of the sight of the horse, eviscerated, lifeless, dismembered. But he could close his eyes for a few seconds and imagine. As the scrawny lad dropped the hooves and bones of another slaughtered creature into the steaming vat and stirred them around with his long wooden paddle, he tried to imagine the great beast alive again and being ridden bareback across the American plains – perhaps by himself, perhaps by some half-naked Navajo – under magnificent skies and a brilliant sun.

Eric Oswald Knight was ten years old. He was working five nights a week and earning less than a five shillings for his efforts. He toiled with no hope or expectation of anything better – even though he had known far better times. His father, Frederic Harrison Knight, had been a wealthy Quaker diamond merchant and silversmith with smart business premises in Leeds, a holiday home on the Isle of Man, and the stylish country villa where Eric was born on April 10th 1897, the youngest of three boys. The house, built of finest Pennine stone, embodied the Yorkshire virtues of which its people are most proud: strength, understated elegance, and fortitude in a harsh and unforgiving world.

The century drawing to a close had seen an industrial revolution, which had made the rich wealthier than they could have dreamed possible. Cities had grown as a people from rural areas came to find work in the mills, factories and foundries, which had sprung up as symbols of the new age of steam power. Most of these migrants had left behind a harsh country life in the hope of prospering in the new industrial centres. But they were unused to mechanised industry, working indoors, the smoke-laden atmosphere and the cruel demands of mass production. They gathered in inadequate housing with inadequate sanitary facilities and soon succumbed to the diseases that proliferated in densely populated ghettos.

The Knights, however, were untouched by such matters. Their business had flourished from the moment Eric's grandfather, Joseph Harrison Knight, began trading as a toy dealer, hardware merchant and Birmingham and Sheffield silver-goods purveyor from premises at 3 Lowerhead Row, Leeds. He had been lucky. An apprenticed silversmith, he married the daughter of his employers, the Awmacks, who already ran two glass and china shops. By 1872, Joseph Knight had added a jewellery and watch-making business and moved to larger premises at number 4, then opened a shop at 47 Boar Lane – Leeds' most prestigious commercial street. He moved his family to the impressive Winscombe House in Hollin Lane, Headingley. It was while living here he noticed an opportunity to expand further, opening a hardware shop and wholesalers at New Briggate House in partnership with a Mr. Day, trading thereafter as Knight & Day.

Joseph's businesses were taken over in 1888 by his son, Joseph John. Trading as John Knight & Co, he moved into wholesale jewellery and opened a new shop in Albion Street, then, two years later, to even bigger premises at 23 Clarendon Place. By now, his brother Frederic was in the business as a hardware merchant. Already an independently wealthy man, he was about to benefit from his father's will. His inheritance and substantial income meant he could move into the imposing house in Menston in which Eric Oswald Knight and his two older brothers, Frederic and Edmund, were born.

The family was doing well, but tragedy was never far from the lives of late-Victorians, and it would strike the Knights when their fourth son, Noel, died at only a few weeks old. The Knights were supported in their loss by an unusually extended household comprising Mrs. Knight's younger and pregnant sister, Ellinor (Nell) Harrison, her infant daughters, Georgina and Freda, and her husband Frederic's teenage daughters from an earlier marriage, Margaret and Jane. The mother of the older girls, Mary Stewart-Muir, had married Frederic Knight in 1882 and died in childbirth in 1884. Her bereaved husband hired a succession of nurses and maids to care for the girls, before he re-married.

Marian Hilda Creasser knew about gracious living. She had been Governess to the children of the Russian Royal Family, who kept a fine house in Harrogate where they took the waters each summer. Marian's parents had for a time run a druggist's shop in the East Yorkshire market town of Great Driffield. By the age of nineteen, after two years with the royal household, she became Frederic Harrison Knight's wife and step-mother to his girls, who were not much younger than she was. The grand house in the quiet lane on the outskirts of the leafy village was the perfect place to raise a family. It was easily big enough to accommodate as many children as the Knights might produce at a time when families of ten or more were not uncommon. The house had huge rooms into which the sun shone through enormous windows, two drawing-rooms with a retractable partition and a sprung floor specially laid for dancing. It had an extravagant staircase, and, living longest in Eric's memory, expansive gardens with views across the rolling fields to the hills and dales beyond. This was privilege, luxury, opulence – but it was to be short-lived.

In 1900, forty-six-year old Frederic Harrison Knight left the family home. He told his wife he was going to fight in the Boer War. 'One morning,' Eric later recounted as one of his earliest memories, 'he wasn't there. I never saw or heard from him again.' Knight had sold his house secretly, leaving his wife penniless. His brothers saved Marian and her sons from the streets or the workhouse, but their generosity did not stretch to maintaining a large house, so the extended family moved to a terraced dwelling in Menston's Main Street. The property, known as West Bank, was never going to be big enough to house all the family, certainly not Nell and her children, nor indeed those from Frederic Knight's first marriage. Unless she could persuade someone to help, Aunt Ellinor was to be homeless.

Nell was two years younger than Marian and an overlooker with a Leeds furniture manufacturer. She had been lucky to have lived in such a fine house and to have had someone to care for her children while she earned a living. She held an unusually high position for a woman and one she would probably not have attained had not the Boer War robbed the factories and mills of so many of their men. Even more unusually, the business was owned by a woman, Mrs Miller, who had taken the reins of the business after losing her husband to consumption. Marian too had briefly been employed by her.

On hearing of Nell's plight, Mrs. Miller found her a job at her mill in London. It came with a tied house large enough to accommodate not only her family and the older girls but also Marian and the three boys. The two families' belongings were packed up and loaded onto a railway wagon at Menston station and the entourage journeyed south.

The 1901 census shows the women and their children living together under one roof at 206 White Post Lane, East Ham, then in the county of Essex, but without Frederic's daughters from his first marriage. The family appear to have survived on one meagre wage for a while, but by the summer of 1902, Menston parish records show the house in Main Street once again occupied by Marian Knight with her three boys enrolled at the village school. The East Ham sojourn had come to an end, but though Marian had a home, she desperately needed a job.

Despite these shifts of fortune, life in Menston, even without their father and the big old house they had known, was sweet for the Knight boys. Young Frederic, Edmund and Eric wandered the hills with their dogs, played in the streams, slept the afternoons away among the bluebells, shot at crows with their air rifle and, in Eric's case, observed the people of the mill village. Much of the land they played on was on the estate of Lord Halifax – but that was just a name to young Eric. Besides, his mind was already preoccupied by thoughts of another land, far away. At school, there was a large map on the wall. The headmaster would strike it with his cane, circle North America, and tell the class, 'From here come tobacco and savages whose heathen ways have been tamed by the great conquering pioneers from England who have been cruelly robbed of their prized jewel.' Eric didn't know why, but he felt more sympathy for the *'savages'* than he did for their conquerors.

Menston was green, despite its mills. It rested its Yorkshire stone dwellings at the foot of sheltering hills, which represented to young Eric a playground paradise that would live in his memory and sustain him in later life. The boy listened, too, with a finely tuned ear, to the local dialect – using it in the streets and in the company of his brothers but never within earshot of his mother.

Eric Knight was at peace in these idyllic surroundings, but the tranquility was about to be shattered and his family wrenched apart as his mother faced a heartbreaking dilemma. Her former employers, planning to return to their homeland after the restructuring of the Russian constitution, told her she could take up her former post and return to St Petersburg with them. The children, however, would have to be left behind.

Marian chose to leave. Fred and Ed, as they were known within the family, were to return to East Ham, where they at least would be among familiar faces. For Eric, however, there was no room in London. He had already lost his father and a baby brother, and was now to be separated from his mother, his home in the country and his older brothers.

He was eight years old. He stood on a bitingly cold rain-soaked platform at Leeds railway station. He clutched the air-rifle the boys had decided he should keep and waved bravely to his brothers as their train laboured away. It was the second time in a week he had lived through this nightmare, for his mother had departed in just the same way only five days earlier. He held tight to the hand that would raise him as lovingly as any mother's, the hand that would tuck him into a warmed bed on cold winter evenings and lead him on walks through the bluebell woods on Lord Halifax's estate. The hand belonged to Eric Knight's Aunt Kit.

Kit's husband, Richard Henry Hallas, stood beside her on the station platform, his huge labourer's arm around the boy's shoulders, steadying him as they would in the years to come against life's challenges. Eric's brothers were gone from sight, but still he waved, and still he sobbed, and still he did not understand why those he loved had left him.

Marian had exchanged potential poverty and the company of her own three boys for the wealth of a Royal palace and the charge of its children, but the family into which Eric was about to be welcomed would imbue in him a spirit he would later define as 'Vital, typical of Yorkshire people, good, kind, honest, hard working and willing to make the best of a bad job because that's what Yorkshire folk do.' He understandably felt desperate on the departure of his mother and brothers, but from this apparently irredeemable disaster came a light that would illuminate the remotest corners of his already searching mind, and a loving warmth he would never forget.

o0o

Aunt Kit and Uncle Richard lived in a small, gloomy back-to-back terraced house in Spread Eagle Yard, just off the Dewsbury Road in Hunslet. They had married in 1903 when she was a twenty-two-year-old mill worker. Richard, who had survived the Boer War, was a carter with what Eric called a 'sudden and furious temper', but not one that he exercised upon his new charge. 'To me he was the kindest and most loving man who ever entered my life,' Eric would say later.

Aunt Kit always wore black – mourning perhaps for Frederic James, the seven-month-old son she had lost in the summer of 1901. She and Richard never had another child. There, on that railway station platform, her lace hem grew blacker as it soaked up the cold Yorkshire rain that clung to Richard's heavy tweeds and dripped from the rim of his brown derby hat. His great hand clutched the boy's as they left the station to walk the streets to their home. 'We'll look after you, lad, worry not,' Richard said. 'It'll not be long afore ya see ya Mam an' Auntie Nell and them brothers o' yours agin. And by gum, what a grand time we'll 'ave on it, you an' me. Come on, lad, I'll carry ya all t'way 'ome. Ay, and at a trot!'

With these words the great man lifted his charge into strong arms as together, man, wife, and boy, they raced home across the rain-slicked cobbles beneath a smoke-laden sky.

Richard Hallas was as good as his word. Eric knew he would be, for already he recognised his uncle as the archetypal Yorkshireman, a man whose word was good.

The house in Spread Eagle Yard boasted no plumbing – save a cold water tap in the scullery – but it provided that one priceless commodity that Eric Knight realised later had been missing from his life, love. His new home was a back-to-back, but at least it didn't have the usual earth closet at the end of the street. The Spread Eagle Yard lavatories stood on one side of the passageway, or *ginnel*, the houses on the other. The ginnel was a narrow thoroughfare down which all traffic passed; it was also the playground, and the place to hang out washing.

A flight of five stone steps – all meticulously scrubbed on a Saturday morning – led from the ginnel to the front door. A second, low door beneath the steps allowed access to the coal cellar. The ginnel was a grey place even on the sunniest days, and those were rare, for the smoke from thousands of chimneys almost always covered the sky. Inside the house the immaculately blacked grate in the tiny sitting-room-cum-kitchen flickered its light across a bare floor. Beside the fire was an oven, from which Aunt Kit pulled a succession of wholesome pies and stews.

Here young Eric would sit, watching her prepare the evening meal, swishing into the scullery with a pan for draining, its handle swathed in a muslin cloth, the steam clinging to her hair. He would watch her quick hands kneading bread dough and wonder at the thousand tasks they performed. She had made the dress she wore and the apron that protected it against flour as she baked. Her hair was washed every Sunday morning in cold water from the tap, it was dried with a towel before a fire, which burned year-round, and piled into a neat arrangement of plaits which shone in the candlelight.

As he watched the Sunday ritual, Eric would mount great battles on the polished floorboards between opposing armies of lead soldiers or, more often, capture his aunt's features in detailed portraits, using the only pencil the family owned, the one that Richard wore behind his ear. Eric, it seemed, was a natural artist.

The evening meal over, pots and pans washed and put away, the three would sit, talking endlessly on any subject to hand. Richard would tell Eric of his war service, the 'bloody pointlessness of it all' and the bravery of men who stared certain death in the face. He would make up stories, too, from his rich imagination. And it was here, for the first time, that Eric Knight gave voice to his own imaginings. He countered with stories of his own, of giants roaming the Yorkshire Dales, magic spells that turned people into animals, dogs and horses who took on human form to perform great deeds, poverty-stricken mill workers who awoke to find great riches had miraculously appeared in sacks at the foot of their beds, and men who could soar like birds. Even at this stage he was bringing into his stories a character called Sam Small. Eric would later claim that Sam had always existed. Whether he was a local folk-hero, or the creation of his Aunt Kit, has never been established, but it is a matter of record that when young Eric misbehaved she would warn him, 'I'll be tellin' Sam Small about you.'

Hallas applauded the stories and encouraged his nephew to make imaginative leaps, always asking him, 'Then what, lad, then what, what 'appens next, what'll ya do then, lad, what?' He compelled the boy to think through his burgeoning plots until finally the story reached a conclusion, or was 'almost nearly perfect', as Eric would later put it.

'Finished', however, was not a word Hallas ever used in reference to any tale. 'They're never done,' he said, 'not while there's a man alive to add a bit o' their own.' So it was here in this kitchen that real life became entangled with fantasy and Eric first realised that no story should ever, or could ever, be 'finished' and that a good storyteller always added and subtracted detail to suit the audience and continue to build it. He also learned from his Uncle that, once written down, the story was 'dead', leaving no opportunity for it to be expanded or improved upon. But that presented him with a paradox. 'If I don't write it down,' he said, 'and I die, it'll be gone forever.' So he reached a compromise and called them 'telling stories'. When told in the traditional way, by word of mouth, they varied, and since all audiences react differently to various elements of the story, the written down version was constantly altered, their inventor never knowing which was best.

So consumed was Eric by his own imagination and the need to record his thoughts, and so encouraged by his uncle, that he began to think of his stories as entities with minds and souls and lives of their own, stories that had planted themselves in his head because, as Richard had said, 'They've found a spot they can grow, just like seeds do, and you must water 'em, lad, so they blossom.'

CHAPTER TWO

The 1905 Factories Act had outlawed child labour altogether, over-riding the 1888 Act which had restricted the hours of ten to twelve-year olds to 'not more than forty-six per week'. However, the law had limited influence in the back-streets of Leeds. Factory inspectors did not work nights, so any child who looked as if he or she might be thirteen, the new legal working age, had no trouble finding a job – so long as they worked after dark.

Most of the child workers did not attend school at all. But Eric did, arriving home from his night-shift in time to eat a breakfast of bread and dripping before making his way to his lessons. 'Life was often hard,' he would say later when recalling his boyhood, and life in the Hallas household became that much harder when Richard fell ill with tuberculosis and was confined to bed. The burden of responsibility fell on the shoulders of a ten-year-old boy who thought himself luckier than most: he was after all receiving an education.

Eric had won a place at the Bewerley Street School for Boys, only a short walk from Spread Eagle Yard. 'The Bewerley' was Leeds' first Board School, being run by a Board of Governors appointed to ensure that children from even the poorest families might attend for no fee – provided they could pass a rigorous exam.

School for Eric Knight was easy. The joy of learning never left him. He remembered best the geography lessons. He had heard a little about America from his old headmaster at Menston but found his new teachers more informative. 'They made the place sound exciting, different, and romantic,' he said. But the teachers Eric loved best were his uncles. He would sit enthralled for hours as they talked, and one, Harry Percival Creasser, would relate the family history as if it were as vital a lesson as any taught at school. Percy was brother to Eric's mother and his Aunts Nell and Kit, all of whom the boy knew – and also to three others, around whom

13

there appeared to be some mystery.

Aunt Ada, the eldest of the Creasser family, had disappeared in 1883 when she was sixteen, having been a domestic servant to the Butterworth family of Wortley in South Yorkshire from the age of fourteen. She would later reappear in Hartlepool as the wife of a James Wilson, but the boy's Aunts Marion and Harriet were the subject of much debate, mainly because their whereabouts were, by the early 1900s, not known.

That one child should be named Marian and another Marion was not that unusual. Children of the same family were often given similar or favourite names at a time when not all were expected to survive into adulthood. Marion's arrival in 1881, however, had coincided with the departure of six-year-old Marian to Portsea, Hampshire, to stay with her Grandmother, Mary Dobing.

Harry Percival Creasser – Uncle Percy – and Aunt Emily lived nearby and spent much time with their in-laws. Eric looked forward to their visits with great anticipation, for Uncle Percy – a man with an imagination equal to that of Richard Hallas – had served in the Boer War. And it was not only family history that echoed across the kitchen table, but great stories of adventure and daring, all of which worked their magic in Eric's mind. He would imagine taking some heroic part in a war where he would fight alongside his brothers just as his uncles had done, and just like them he would relive their great adventure for the benefit of wives and children when the fighting was over.

The stories held the boy spellbound, but Uncle Percy possessed another great attraction for young Eric Knight, for he had lived the greatest adventure of all – he had been to America. Percy Creasser had sailed for the United States in 1886, aged fifteen. He had worked as a stevedore, a builder's labourer and, most romantically in Eric's mind, as a cowhand. The outdoor life had lured him as far west as California and as far north as Canada, where he had been a lumberjack. All his stories lived in Eric's imagination like moving pictures. He would run them over and over again, placing himself at their centre. But the stories that overtook the boy and dragged him along in their wake, almost consuming him completely, were those about the Navajo Indians. Percy had lived with the Navajo for many months; he told his nephew he had traded goods like the trappers of old, made bows and arrows and slept in a tepee. 'What are they like, Uncle Percy,' the boy pleaded, knowing his enquiry would be met with a response that never failed to thrill his very being.

'They're a lot like us Yorkshire lads, Eric, they're grand folks, kind and 'onest and 'ard workin' and they mek ya welcome, once they know you mean 'em no 'arm an' that you've come 'alf way round t'world to be wi' 'em.'

Eric heard how Percy had learned to ride bareback, make a fire without matches, skin a deer, kill a snake, and, most vitally, obey the laws of nature.

'T'sun tells 'em when to reap and when to sow,' Percy related. 'T'moon sez when to slaughter a beast and every new bairn gets 'eld up for 'im to 'ave a look at… An' every man-jack of 'em lives in 'armony wi' mother earth. They're a proud lot,' Percy would assert, 'not always at peace wi' their neighbours, t'neighbours fault, not theirs, but they'll not give in, not a inch, they 'ave their land and they believe it was given to 'em by their gods and it's theirs for all time. They 'ave their beliefs an' there's no budgin' 'em.'

If the similarities between these far-distant people and those of his native Yorkshire had not been pointed out to young Eric Knight, it would not have mattered; he made the association without prompting. He promised himself right there, as a ten-year-old with no prospect of ever travelling further afield than Halifax, that he would one day visit those Native peoples.

Uncle Percy's joyful visits inspired Eric's active mind and sustained him, as he later recalled, through long hours of hard labour, which began when he was ten. Eric was tall for his age; he needed to earn a living and he knew which factories and mills took on under-age lads. One such was Lax & Shaw's bottle-works, half a mile away on Belinda Street. Eric started work there at the age of ten. The work was hard, conditions were filthy and hot, but the few shillings he earned helped keep the family afloat.

As the youngest employee, Eric was charged with sneaking out to buy bottles of beer and Cornish pasties for the men in the factory. The doors were kept locked in working hours, so a couple of planks that formed part of the warehouse wall were levered apart to allow a slim lad to squeeze his way in and out without detection. It was worth the risk: the 'pie-boy' earned valuable farthings for his trouble.

After a year at Lax's, Eric found a similar position at the Crown Bottle-Works on Jack Lane, only a few yards from his home and school. The work and the pay was the same, and as he laboured in the stacking shed he dreamed his dreams and plotted his stories, always calling upon his older workmates for characters, many of whom would appear in the Sam Small tales which were constantly 'making themselves up' in his head. On his arrival home he would try out his stories on his bed-ridden uncle who, through the pain of violent coughing fits, would chuckle at his nephew's invention.

Eric could never say for whom he next worked, for the stinking yard at the rear of the bottle-works had no name, save that by which it was known by those who worked in and lived around it – 't'knacker's'. He was given a man-size leather apron, which he had to hold up with string to stop it trailing on a floor sticky with the 'purple' blood of butchered animals. Fellmongers would lead in old horses, none of whom had ever enjoyed the sun on their bare backs or the sweet meadow beneath their hooves. Most were lame or had colic; many had been mercilessly beaten. Death for these creatures was release, and Eric often worked with tears in his eyes.

One fine mare touched him so deeply she would appear over thirty years later as the heroine of an adventure in which the horse proved itself to be cleverer than its owners. *The Dumbfool Josephine*, a short story which appeared in *Argosy Weekly* in May 1939, told of how a cavalry officer's horse, 'in its stupidity', refused to leave its stable on the day of a great battle. The fighting was fierce, every man and horse died, except the 'stupid' Josephine, who remained, unharmed, safe in her shelter until being released and retired to pasture. The model for Josephine was a fine, almost-white cart-horse, whose owner took her for slaughter having, as always, meticulously groomed her. He fed her one last apple as she kissed her owner in grateful thanks. The man, Eric recalled, was huge, with the hands of a giant, a great square head and massive shoulders rounded from a lifetime of coal-carrying. 'He looked as if he could have knocked down a row of houses with one punch,' Eric said, 'but he cried like a child as he bade farewell to his faithful servant of eighteen years'.

The mare stood perfectly still in ignorance of her fate as the great yard gates closed behind her owner. The man had refused the usual payment for the animal, saying, 'Nay, I cannot tek owt for slaughtering me dearest companion. May God 'ave mercy on 'er. Ay, an' on me for this wicked deed.'

The slaughterman lifted the heavy metal spike to the huge mare's forehead and nodded to his assistant to strike it home. The animal fell heavily, shaking the cobbled yard and sending a lad in an oversized leather apron into uncontrollable sobs. The foreman put a hand on his shoulder, 'It's t'way o' things, Eric, lad, we all 'ave to go. Would that we could all go so quick an' painless an' wi' no time to dwell on t'past.' Eric Knight could not know what name the fine mare had carried through life, but when she reappeared as 'Josephine' she would, he said, 'live forever'.

oOo

So the seeds of stories found a place to grow, and were watered with an imagination far beyond the years of the boy who carried them home like precious jewels to share with those he loved.

Summers were more tolerable for the lad. Separated from his brothers, he had for company the children of his Uncle Lewis Edwin Knight, a partner in the jewellery business. The youngest, Eric Glencoe Knight, was only two years younger. In summer there was no school and Eric worked in the early mornings, either stirring the boiling bone and hoof vats or, if he were lucky, helping load bottles onto railway wagons. Having earned his few pennies he would hop aboard for a free ride, something his Uncle

Percy had done in America. His favourite stop was Malton in North Yorkshire. Malton is only fifteen miles from Great Driffield where he had relatives, but Eric noticed that the accents were quite different there from those of his Aunts and Uncles, an indication of how keenly he had tuned his ear, for the two are indistinguishable to most. Malton, rich with natural springs, had been a brewery town for almost three centuries when Eric visited it for the first time. The sparkling waters were also perfect for the manufacture of lemonade and the town had four such factories, all using bottles produced at Lax's.

Days out spent entirely in pleasure were rare and precious things in those times of huge industrial demand, poor wages, and inadequate living conditions. The typical working week comprised seventy hours of back-breaking labour in an environment that seemed to have been designed specifically to shorten the lives of employees. Seaside holidays were rare, though Eric later talked of having once visited Bridlington and nearby Flamborough Head, with its high white cliffs and breathtaking views. Mainly, however, the folk of the towns and cities took their pleasure where they could find it. A journal entry from young Eric's diary notes:

'On the 9th day of April, 1908, the day before I was eleven years old, I dreamed about Indians. It was a beautiful dream. I was lying in Middleton Wood, a few miles off Dewsbury Road, across Hunslet Moor from Leeds, Yorkshire, England. The reason I was there was because I was crazy over Indians. I used to practise woodcraft on the gamekeeper. This consisted of letting the gamekeeper see me go into the woods and then lying snugly in the deep bracken and the long-stemmed bluebells while he crashed around, looking for me. I would think that most any Indian tribe would be glad to have me for a member.

I lay there, with the wild hyacinth scent hanging heavily in my nostrils and the throstles singing loud as locomotives, and my mind saying words like wigwam and moccasin and wampum and squaw so loudly the birds lost the competition. I knew there was nothing I wanted more in the world than to go to that Wild West and be among those Indians—and some day I'd do it.

Later that afternoon I picked hundreds of hyacinths and bluebells because my Aunt liked flowers, and I went home in the dusk beside the beck that was stinking and muddy from the Middleton Pit, and then across the moor. Only it was a trackless prairie and not a moor. And as my feet came down I sang, both inside and outside me, a song…

> *Way down in the sandhills of New Mexico…*
> *Me and my Nava—Nava—my Navajo.*
> *I have a love for you that will never go…*
> *Oh Lord —the sandhills of New Mexico!'*

By now, Aunt Kit had become the mother he had almost forgotten, the friend who took the place of his absent brothers on treks across the moors, the person he loved most in the world, and the one who would soon need a strong shoulder to cry on.

Tuberculosis – or consumption – killed almost ten thousand Leeds citizens between 1880 and 1920, and Richard Hallas was about to become one of that number. He was buried in the same tweed suit he'd worn all those years before on Leeds railway station, his prized brown derby hat resting on his chest. As Richard's coffin was lowered into the sodden earth in Leeds' Beckett Street cemetery, Eric squeezed his Aunt's hand. Tears rolled down beneath her modest black veil. Passing carters halted their horses as a mark of respect to their late colleague. 'There was silence,' Eric remembered, 'a rare thing in Leeds, day or night.'

Raindrops collected on the brass plaque bearing the name, Richard Henry Hallas, blurring it, washing away the life of a man who had been the father Eric had not known. 'Tha'll be t'man o' 't'house soon, Eric, lad,' Richard had said only days earlier through desperate gasps of breath. 'You must look after yer Aunt Kit just as she's cared for thee. She'll need thee now, lad, you'll not let me down.' Clutching the boy's hand with the last of his strength he added, 'An' don't forget to mek her laugh, lad, we've 'ad many a laugh, us three. I don't know what's in that 'ead o' yours but by gum, it's a varry wonderful thing.'

Eric's future was now clear. He would love and support his Aunt Kit, and make her laugh, if he could, but for the rest of his days he would be the man of the house at 48, Spread Eagle Yard, Hunslet. For the next six months he would work 'half timing' – from six o'clock in the morning until two in the afternoon, beside his Aunt Kit, as a bobbin setter at the mill. Five hundred looms clattered out their deafening beat and men, women, girls and boys learned to lip-read in order to carry on conversation against the unrelenting noise. After work, Eric attended school, where silence reigned. All thoughts of the Navajo, he determined, would be swept from his mind forever – 'forever,' he repeated, knowing he had set himself an impossible ambition.

CHAPTER THREE

Eric Knight felt his life had come to a sudden halt when Richard Hallas died, though death was common enough in that neighbourhood. 'Barely a day passed,' he would recall in his thirties, 'when the iron-rimmed wheels of the funeral bier were not heard in the cobbled streets. I hear them still sometimes in the cold of the early dawn, just as I heard them the day they rolled no further but stopped outside my door in the ginnel.'

Richard Hallas's coffin had lain on the kitchen table that doubled as baking board and ironing platform and at which joyous meals had been taken in laughter, not mourning. The pall-bearers had struggled with their heavy burden while Aunt Kit fussed about making sure the coffin was properly handled. At the bottom of the five stone steps leading to her door, she had reached out a hand one last time to her beloved husband as he was borne away. The bier was pulled by four black-coated men in top hats with long black ribbons curling in the wind. It was followed by a procession of weeping women and stout men. But his Uncle Richard had told Eric he was the man of the house now, so he swallowed his tears.

After the funeral, a traditional ham tea was provided at Spread Eagle Yard. Women in heavy mourning and men in uncomfortable suits and newly-shone boots said warming things about Richard. All wished Aunt Kit their deepest sympathies and sincere condolences, words and sentences that, Eric noted, sat awkwardly with the broad Yorkshire dialect.

That night Eric and his Aunt Kit spent the night sobbing out their grief while curled up together in a rocking chair in the kitchen fire's glow. Then there was the day's work to be done, as normal. Afterwards, Eric arrived home full of dread. But as he opened the door he was greeted by a scene which signified to him comfort and love: 'The kitchen was so warm it made my cheeks shine and the lamp was lit and the place smelled of hot tea and bottom loaf set out to cool.'

As time passed, life without Richard became normal, even if the dead man's second-best boots continued to rest, as they always had, by the fire grate, polished and ready for their next outing. They would stay there four years – long enough for a boy almost, but not quite, to grow into them.

When Eric made his promise to his dying Uncle it had been a hard one; he had after all already promised himself he would one day go and live with the Navajo. He may have been the man of the house but the boy within him was not ready to consign his future to the mill, regardless of the love he felt for his Aunt. His dreams, however, were about to come true by dint of a happy and totally unforeseen circumstance.

Eric's mother had gone to St. Petersburg three years earlier. She was now, miraculously, in the very place her youngest son most desperately wanted to be, America. With the growing unrest that followed the Russian army's defeat by the Japanese in the 1904-5 war, Princess Xenia was taking refuge in her summer home on Long Island, and Marian had gone with her. There she soon met Sonia Francis, the daughter of a wealthy financier, and was offered the post of Governess at her home in Philadelphia. Unsure that the Princess would remain permanently in the US, she accepted. Within months she had met and married a German immigrant, Simon Kahn, head waiter in a classy restaurant. She sent for her eldest son Frederic. Edmund arrived soon after. It took some time for this news to reach Eric, and on hearing it he assumed that he would be the next to be summoned – but all he received was an invitation to join the family 'provided I could pay for my own ticket'.

If the invitation was designed to deter the lad, it wouldn't work; his mother could not have known that he was already obsessed with America or that his plans to go there had been formulated years before. It seems unlikely that the new Mrs. Kahn intended any offence. Mouths had to be fed and money was short. Fred, at the age of thirteen, would soon be able to earn a living and it would have been nothing short of cruel to separate him from the younger brother he had grown up with, while Eric hadn't seen his siblings since they left Leeds for East Ham. Far from being offended, Eric simply promised himself he would go, but only with Aunt Kit's blessing. He had, after all, promised Uncle Richard he'd make her laugh if he could, and if he could not, he was not about to make her cry.

By 1910, Eric Knight the boy was becoming Eric Knight the man, though still not big enough for his late uncle's boots. His schooling would come to end on April 10th, and once his Labour Certificate was signed he would be a man in the eyes of the law, the document entitling him to 'Total exemption after thirteen years of age'. In other words, he would be legally entitled to work full-time. It was a momentous occasion in the boy's life and one that, in this case, coincided with an offer of work from his mother's youngest brother, twenty-two-year-old Ewart Vernon Creasser –

and with Aunt Kit's decision to remarry.

Creasser and his brother Edwin worked at JB Farrar's worsted mill, in Halifax, where there was a job for Eric as a doffer and setter, 'if he wanted it'; and because he had already served his 'apprenticeship' in the Leeds mill with his Aunt he would be in charge of six bobbin setters. This arrangement had been contrived by the Creasser brothers who reasoned that their sister would want to start newly-married life with her husband alone.

The Creasser family lived in Skircoat Green, a village less than a mile from the town centre, and were planning to move to a larger house where they would take in theatrical lodgers. So 30 Wellington Street South became home to Edwin, his Irish wife Emily, Vernon and his wife Sarah, and Eric – plus an ever-changing gaggle of 'theatricals', all of whom would have a remarkable influence on the youngest resident of their digs.

Eric said farewell to his Aunt Kit and his new Uncle, Harry Sanderson, in June 1910. He tried on his late Uncle's boots, decided that they might just fit him before long, and packed them up. Then he journeyed the few miles to Halifax. He arrived on a brilliantly sunny day, dust rising from the streets, ladies in summer outfits carrying parasols, and the calm of a Saturday afternoon on the mills. He made himself at home, enjoyed a specially prepared meal of home-grown salad and a freshly boiled ham, and explored the area for possibilities. In characteristic form, he decided, though he was not obliged so to do, to enrol in a nearby school, despite having been legally released from education. He attended first Halifax Parish Church Day School and later St. Augustine's, all this while working nights as he had done in Leeds.

After a few weeks, however, he approached the Halifax Corporation garage to ask about apprenticeships. He was accepted, but lasted only two weeks. 'It all came to an end,' he said, 'when they went on strike. I made a very good striker, I never went back.' He returned to the mill and persuaded the manager to take him on again. The work was hard and occasionally dangerous among the flailing looms, but no worse than the bottle factory and a great deal more pleasant than the knacker's yard. It suited him fine. He could pay his way and save for that one-way ticket to the land of his dreams, depositing what he could afford, week by week, in the Yorkshire Penny Bank.

'I made up my mind that when I was grown and strong and powerful, the first thing I would do would be go and live with the Indians,' Eric wrote, but the fascination for now was with his Aunts' theatrical lodgers and the lessons of life:

'I learned the change in dialect here, put down any lingering pretensions of a more polished life learned in childhood and worked full time and took charge of a bunch of lads in their first long trousers. The days were long and mainly I was bored. I remember grubbing for coal during strikes, being hungry, the shame of poverty. The sights and smells and accents and the actions of the people are stronger to me than things that happened yesterday …and there were always the lodgers…'

The 'theatricals' would enthral the lad with their stories of lives lived on and off the stage. 'They were,' Eric said, 'dual beings, people with two lives, equally convincing in both'. The actors would occasionally sneak him in by the stage-door of the Victoria Hall where he stood in the wings as people who had been 'ordinary' only ten minutes earlier became, in his words, 'godlike, like dreams come true' as they played out their parts.

Life in the Creasser household, with its regular turnaround of exotic and eccentric guests with stories of the hundreds of plays in which they had appeared and the characters they had known and played, filled Eric with a love of the theatre. He still wanted to live with the Navajo, or be an artist, but if that did not work out, he said, he would 'be an actor, or better still, write plays for actors to perform'. The lodgers always had lines to learn so there were plenty of play scripts lying around to be examined by the enquiring eye – and plenty of hands to applaud the stories he continued to tell.

For the first time, Eric Knight harboured the ambition to write. Perhaps his 'telling stories' might become 'acted stories' with real people playing the parts of those characters he had invented or who had made themselves up. His fictional characters could take human form. 'They could live,' he said. 'They will live!'

Like millions of other boys, Eric had dreams born of hardship – the goal being escape to a better life. Though he was very well aware that there were many for whom life was a great deal worse that it was for him. He might have contented himself with his lot and remained a mill-hand all his life, and in many respects the Sam Small stories he would later commit to paper represent the eternal struggle between contentment and aspiration. He was aware however, even at fourteen years of age, that dreams were often no more than a distraction from life's hardships and that pinning your hopes on them could lead to disappointment. So while his friends talked of their dreams, he felt they would do nothing to make them come true while he, encouraged by the adventurous spirit of the Creasser household, would. The thought would appear years later in a story about the Navajo, written at a moment in his adult life when he was in a position to make almost any dream come true: 'What do we chase dreams for? How long does it take us to learn that a dream is beautiful not because we chase it, but because we never catch up with it? If you catch up with it by one chance in a million it isn't a dream any more.'

CHAPTER FOUR

The newspapers were full of stories of the 'unsinkable' *Titanic* making her maiden voyage. There was a feeling in the air of great optimism for the future and there was much rejoicing at the completion of the world's greatest feat of marine engineering. But in Halifax, Eric Knight was reliving the heartbreak of his mother's and brothers' departure, only this time it was he who was leaving behind tearful relatives. 'It rained,' he wrote, 'like it always does when people leave. Grey sky, grey rain, grey houses and factories. I was glad. I felt grey.'

The lives of those whom Eric left behind would go on in the way they always had, albeit without the unending chatter and constant invention of a lad with a head full of stories. Eric's life, though, would never be the same again. He had worked hard and saved his shillings in the Yorkshire Penny Bank. He had bought his ticket and was going to America.

Eric sailed into Philadelphia on April 12th 1912, two days after his fifteenth birthday, and was greeted with the news that the *Titanic* had been lost in the early hours of the morning. As news of the tragedy spread, a feeling of sadness and disbelief tempered his impressions of his new surroundings. Here was America, and it seemed it would be everything he had expected it to be. The sky was a shade of blue he had never seen before; the buildings were unlike anything in smoke-blackened Leeds or Halifax with their great flat roofs and cream-coloured bricks. He could see from the deck of the ship that the roads and sidewalks were wide and sunlit. The dockhands wore a fabric he discovered was called denim, there were more cars in one place than he believed existed, and the shouts rising from the quayside echoed around his head in a hundred tongues.

'The very air smelled new,' he said. He knew America would be different from everything he had known – but the speed at which the differences hit him almost confused his senses. 'Even the birds sing a different tune,' he remarked to a fellow passenger. He had left the industrial north of England behind; he had left the bottle factory and the glue-works and the mills – and everybody he loved. But this was America, and Eric knew that everything was going to work out just fine. 'Sure,' he said, 'the Titanic had sunk, but there would be few if any fatalities; she was after all the best-equipped ocean liner on earth. Thank goodness I was sailing to Philadelphia rather than New York, otherwise I'd have got my feet wet.'

These earliest observations of life in America would provide the backdrop for his first book, *Invitation to Life*, still twenty-two years away, but the experiences of his very first day there would also appear in his story about the Navajo, a work which would not be written until 1942. Eric's account of his arrival in America describes a formality more usually employed in the greeting of strangers. He felt that perhaps he, with his Yorkshire accent and heavy tweeds, did not live up to his mother's expectations, or that she somehow felt more estranged from him than her other sons. Whatever the case, we may be sure that the emotions he felt on that momentous day were accurately recounted in his later work. His mother's demeanour was unsettled, her attitude cold. As to his disembarkation, he later wrote: 'There, just off the boat, in the Customs Service, I met the most discerning man I have ever known. He wore peg top trousers and yellow shoes. And when, in my luggage, he saw my air rifle, he smiled. *'Sonny,'* he said, *'I guess you've come to shoot Indians.'*

Eric protested he had not come to shoot Indians, quite the opposite, but the man just laughed and stamped the boy's papers. *'They don't do that no more,'* he said. *'If they did, I wouldn't be here, would I?'* Eric had met his first American, and his first Indian. He would meet many more of both and would always know with which he felt more comfortable.

The name on the ticket he had purchased to the USA read 'Eric Oswald Knight', but the middle name he gave upon arrival was Mowbray. 'Why not start a new life with a new name?' he told his mother. But Mowbray was not plucked from the air, it came from the deep sense of tradition that permeated Eric Knight's very soul, and he wanted to carry it into his new future.

His paternal great-grandmother, Sarah Johns, had been born in Melton Mowbray, Leicestershire, in 1824, while his maternal grandfather had been Wilson Mowbray Dobing, born in County Durham on June 7th 1812. Wilson took his middle name from his mother, Margaret, and her father, Anthony Mowbray, born in Stockton in 1750. Eric was aware from Percy's teachings that the same name existed in both families and changed his middle name in an effort to tie himself to both. More importantly, he chose the name in honour of the little brother he had lost and who had been christened Noel Mowbray. Eric's name change, however, was never a permanent feature, his 1932 passport still showing his middle name as

'Oswald' while inside the document is printed: 'Also known as Eric Mowbray Knight'.

After the encounter with the Native official, Eric assumed his mother would take him straight home to be reunited him with his brothers. She didn't. 'First,' he said, 'I had to look like an American.' He was taken by his mother and her new husband for an American haircut, and from there to a store to buy some American clothes. As a young man who had grown up wearing hand-me-downs, having his hair cut by his Aunt, and now, finally, wearing his late uncle's boots, he might have seen a trip to a huge department store to buy a brand new outfit as something of an adventure. But he had made a great effort to look smart, only to find it was not good enough. He was proud of his full head of auburn hair, but now it seemed it had to be cropped close.

He thought his mother would be proud of how tall he had grown and how much like a man he had become and how he'd saved his money for the ticket and how much he already knew about his new home – but if she was, she never showed it. 'I had a feeling,' he said 'that I was supposed to forget about being a Yorkshireman and become an American. I couldn't.'

His step-father too was cold, distant, stiff and superior. His formal handshake felt perfunctory and did nothing to reassure the boy in the way Richard Hallas' strong arms had on the day he started his new life in Leeds. When he finally arrived at his mother's house, the atmosphere was flat, and there was a surprise for which nothing had prepared him. Eric was delighted to meet his two-year-old half-brother Adolph, but shocked to discover that the house was also home to Simon Kahn's sons, Jacob and Gustav, from his first marriage. 'There was an unease,' he said. 'I put it down to the distraction that was young Adolph and the Kahn boys, Mother being preoccupied with a small child and new stepsons. It just wasn't what I'd hoped for. Fred and Ed didn't feel like my brothers any more.'

Adolph had arrived in 1910; he would grow to be more like a brother to Eric than Fred and Ed now were, and would change his first name to Ed in the late thirties when bearing the name *Adolph* became a source of embarrassment – and when anti-German feeling began to affect his job prospects he would become Ed Knight.

Eric realised immediately on his arrival that America was full of people like him, immigrants. After only a few weeks he could spot the Germans and the Poles and the Russians, none of whom appeared willing to part with their identity. All of them, he noted, felt about their homeland as he did about his. Even so, within a few weeks Eric felt that all he had left of his 'blood and background' was the one thing his mother could not alter – his Yorkshire accent. 'They don't get me,' he told her, 'they think I'm Canadian. I can't wait to meet a Canadian, they must sound Yorkshire.' The accent would, perhaps of necessity, disappear with time, but only in general use, 'Yorkshire' being always just beneath the surface

Eric's first job on American soil was as a hotel elevator operator; thereafter he worked as a labourer, first in a carpet mill and then a lumber yard. Working nights and at weekends allowed plenty of time for schooling, and again he proved himself an accomplished student. Once again, he registered in a school, and did so well his headmaster put him forward for a scholarship to the Latin School in Cambridge, Boston. Two hundred boys sat the scholarship exam for the one place available. Eric, however, had already told his family, 'I'll win it, I know I will'. So, we may assume he was not surprised when the school was told at morning roll-call that the scholarship was to be awarded to him.

In the autumn of 1914 he entered the white-columned portals of 'the Cambridge', feeling very much at home in both the city and his lodgings in a leafy street opposite a tree-covered park. Throughout his life, Eric Knight felt happiest in surroundings that reminded him of Yorkshire, or when in the company of people who reminded him of those he had left behind. There is no doubt that the education he received at this time set the pattern for his literary career, for it was here he studied the works of those whose lines he would borrow for the titles of his books and stories.

Gertrude Stein's *Three Lives* impressed him greatly and reinforced his fascination with duality, while Robert Southey's ballad, *The Battle of Blenheim*, would inspire him to works of military semi-fiction, which included '*The Dumbfool Josephine*', the story featuring the white mare from his boyhood. Shakespeare featured heavily in his education, as did Joseph Addison and F.W. Faber, who would provide the title for *The Happy Land*. W.E. Henley was also a favourite – a line from *England, My England* providing not only the title to a Knight novel but words that would be called upon for comfort in its author's darkest days:

> *Life is good and joy runs high*
> *Between English earth and sky:*
> *Death is death; but we shall die*
> *To the song on your bugles blown,*
> *England –*
> *To the stars on your bugles blown!*

Song On Your Bugles would not appear until 1936, by which time the lines had been recited a thousand times by Eric, often silently, but always in times of greatest spiritual need. For Part II of *Song On Your Bugles* Eric called upon another English writer, A.C. Swinburne, for his lines:

> *O Friend*
> *Will make death clear or make*
> *Life durable.*

His choice is testament to the fact that he read deeply as a student and with an understanding far beyond that of a boy who had received only a standard education.

His departure for the Cambridge Latin School relieved three problems at home. The arrival from England of Aunt Nell and two of her three children had put pressure on the available accommodation. They travelled to the US after Nell's husband died, leaving her with not only the older girls who had shared the Knight house in Menston but also Edwin John, aged ten. She had been lured to the States by the promise of a place to live, a desire to reunite the family, and to find work. Eric would say later that he fell in love with his cousin Marjorie, Nell's sixteen-year-old daughter, and that leaving her to go to Boston had been his first 'romantic heartbreak'. Marjorie would become immortalised – as so many real-life characters did in Knight's works – as the heroine of *Song on Your Bugles*.

The second problem centred on oppression. 'They scrubbed the dialect out of my tongue,' Eric said, 'and even tried to put me in knickerbockers. Then I shipped off to school. It didn't matter, we were pretty much strangers, and anyway, I was with my family, but I was still homesick for Yorkshire.' The third problem concerned a continued tension between Eric and his brothers, which persisted despite all his efforts to overcome it. He realised that the arrival of Adolph was not to blame. All three brothers doted on the boy. It was a problem upon which he would ponder in quiet moments and one that would cause him great sadness. The truth of the matter would out, but that day was almost twenty years in the future.

Nell brought news from home that Eric's beloved Uncle Percy intended to re-enlist if, as seemed likely in 1914, war broke out, a promise he had made good by the time the lad took up his studies at the Cambridge. Vernon would also serve, as would their oldest brother, Edwin, who was determined to fight despite being forty-five years of age. Uncle Frederic Creasser, also keen to be back in uniform, would serve as a Military Police Officer in Egypt. Eric's mother, while delighted to see her sister, was distraught to hear this news. She had lost her husband in the Boer War and feared her brothers, indeed her own sons, would suffer the same fate. 'Percy and Fred have served their country,' she reminded her sister, 'Why fight in a war when you don't have to? It doesn't make any sense.'

'The war in Europe seems far away from Boston, like it is happening in a dream,' Eric wrote, and buried himself in literature. He decided he wanted to be a journalist – always assuming his previous desires to be one of the Navajo, an artist or script writer came to nought. This new goal was fostered by close study of those upon whose words he would one day call for titles and inspiration, for all had followed that occupation. He told a friend:

'It is possible to begin as a journalist and end as a novelist. It is a natural progression. I used to think that if you were one you couldn't be the other and that journalists were looked down on by writers of books. But that is not the case. It seems it is possible to be both at the same time.'

He had reached this conclusion through biographical study of the writers he most admired. He discovered that Joseph Addison had written for the *Guardian* and the *Spectator*, Goldsmith for *Griffith's Monthly Review*, Henley for *The Scots Observer* and the *National Observer*. But the man whose work most thrilled him was AC Swinburne. Though not a journalist, Swinburne had been a friend to Dante Gabriel Rossetti, his sister Christina and others of the Pre-Raphaelites, a connection that embraced Eric's twin passions of art and literature. Swinburne had also been influenced by Greek tragedy, an area in which Eric read widely – and had endured a tragedy of his own, alcoholism, a weakness that would afflict the adult Eric Knight, and which he would overcome.

Eric was seventeen years old in 1914. He was attending a prestigious school on a hard-won scholarship. He was studying the literature he loved and making friends, all of whom were captivated by his charming accent and direct manner. Boston reminded him of Yorkshire, he was well fed, living in comfortable lodgings and paying his own way through a variety of jobs, most notably that of hotel washer-up, a profession he held in common with George Orwell who, during his year as a down-and-out in Paris, also became a *'plongeur'*. Knight never failed to include mention of this time in conversation – and in later years his friend Ernest Hemingway regularly introduced him as 'Eric Knight, the man who dish-washed his way through the Cambridge Latin.' Despite all this, the young man was not entirely happy, as his diary notes:

'Boys younger than me are fighting in a war, getting killed, for reasons they don't understand, reasons I don't understand. And I'm here, acting as if it wasn't happening at all, like some bad dream to get over. It feels unreal.'

He feared news that one of his uncles had been killed: 'I keep expecting that letter from my Mother, and when it doesn't come it makes it worse, so many are dying, how can they survive?'

But the letter never came and his studies continued. He immersed himself in the study of poetry, Greek myth and legend, and the history of English literature, and acquired a knowledge of writers from Shakespeare to Mark Twain. He exercised his mind in comparative studies of English and American writers working in the same periods: Hawthorne and Dickens, Stowe and Brontë, Twain and Morris, and found in one, Henry James, the embodiment of the Anglo-American writer he would one day become. The nature of James' work reinforced Knight's growing obsession with duality – the ability to be either of two personalities at any time. Here he realised for the first time that the Sam Small stories that occupied his mind in idle moments contained strong elements of the dual beings explored so deeply in the Gothic literature of the late Victorian era. Bram Stoker's *Dracula* was a dual character, as was Robert Louis Stevenson's Dr Jekyll while Mary Shelley's 'monster' was a manufactured creature locked in an internal struggle between the many sides of its manufactured personality.

Stevenson's friend, Henry James, however, had presented characters in *The Turn of the Screw* upon whose true identity the reader was obliged to make the final decision. They were many-sided and open to interpretation, lending themselves to constant re-reading, a quality that appealed greatly to one who believed this to be the most vital element of any story. Knight still believed that a story was 'dead' once it was written down and would go on saying so, but his studies of both Gothic and Modernist literature imbued in him a belief that he might present them in a way that would embody both genres by allowing the reader to take part in their plot, participate even, yet still read them over and over, always with a new response. He reasoned that the purpose of 'telling' stories was to involve the listener, captivate and enthral them, and now he believed he could send readers away reliving the tale, always adding to or conjecturing upon it.

From this time on he became increasingly interested in analysing the writer's motivation, deconstructing their work to discover those elements present, working out which route the writer had taken to get their message across – or if indeed any message was present. He had discovered through reading Joyce and others that a story could simply be a story and not only have no ending but no beginning either, just a 'snapshot' of life. And there would be no better time to do it; literary output and content always changed most rapidly at the turn of a century or in the wake of great conflicts.

Modern writers, he discovered, were adopting the role of observer and reporter on what they witnessed, even if the action had taken place wholly within their imagination. A technique would evolve through his consideration of these points that would find its unique place in literature, but almost twenty years would pass before he would begin to place any faith in that technique.

His studies did not, however, change his mind about Sam Small. Indeed, he made a point later of saying, 'I never said that nobody else should ever write a Sam Small story', and repeatedly refuted his 'ownership' of the character. And while we are invited to enjoy Sam's adventures in the Modernist sense of the work, they remain essentially 'telling stories'.

One author whose literary influence was felt on both sides of the Atlantic was Sir Arthur Conan Doyle. Best known for his *Sherlock Holmes* stories, Conan Doyle's passion was actually historical fiction, but it was his story telling ability that appealed to Eric Knight. Not surprising, perhaps, as the two had similar backgrounds. Both had been encouraged by uncles who recognised their nephews' imaginative abilities, and both believed in the tradition of word-of-mouth story-telling. Conan Doyle had grown to despise his hero and had killed him off, only to be persuaded by a huge cash sum to resurrect him. Knight would never face this dilemma but would suffer a similar fate, posthumously, in being recognised only for one creation. He could not know it at the time of reading Conan Doyle but he too would be published in both *Strand Magazine* and *Collier's*, publications that had recognised Conan Doyle's early potential.

Despite concentrating on his studies, Knight's unsettled feeling would not go away. As he wrestled with the dilemma of whether to continue his studies or fulfil his childhood aspirations by doing his duty for his country, another opportunity arose: 'Fancy coming to New York with me, Knight? I'm off to join the Art Students League.'

The invitation came from a friend Eric only ever referred to as Seaford, a Canadian student with a reckless streak. It was the summer of 1916. Eric was about to enter his final year at the Cambridge Latin School and had just won the coveted Sydenham Medal for drawing. His uncles had so far survived the war and he had managed to resist the urge to return to England to sign up. Perhaps Seaford's plan was simply irresistible, a youthful, spur-of-the-moment adventure, but Eric's actions in leaving Boston and his education when so close to graduating with honours is uncharacteristic of him. Perhaps Seaford exercised some hold over him that has never been explained. It may be that Eric, on the other hand, had said so often he wanted to be an artist, he felt unable to refuse the invitation when it came. One thing is certain, as the train rattled on through New Haven, Hartford, Stamford, Darien and Fairfield toward Long Island, Eric realised that his American dream had come true and he was about to fulfil another – that of becoming an artist.

CHAPTER FIVE

Seaford and Knight rented a small apartment at 854 West 181st Street and enrolled at the Art Students League at 108 Fifth Avenue. Founded in 1875, the League resulted from disillusionment among students concerned that the National Academy of Art and Design was no longer serving an increasingly avant-garde artistic community. While it would later count luminaries like Jackson Pollock among its alumni, it was at that time a membership organisation whose applicants underwent a selection process before being invited to join a small but elite society. Candidates had to display artistic qualifications, to demonstrate that they were of 'acceptable moral character' – and had the means to pay their fees.

The atmosphere was contrary to that of the Academy and most other art schools in so far as it embraced a more European attitude to its practices, which were very informal. Eric and Seaford attended afternoon sessions, which they booked on a monthly basis, never sure of being able to support themselves in the long term. Eric took what work he could find – as a lumber-yard labourer, a mill hand, then as a newspaper vendor, calling out the day's headline from street corners.

Applying to join the League, Eric had taken with him, as proof of his abilities, pencil portraits of his family and friends, most poignantly one of his Aunt Kit, made on his last visit to Leeds before leaving for America. Relieved to be accepted, he threw himself into his studies, but there was now a new distraction in his life. Dorothy Caroline Noyes Hall was two years younger than Eric. Like him, she was an art student, and like him she had come to New York from Boston. Her father, Frank Willis Hall, was a Londoner, her mother, Mary Aiken Noyes, a native of Staten Island. Dorothy was slim, dark-haired and beautiful, also educated and artistic. Love blossomed, but events – most notably America's entry into the war - were about to overtake the pair. Eric might well have sat out the conflict had not his brothers, Fred and Ed, joined up. Both were now serving in King Company, the Pennsylvania Light Infantry, and while this may have been the only motivation Eric needed to enlist, there were other considerations.

Firstly, Seaford announced his intention to quit his studies, return to Ottawa and join the Canadian army. In a letter to his mother long after the event, Eric said: 'Seaford told me he was off to Canada to sign up. If I were interested I could do the same, so I strung along with him.' Secondly, Dorothy was pregnant – and Eric was not ready for the responsibilities of fatherhood. 'It wouldn't matter. I knew I was running away but it wouldn't matter, we were all going to be killed anyway,' he would say later. He expected to enlist and, after basic training, sail for France, from where he did not expect to return. Dorothy's mother, however, discovered Eric's plans, boarded a train with her heavily pregnant daughter, and arrived on the young soldier's doorstep with marriage plans drawn up. The wedding would take place within forty-eight hours.

2265657 Knight, E. M. enlisted in the Canadian Signals Corps on June 13th 1917 giving his occupation as art student. His medical history sheet states he had no small-pox marks, that he weighed 147 lbs and that his height was a little over five feet eight inches. His chest measurement was thirty-two inches, his vision 20-20, his physical development 'good' and his four vaccination marks clearly visible. He was therefore declared by Medical Officer I.M. Shillington of the Toronto Mobile Medical Unit 'FIT FOR SERVICE'.

On the Attestation Paper he named as next-of-kin his mother, Marian H. Kahn, but this has been crossed out and in its place the name Mrs. E. M Knight added. Marian's address, however, remained, although it is unlikely that Dorothy ever lived with her mother-in-law, preferring instead to remain with her parents in Boston. In any case, Eric wanted his mother to be informed first of what he described as his 'inevitable annihilation'. He and Dorothy were married on July 28th 1917 and four days later Isobella, known as 'Betty' from that day forward, was born.

At that time, the stigma attached to having been conceived or born outside marriage was such that the fact was often covered up. In Betty's case a year was deducted from her age when she started school. Eric would see his daughter in breaks from basic training before he departed for England. When he sailed, he did not expect to see her again.

Knight and Seaford stood on the freezing deck of the *SS Megantic* under a November sky. Goodbyes had been said long before; tearful wives and children were not allowed on the quayside. There was no ceremony, no marching band. The screech of circling seagulls and the rhythmic beating of the ship's engine as it nosed out into the wide Atlantic were the only sounds of farewell.

The prospects facing any infantryman bound for France in 1917 were daunting. At Passchendaele alone, there had been 475,000 casualties. Those in signals regiments had cause to hang on to their jobs, keep their heads down and avoid the front line by any means possible. The heavy losses suffered in the taking of Vimy Ridge, however, left the Canadian Corps seriously short. One-third of their number had been killed. Volunteers were called for to replace those lost, and the response was immediate. Jostling in the queue were Knight and Seaford who, along with their comrades, had spent eight months under further harsh training at Bramshott Barracks in Hampshire and were keen to play their part.

'They show us how to aim a Lee-Enfield at a man, and how to pull the trigger to extinguish his life. They show us how to hurl a grenade to blow a man's life and limbs apart. They show us how to stick a bayonet in his guts and how to twist the life of him, and the PT bayonet training man is the only one around here with any compassion for us who are going over the top. But they don't tell us how to look the enemy in the eye, and they don't tell us why, and they don't tell us how to die. Perhaps we will die before we have the chance to kill some other innocent.'

Eric and his pal were among the first to transfer to the Princess Patricia's Canadian Light Infantry. The trivialities of camp training were soon forgotten in the mayhem of the first action. Eric was touched by the noise accompanying the battle. 'It was,' he said, 'both its terror and its redeemer'. He likened the noise of machine guns to the sounds he'd been used to in the bottle factory, 'a constant almost rhythmic rattling, like the crates of bottles on the train,' he said, 'only with great explosions and the cries of dying men, men who had been full of life only moments before. If the noise stops, you're dead.' This was his first battle on his first day in the front line, and all was confusion, mayhem, and terror. Despite the months of preparation none of the men around him were ready for that first day.

He recalled seeing a young soldier's head explode after being hit by a grenade: 'Why am I still here? He was only feet away. I felt nothing, physically or mentally, until I closed my eyes to sleep many hours later. All I could see was the face he'd once had. I still see the face he once had. Why should I survive? It doesn't seem fair.'

'The stench of the dead in the trenches,' he said, 'reminded of the knacker's, but even that could not erase it from my mind'. It would be the noise of war, though, that he would most vividly recall. It featured in his mind to the exclusion of smell or colour, and as an artist he found this odd. He was musical and would later learn the piano accordion, but the artist in him wanted to remember the colour, not the sound – especially the screams of dying soldiers. Many years would pass before his audible and visual memories would come together. They would give him a unique outlook on life and everything in it.

Between August 6th and 15th, he and Seaford fought side by side in the Battle of Amiens, Eric always repeating the Henley poem as the Captain blew the whistle which sent their men over the top: 'Death is death but we shall die, to the song on your bugles blown...' Ten days later they embarked on the cruel two-week engagement that was the Battle of the Scarp. Thereafter came a brief respite, but on September 27th, the Battle of the Canal du Nord began and lasted a week. In the eerie quiet that follows every battle Knight received devastating news:

'The Adjutant sent a messenger. I knew it would be bad. My first thoughts were for my brave uncles. My mother's words came to me. She was right, why fight in a war when you don't have to? Why fight in a war when you do?'

Eric's uncles, despite fighting in the fiercest theatres of the war, would survive, one long enough to witness the outbreak of the Second World War – but his brothers would not. Fred and Ed had been killed in action on June 28th – neither knowing of the other's death. There had been several days of bitter fighting before a daring night attack took place in which the brothers were leading their men across the Ourcq River east of Paris when they were mown down by German machine gunners. They died only moments apart.

It seems the brothers had joined the army with a friend, their service numbers being but a single digit either side of his, but such is the confusion of war that the two were not even reunited in death. Their final resting place among 6,010 others in the Oise-Aisne American cemetery is in separate plots divided by dozens of rows of white crosses, every one of which marks the sacrifice of a young man who gave his life for his country in the few seconds of withering fire that ended the lives of two Yorkshiremen, Sergeants Frederic and Edmund Knight. 'I had a couple of brothers once, I don't remember much about them,' Eric would say later, once again hiding the emotion of tragic loss.

During the first week of November 1918, days before the end of hostilities, Eric's unit was pinned down in a wood where they took refuge in a row of ruined cottages. Contorted blackened trees, branches severed and splintered by exploding shells, leaned on each other for support as the ground around them steamed and smoked in the mist. Having been blown out of the ground, some rested on the roofs of the cottages, their leafless branches acting as a target for canon fire in an otherwise treeless landscape. In the corner of one cottage there stood a roughly built wooden shelter, under which, undamaged, stood a pianola. The instrument played only one tune. *Meet Me in the Shadows* rang out its plaintiff notes to a counterpoint of German machine gun bursts, as the Canadians tried yet another advance. After each attack came the ritual of burying bodies in shell holes in the uneasy lull. It became a macabre game, soldiers winding up the clockwork device before attacking, the enemy responding with applause of bullets. The soldiers even played the machine when stood down, once again drawing machine-gun fire. Eric came to loathe the instrument.

When reinforcements arrived to take up the advance, their horses were stabled in the cottages while the men slept under canvas. A new crop of recently rested officers played the machine and once again drew enemy fire, all of which they considered quite entertaining. Finally, the order came to begin a decisive attack and the units moved out en masse, spurred on by a growing conviction that the end of the war was near.

Eric and Seaford hung back as the men advanced along the trenches. When they were sure they were not being observed, Eric produced a Mills bomb he had secreted under a pile of logs. The two dived for cover as the bomb destroyed the pianola. They congratulated one another and prepared to rejoin their comrades in a feigned panic of having almost died under German attack. But Seaford had another kind of 'bombshell' for his friend.

It had been his idea to join the Artists League, and his suggestion they enlist in the army. Now he proposed the execution of a plan he had made even before the two men were posted to France – to desert the regiment. This was where Eric drew the line on loyalty to a friend over loyalty to his country. He would later write an account of a day off from training in England during which Seaford talked of his desertion plans:

'We went to a cliff top, the Harvard student and myself. And talked over his plan. We decided that England was still the England of our story-books. We listened to the guns in France and lay in the grass. He was a remarkable chap. I can still hear him saying: *'Knight we've made a bad mess of the war, and only intelligence can rectify it. We enlisted to kill a disease called Prussianism, and we've become part of a system we started out to kill. I shall desert the first chance I have, and if Germany has a better reason for fighting a war I shall go into the German army.'*

When they first met at the Cambridge Latin School, Seaford claimed he had been a Harvard student and that his family were wealthy Canadian oil producers. He was most likely lying. No trace of him may be found at Harvard or in Canada. Seaford – if that was his name – did desert, and did go to Germany. He spoke fluent German so perhaps his true identity secretly rested there. Knight heard from him only once more:

'I got a curious letter from Seaford a year after he deserted. It came from Ireland. He apparently didn't like Germany and had joined Mickey Somebody's party to fight for honest freedom. He said he'd taken two British revolvers to the Irish as his contribution. I never heard from him again.'

Some fifteen years later, Knight pondered this and another, deeply poignant memory of the final moments of the war. He was working scattered pieces of material into a story based on these wartime memories. He recalled how he sat under the shelter of trees, behind a flood bank, a few yards from a bridge over which Canadian soldier George Price was advancing. The sound of a single shot echoed and died in the mist. Every serving soldier knew that sound, he had heard it ten thousand times. It was the sniper's rifle. 'We never fired a single shot after midnight on the tenth. But the Germans kept on throwing everything at us – and killing lads who'd have otherwise survived – right up to the stroke of eleven. Why? They were beaten, there was no point, but they fired anyway.'

The bells of Mons rang out their eleven o'clock chimes on the eleventh day of the eleventh month. They were the last sound George Price heard. He died moments from safety and only four hundred yards from where John Parr – the first soldier to die in the conflict – had lost his life to a sniper four years earlier. 'To the song on your bugles blown,' Eric repeated as the bells rang and the body of George Price was covered with a rough army blanket. It would be twenty-five years before he could allow himself once more to speak these words aloud.

The story based on these events, *Meet Me In The Shadows*, appeared in *Story Magazine* in 1935. Wisely, he removed himself from blame for the Mills bomb and Seaford from any IRA involvement. He added a description of the manure left by the cavalry's horses, propelled in every direction by the explosion which destroyed the building, a thinly disguised parallel between the resulting 'shower' and the utter pointlessness of war.

Knight's literary career took him a long way from those dark days, but everything he would write would be coloured by his experiences. He could never accept death lightly, even in a work of fiction; it was always a tragedy.

The Pats remained in France until February 13th 1919 when they returned to Bramshott to prepare for the wedding of HRH Princess Patricia to Commander Ramsay, an event that every remaining member of the regiment attended. Eric used his three-week leave to travel to Yorkshire for a joyous reunion with his uncles in Halifax. The five survivors sat around the kitchen fire with its steaming kettle and glowing coals, Eric in his rough serge uniform and knee-length puttees, the others back in civilian clothes. The older men, once uncles but now comrades-in-arms, talked out their war as Aunt Emily sang and kneaded dough. As for Eric, the tales he had dreamed of telling when a boy were as dead as his two brothers. He wrote:

'The stories only exist if you and those you love survive. Even my uncles just wanted to forget. The horror was too much for me, and I was only involved for a few months. Their four years of hell are unimaginable. That we survived is not the miracle, the miracle is that anybody survived.'

If the Boer War had sounded romantic to the boy in the kitchen at Spread Eagle Yard, the reality to the man he had become was one of unbelievable and irreconcilable horror.

For the second time in seven years, Eric Knight boarded a ship at Liverpool bound for the other side of a world now changed forever. Six days later the regiment mustered in Ottawa where their newly-married Commander-in-Chief performed her last official duty in taking the salute at their final parade, after which all the men were officially struck off the strength. After years of relying upon each other absolutely for their very survival, they were once again individuals. No longer in mortal danger, and with the common cause won, they set about rebuilding their shattered lives.

Knight would do what many others did and throw himself into life as a married man and a civilian. Like all the others, he determined to put his army service behind him and to this end kept no contact with any old comrades. He would revisit his war experiences many times through his 'fiction', through humour, through his anger at the trivialisation of the kind of deaths the movies portrayed, through his articles concerning social injustice, in letters to friends, and through bouts of depression. His last words on the subject of the First World War would be contained in a story about his childhood; they would represent his last word on any subject. And despite the passage of much time, their poignancy in recollecting the period of his greatest desperation would not be dulled:

'I cried inside myself as Englishmen have cried in no matter what corner of this vast, foolish world.'

CHAPTER SIX

If there was animosity between Eric Knight and his mother-in-law it was hardly surprising; he had, after all, committed one sin in getting her daughter pregnant and another, greater one, in deserting her. None of this would have mattered if he had died along with the millions of others. But he had not. And, he was determined to make a go of his marriage despite the 'dark moods' he now suffered. He doted on the daughter whose first words and first steps he had missed, but who would grow up with no memory of her father's absence.

Mrs. Hall's determination matched Eric's, and in seeking to secure a future for her daughter she had set her up in her own infant school in Fairfield, Connecticut. The school, however, was not totally funded by Mrs. Hall. Isadora Duncan, the dancer and socialite, was already an extremely wealthy woman with an altruistic and bohemian approach to life and education. She had lost her own two children in 1913 when they drowned in a boating tragedy, after which she founded many schools in their memory, all based upon the ethos of 'spirituality and movement'.

The Fairfield school, known as St Elizabeth's of the Roses, was one of them. The school benefited from Dorothy's passion for art and dance and was popular – but it would not meet all the needs of the family. Eric needed a job. 'But what does a man do,' he reasoned, 'whose previous jobs include bottle-factory labourer, glue-works vat-stirrer, mill boy, lumber-yard hand, failed Latin scholar, failed art student and soldier?' The answer may not have been obvious to many, and took some time to occur to him, but after a brief unsettled period of casual work and the study of his new surroundings it hit him like a thunderbolt. 'The town didn't have its own newspaper. I had the top floor of the school, a passion for words and time on my hands.' *The Fairfield & Stamford Sun* was born – but not before he had done a stint as a machine-hand in a factory, which would spawn one of many myths that would forever circle around him.

In later life, when questioned about his education, or when he felt like boasting a little for the pleasure it brought him, or when talking to Hollywood producers – 'so drowning in bullshit that they couldn't tell truth from fiction if their lives were at stake' – he would casually say, 'I was at Yale, you know. I studied art.' People accepted his word; the myth was perpetuated and has since been repeated, even by scholars. Eric Knight 'was at Yale'. The university in New Haven, Connecticut, however, holds no record of Eric Knight's attendance at their School of Art or any other School. The key to the Yale myth may be found in the *Stamford City Directory* for the years 1921 and 1922. Eric M. Knight is listed in both as working for Stamford's largest employer –Yale and Towne Manufacturing, makers of Yale locks.

In those editions of the directory Knight also described himself as an 'editor', his own small operation already producing a weekly news-sheet that he compiled in the evenings while working a day-shift at the factory. By 1923, he was 'Editor – Towne & Co.'s in-house newspaper, article writer - the Bronx Home News, News Editor - the Norwalk Sentinel and the Darien Review'. Norwalk, Darien, Fairfield and Stamford were neighbouring towns. There was no mention now of machine operating.

The articles he wrote for those newspapers survive in typed copies of the originals, carefully preserved in the Knight Archive at Yale's Beinecke Rare Book and Manuscript Library – their presence in 'the world's most important manuscript depository' lending weight to the myth that he had once been a Yale student. The copies provide evidence of another abiding passion, the movies. He was an inveterate, almost obsessive, movie-goer already formulating views on films and film-makers, which would lead to his becoming America's most celebrated, most feared, and most scathing critic of actors, producers, directors, studios, and film content.

That he was submitting film reviews to newspapers in the early 1920s places him in the vanguard of movie criticism, and in the opinion of some makes him America's very first film critic. Films had been part of everyday entertainment for years before newspapers began printing criticism and Knight struggled desperately at first to have his views accepted, but he mounted a very plausible argument in support of his work. 'If your newspaper runs literary criticism, then it should also carry film criticism. Most films are after all based, albeit loosely, upon literary works, most of which I have read, which places me in an ideal position to offer critical remarks.' Many editors were impressed by both the argument and the man raising it. But then, most believed themselves to be dealing with a Yale scholar. However, nobody was willing to run his reviews.

Little by little, Eric Knight became proprietor, editor, reporter, and – after purchasing a second-hand press – printer of his own newspaper. He visited Stamford's businesses to solicit advertising copy, reported on births, deaths, marriages, court proceedings, fires and accidents, anything he could turn into saleable newsprint. But there was a problem. 'Any fool can produce a newspaper, but how the devil was I going to sell it?'

Stamford and Fairfield street corners soon echoed to a now fading Yorkshire accent proclaiming the latest headlines. Even when the *Sun* could afford paper-boys, Eric would still go out to his favourite 'pitch' where he became a feature of the townscape. He would use these occasions to gather news stories from his customers or pick up valuable advertising clients. 'I made more friends on street corners that most good-time girls,' he joked later.

As the paper grew, so did the Knight family. Winifred was born on 27th July 1920, and Jane – known as Jenny – on September 9th, 1921. Betty had been enrolled in school, having had a year deducted from her age, but all the girls attended lessons whether they were actually old enough or not. Knight admitted that he did not spend as much time with his daughters as he would have liked but seemed unable to prise himself away from the work of editing Yale & Towne's in-house publication and running his own newspaper while writing articles for others. And since the summer of 1921 there had been a new demand on his time – the National Guard of Connecticut.

Despite saying 'never again' after demobilisation in 1919, he spent part of his next five summers at Fort Sill, Oklahoma, as a Captain in the Field Artillery School. In his subsequent writings he justifies his retaining pacifist views while teaching young men how to fire cannon. 'If war was inevitable, we should teach young men how to survive, not how to die'.

After a brief period of success, Eric's newspaper went bust. Thereafter, he taught English at the school while Dorothy concentrated upon art and dance, apparently to the satisfaction of its founder, who gave the school her approval after a visit. Though he loved teaching, it is clear that the newspaper business had captivated Eric Knight. He was anxious to find a regular job with an established paper. Throughout his life, he would get almost every job for which he applied. No doubt his unusual accent charmed many, but his impeccable 'Yale' education and his obvious intellect simply overwhelmed prospective employers.

The editor of the *Brooklyn Eagle* newspaper in Long Island fell for the Knight charm and offered him a job as a reporter, whereupon the family was uprooted from Stamford and relocated to an apartment in New York. It could not have been further removed from the rural life they had known and the comfortable home they had shared with Dorothy's parents and brother, Caral. Eric worked not only for the *Eagle* but also for the New York City News Association. He contributed further to the *Bronx Home News*. But despite it all, the move to the city and the obvious unhappiness it caused within the family was closely followed by the failure of the Knight marriage, and though he never wrote directly of the reasons for the break-up, it is likely this upheaval was largely to blame.

Eric Knight recoiled from all failure, particularly that of his marriage. He lived at a time when failure was not discussed, his Yorkshire upbringing forcing him always to 'stick it out as best you may and wait for better times to come'. He suffered a severe lack of confidence following his marriage breakdown, however, and there is every indication that his post-war years carried with them more than their share of troubles. He was beginning to exorcise the demons of the war, the manifestations of which were perhaps more than many women could be expected to cope with, especially when they are coupled to an uprooting of the family to what must have seemed a hostile environment. Most veterans would never refer to the most harrowing elements of their time in service. Most would also have been too proud to blame any later personal failure on their experiences, but Knight's newspaper had folded because the ability to concentrate was, for a time, lost to him. It would take until 1937 for him to voice the thoughts that had been racing around his mind at the time of his marriage breakdown:

'After the war I drifted into the American army and became a good artillery expert. I found that something had happened to my memory. I can't remember people's names though I can remember faces. I can't remember what I write and what I read. Curious, I can remember everything that happened before the war – every last boy in my class, everything I read, everything I had stuffed into me between 8 and 10. Yet I can't remember a thing I read after the war. It's a hell of a short life though... and possibly a damn good one. I decided that all the rest of my life was velvet to which I had no right.'

In truth, Eric Knight was suffering the guilt of the survivor. His business venture and marriage could be added to the list of those elements of his life he labelled failures. He tried returning to his love of art but was diagnosed, for the first time in his life, colour-blind. Suddenly, the 'purple' blood he had remembered flooding the floor of the knacker's yard and the blood he had seen mingling with the mud of the trenches made sense. It had of course been red, just as the dales he had wandered as a boy had been green, but to him they had both been varying shades of purple. He realised that he did not see the world as others did, and in a strange way this countered the disappointment of his realisation that he could never be the artist of his ambitions, for what he saw and what he thought became aligned for the first time. He had, after all, never 'seen' the world as others did; his view of people, world events, philosophy and literature, art, social conditions and the political system had always seemed at odds with the general mindset. He had an individual outlook on life, and though the break-up of his marriage would lead to great pain and later bitterness, it was the catalyst for unprecedented and unexpected change.

He was, though he could not have known it, embarking on yet another journey, one that would bring him to close friendships with a community of like-minded artists, writers and actors who would witness the emergence of an Eric Knight previously hidden from view, a man unafraid to mount an argument with anybody, to state his views, to assert his intellectual credentials, a man with the confidence to do what Yorkshiremen are renowned for doing the world over – calling a spade a spade.

One such friendship would be with Peter Hurd, one of America's most respected artists. Hurd would crystallise Knight's actual view of the colours of life – and the world's view of him – in a portrait that exhibits a surreal use of colour, seen as an impressionist interpretation by those unfamiliar with the lives of either artist or sitter but which is actually a representation of the colours Knight saw, mostly at the purple and vibrant blue-green end of the spectrum. In the work, Knight is portrayed as movie stars were at the time, broad shouldered, square jawed, handsome, utterly relaxed, oozing sexual allure, wearing a sweater and no shirt. And in its depiction the portrait exhibits a third element, one of irony, for Hurd knew well that his friend loathed the male Hollywood image as served up by the publicity men responsible for creating 'stars'.

The Hurd friendship was some years in the future, however. For now Eric committed his own artistic impressions to paper in charcoal, pencil, or pen and ink, mediums without colour and therefore without the errors commensurate with the work of one unable to distinguish reds and greens He would contribute many illustrations to various magazines and leave behind a legacy of outstanding artworks, some of which *are* in colour, the need to overcome his visual disability never quite leaving him.

His love of words had deserted him temporarily because, once he had written a piece for a newspaper, he would forget it. His inability to recall which subjects he had written about, or what he had written, led to his keeping meticulous records lest he submit an idea repeatedly. Life was easier as a news reporter. If he concentrated on stories that needed no follow-up piece, he did not make errors. Thus he sustained himself, often consoling himself in his cramped apartment with thoughts of home and the Sam Small stories still occupying the part of his mind that permanently resided in Yorkshire. The stories would not be published for ten years, 'But they were there,' he said, 'making themselves up, slowly but surely'. Knowing that his spirits were as low as they had been at almost any time, and beginning to find more solace than he knew was healthy in liquor, he prescribed for himself complete change. He decided to return to the remnants of his family in Philadelphia.

In the summer of 1926, and for the seventh time in his twenty-nine years, Eric Knight was starting from scratch. Quitting his job, he used what little remained of his last salary cheque to rent an apartment at 222 Spruce Street and did what he had done so often before, set about finding a job. He claimed later to have had no plans, but in taking his apartment he had placed himself conveniently close to the offices of the *Philadelphia Public Ledger*, which occupied newly-built premises at 620 Chestnut Street, in the heart of the city. He read the newspaper closely and followed up on a story it published. A Polish woman had stabbed her husband to death and been given life imprisonment. To find out why she did it Eric visited the woman in jail.

The *Ledger* editor was not impressed with the resultant story. 'They weren't interested in any stories about women,' he said, 'but the next time I saw him with my movie criticism he remembered me, and turned me down again.' The impression had, however, been made, and though America was descending into the grip of financial crisis, Knight was eventually summoned by the editor who rewarded his persistence with the offer of a job. For a man who had run his own newspaper and been a National Guard officer it must have been hard to start at the very bottom, but that is what he did, as a copy-boy running errands normally reserved for a fourteen-year-old.

For more than a year he submitted ideas for articles, and his movie critiques, fruitlessly. He fetched coffee and did the hundred other jobs of the lowliest employee while learning everything he could about the newspaper business. On days off he spent time with his cousins, his mother, half-brother Adolph, and his Aunt Nell, always with the aim of keeping the family together. He lived frugally and sent what money he could afford to support his children. He learned the piano accordion and guitar and fed his passion for the theatre and the movies. He petitioned his editor, arguing that the newspaper owed it to its readership to offer movie criticism, his case being supported by forthright copy written on his own time. His ideas were consistently rebuffed. His views, and his style, were too blunt. He continued to argue his case, that with the huge growth of the movies the public would desert their favourite newspaper in favour of one that did offer comment on this new form of entertainment. In 1928, the *Ledger* relented, and appointed him to the post of theatre and movie critic.

Little of his movie criticism from this time is to be found in the Knight archive. That any record survives is due to third parties who retained the newspapers and magazines in which his work appeared and later donated them to library archives. The nature of the job meant he was constrained to spend much of his time in movie theatres – up to fifty new films were appearing weekly – and the rest in traditional theatres. In many respects theatre and film criticism suited a journalist who was still having difficulty remembering what he had written; they were subjects after all which he would not have to revisit. And though the theatre never failed to thrill him he became increasingly disillusioned with Hollywood's output and often bucked the trend by criticising even the most popular performers.

That no-one else dared attack the stars made no difference to a man who was making friends among Philadelphian actors – some of whom would go on to fame in Hollywood – and finally beginning to deal with the twin trauma of war and his marriage breakdown. He was rediscovering his natural Yorkshire propensity for straight talking in the face of what he described as 'the perpetual idiocy of Hollywood', and he had an editor willing to support him because 'controversial comment makes good copy, and good copy sells newspapers'.

Success was beginning to seem possible, and when his editor called him into the office during the summer of 1929, it was to impart good news. From January 1930, Eric Knight was to become the paper's feature writer. What was more, he was to be given total discretion on his output without the usual editorial controls. 'No writer could ask for more,' Eric wrote, 'a regular pay cheque and the freedom to write what you want to.'

Though Philadelphia suited him in every respect, he could not be completely happy, having by now lost all contact with his daughters. His letters to them went unanswered, and a growing anger toward Dorothy began to cloud his thoughts. He had not been able to afford any kind of holiday for five years, so in celebration of his promotion, and in recognition of the fact that the war had obliterated some of his childhood memories of Yorkshire, he decided to return to England for a vacation. He arrived in late September 1929 and broke his journey in London before travelling to his beloved Yorkshire,

In Halifax, Knight stayed in a public house close to his former home in Wellington Street South. He borrowed a bicycle from a boyhood friend from the mill, George Simpson, who had returned from war service with the Royal Navy mentally shattered and minus a leg. George had been unable to ride his bicycle since his return but had maintained it regardless and was happy to see it put to good use. Eric went on tour, exploring the villages he had known in his youth, staying overnight in inns along the way. Here it was that he immersed himself once more in the warmth of the Yorkshire accent, his own having now largely disappeared except when consciously called upon. Indeed, he allowed pub regulars to take him for an American and to pump him for information about a land they could never hope to see. They wanted to know about the factories and the mills and were apparently favourably impressed by the fact that they differed little from those in which they laboured. When the conversation turned to the weather, however, they became sceptical, especially when Eric spoke of the lack of rain in places like California, '*Ow do thi grow corn?*' was the obvious enquiry. Eric explained that water was piped five hundred miles to feed the crops – which grew six feet tall. Gasps of disbelief prompted him to explain that when Americans talked of 'corn' they didn't mean the wheat that grows in Britain, but maize. It was no use; he was in too deep to extricate himself and no amount of explanation, despite being illustrated with drawings, would persuade the drinkers that 'corn on the cob' was not an invention of his imagination. When he rashly mentioned highways built forty-feet in the air on great concrete legs, one man put his pint on the table, wiped his mouth and uttered the words that would become the title of a Sam Small story. '*All Yankees are liars*' the man said, bringing conversation to a halt.

'*All Yankees Are Liars*' would in fact be omitted from the first edition of the Sam Small stories for fear of upsetting Britain's American allies in the face of impending war, but it would be included in a later edition. As always, the story starts with a quotation, not from poetry on this occasion but from folklore:

> *You can always tell the Irish.*
> *You can always tell the Dutch.*
> *You can always tell a Yankee,*
> *But you cannot tell him much.*

The story tells of a visiting American, a Mr. Smith, who, on a cycling vacation, falls into the hands of a bunch of archetypal Yorkshireman in the Spread Eagle pub. By the time the Sam Small stories were published, Eric had placed the pub in Polkingthorpe Brig, the fictional home of his eponymous hero.

When his visit to Yorkshire was over, Knight would carry home with him an impression of a place and its people that had not changed in all the years of his absence. It would work on his subconscious mind until finally being brought forward to appear in a story being told when he was far from that place, the colour and tone enhanced by the passage of years and a continued longing to be back there.

Sam's stories reveal as much about the author as any work of biography ever could, and a sincerity of purpose is imparted as a result in works labelled 'fiction' or 'comic prose'. The adventures are tailored to an audience capable of deciphering the idiosyncrasies of dialect and metaphor, but may be read simply as a joyful and thrilling adventure told by one whose works display all the hallmarks of the master story-teller.

It remains oddly paradoxical, however, that the Sam Small stories would become bestsellers across the English-speaking world and particularly in America, where it might have been thought readers would be severely challenged by the Yorkshire dialect, but such was his publisher's belief in Knight that changing it was never even contemplated, and the great reception the stories received justified that confidence.

Many years would separate the inspiration for '*All Yankees Are Liars*' and its appearance in print, and some of the influences upon Sam were yet to be experienced by an author who left Yorkshire bursting with inspiration for his new job.

GREG CHRISTIE

CHAPTER SEVEN

'As soon as I got to my desk this morning, the phone rang. He begged me not to print all that stuff he said last night, *I was drunk,*' he said, and he was. He poured poison on everybody from the hotel bellboy to the President. Boy, how I'd love to print it all, but I won't.'

Eric Knight wrote these words the day after interviewing an American literary legend who would become one of his closest friends, a man who would inspire him to write when it would have been easier not to, one who would call him 'The best writer to come out of England in decades.' The subject of Knight's first interview as Feature Writer for the *Philadelphia Public Ledger* was Ernest Hemingway.

He and Hemingway had much in common. Knight had sympathy for the celebrated author's drinking habits and perhaps saw rather more of himself in them than he was comfortable with. Hemingway, though two years younger than Knight, was already a celebrated writer, but he too had been a newspaperman, reporting, as he put it, on 'fires, fights and funerals'. He wrote in *For Whom The Bell Tolls* of waving goodbye to his father at the railroad station when leaving for Kansas to take up his first job, an event bearing striking similarities to Eric's departure from Leeds, an account of which would appear in his novel *Invitation to Life.*

Hemingway's father, like Eric's mother, had been against his joining the army. Eric need not have joined, and Hemingway could have legitimately avoided service due to an unusual and incurable eye condition. However, his friend and colleague, Theodore Brumback – who had a glass eye – had joined the American Field Service and Hemingway did the same, having responded to an advertisement in his own paper for volunteers.

Like Knight, Hemingway was spared none of the horrors of war. An Italian munitions factory exploded on his first day on duty, and his introduction to Field Service was the collection of hideously mutilated bodies, the presence of women and children among the dead being a sight for which he had not been prepared and one which would leave an indelible mark on him. After four months in hospital following a bomb blast that wounded him in the legs, he was promoted to First-Lieutenant and awarded the Silver Medal for Valour. In common with Knight he found release from his real-life pain through his writings. *A Farewell to Arms* explores his love for Agnes von Korowsky, the nurse who tended his wounds while he was hospitalised.

There is a similarity between the works of Knight and Hemingway insofar as both writers explore deep emotions in their work, and while Knight was quick to acknowledge a debt to Hemingway's frankness, he would surpass his friend in adding explicit sex scenes to his account of a Second World War love affair in his 1941 novel *This Above All*. The work also implicates the protagonists in crimes against The Crown, a theme rarely explored even in peacetime. To that point, such activities had been the domain of the villain, but Knight asks his reader to consider that an illegal, unpatriotic act might be justified in certain circumstances and its perpetrator seen as no less of a hero. His bold step drew high praise from Hemingway and many other writers.

It is fair to say, though, that what impressed Knight most about Hemingway was not his friend's bold literary style but his friendships with writers such as Ezra Pound, Ford Madox Ford, and Knight's literary heroine Gertrude Stein. It should be noted that by the time of the Hemingway interview, Knight's problems with memory were being overcome – and that Hemingway, ironically, would end his own life in July 1961 when he too could no longer remember what he had written only hours before.

On June 28th 1930, *Liberty* published Knight's first short story, *The Two-Fifty Hat*. It was an auspicious beginning to a career in fiction: two other literary newcomers made their debuts on the printed page in the same issue, Truman Capote and J.D. Salinger.

The Two-Fifty Hat draws directly on the Polish woman who had stabbed her husband. She appears as an immigrant who 'earns a few cents here and there, sweeping and cleaning' and who is overwhelmed with the need for a little colour in her life. When a Philadelphia milliner displays a red and yellow hat in the shop window, reduced to $2.50, she cannot resist. But the expense means there is no supper for her tyrannical husband, a foundry labourer. In disgust he throws the hat into the coal stove and watches it burn. Mrs. Czernowsky now stands before the Justice, babe in arms, accused of stabbing her husband with a kitchen knife. Her fate lies in the hands of a tired old Judge who is not interested in hearing mitigating circumstances in broken English from a woman who can't afford a lawyer and whose poverty he cannot understand.

Knight learned an important lesson here. The real-life story had been turned down by the editor of the *Public Ledger* five years earlier, but now found its way into print as a work of fiction. So it was possible to tell the truth, so long as you called it 'fiction'. In less than a thousand words, *The Two-Fifty Hat* describes a desperate life – two thirds of which would be spent in jail – an unjust legal system, an oppressive marriage, and an unequal society.

There now began a prolific outpouring of work, which would comprise short stories to be published worldwide and movie criticism syndicated across America, having first appeared in the *Public Ledger* and magazines like *The Town Crier*, a publication carrying the tag line 'Relieving The Tedium Of Philadelphia'. Buoyed by his success, Knight moved to a larger apartment at 1521 Spruce Street at a rent of $50 a month, quite a sum at the time but an indication of growing confidence in his movie criticism, now being syndicated. The first piece to feature on pages other than those of the *Public Ledger* had appeared in *The Town Crier* on February 7th. It concerned the film version of Hemingway's latest novel and the work of Hollywood's most celebrated director, John Ford, already a veteran of the film industry and a man who, by the end of his career, would have 145 movies to his credit.

Knight's criticism was forthright, blunt, cutting and unsparing. He took what he knew was a brave stance and refused to compromise his honesty with the tact he saw at work in his contemporaries. Few film critics existed at the time, and those who did, Knight said, were either 'literary reviewers ill-qualified for the job or young reporters with a passion for movies.' He considered himself, however, to have served his time in the movie theatres and to have read enough to know when a film adaptation of a novel was unfaithful to the author's original intent.

He believed he knew actors well enough to recognise a poor performance when he saw it and considered himself qualified to say so. He also knew from talking with other critics that even when they did loathe a film, they dared not say so publicly for fear of upsetting their editor or their public or Hollywood. 'They're all frightened pissless,' he told Hemingway, and came almost but not quite as directly to the point in his published criticism:

'Frequently, the movie critic does not want to say more than a few Anglo-Saxon words about the movies of today. Instead I will criticise the movie critic. The idea is that when a man becomes a critic a special kind of God gives him sagacity, knowledge and inside information withheld from the masses. And his readers let him get away with it. This is poohbah!

You might enjoy *Men Without Women*, although Hemingway fans will be disappointed if they think it will have anything to do with the book of the same name. John Ford the director clings to convention that started in the days of Bronco Billy and still believes that a pistol is fired from the region of the umbilicus. Hooey!'

It was in this, his first syndicated piece, that Knight made a reference to 'men awaiting death' acting 'amazingly like fat bullocks stolidly standing in a pen at the slaughterhouse'. The line shocked many readers, but at the same time ensured they would read his next column. Even though twelve years had passed since the end of the First World War, the memory of the carnage was never far from the surface and Knight chose to refer directly to it when many others, even those who had served, were avoiding the subject. His fear was that the war would be glorified on the screen, that film heroes would either survive by some undeserved miracle or that their death when it came would be accompanied by poignant words or some wisecrack designed to render it acceptable. He had hoped that the war would be represented in all its horror, and thereby act as a deterrent to further wars.

The way in which movie lives were cheaply and dramatically destroyed would remain a perpetual theme of Knight's criticism. But he was particularly angered by John Ford, whose reputation had never before been questioned and with whom he would later be obliged to work He was equally disgusted by the way the message of a well-written novel could be twisted once the film rights to it had been sold. 'If they can do that to Hemingway,' he said, 'then they can do it to anybody.'

In a further piece of criticism two weeks later, Knight gives away a little more of himself than he intended and more than he ever realised, for in it he divulges, subconsciously perhaps, that he knew more about his own family than he had ever disclosed: *Fanny Hawthorn* is a straightforward film lacking in artifice, all it did was remind me of visiting an Aunt in Lancashire where the sound of the girls' clogs rattled off the cobble stones.' The Aunt in Lancashire would return to Eric Knight's mind two years later, but for now she was just a slip of the tongue to which nobody paid any attention.

His reputation around Philadelphia was growing as the result of his newspaper features, and one cinema manager was quick to profit by it, a fact that Knight noted in his piece of February 28th 1930: 'I think I'm being kidded, I saw a sign outside a movie theatre that said 'To be reviewed – if Mr. Knight has the time'. This is ridiculous, everybody knows a movie critic has no time, just like a Queen has no legs.'

Having gained immediate notoriety from his swipe at Hollywood's foremost director, Knight felt no compunction in levelling equally scathing criticism at one of its leading men: 'John Barrymore has done a lot of terrible work in his movies. I suppose this statement is a treason that ranks along with the disavowing of the sanctity of American womanhood and the supremacy of the Nordic strain.'

'If anyone is safe from criticism,' he argued, 'the critic is not doing his job.' The way he saw it, theatre critics felt no compunction about panning a stage play, so why should Hollywood be treated any differently? This philosophy was based on his love of traditional theatre and Vaudeville, both of which he feared were dying as movie theatres proliferated. 'They are giving up their stars to Hollywood's production-line,' he wrote, and he was not about to let them get away with it, even if over fifty per cent of Americans were visiting the movies at least once every week. He further believed that brevity was vital to his work:

'It costs five cents to see the movie at the Beideker – save your dough!'

'Last week I called 'The Melody Maker' 'The Music Man'. Go ahead, sue me. Who cares!'

'I got sprung. I swore I'd never see or hear Rudy Vallee. My dear, he's just as cute as I thought he would be. Reminds me of my old Scout leader.'

'Baseball has a remarkable hold on the national consciousness, and for a long time I've been waiting for someone to make a rip-roaring film about it. *They Learned About Women* ain't it!'

It is clear that he was enjoying his new position and the fame it was bringing. Nobody in the history of criticism had dared be this direct: 'It is two days now since I saw *His First Command* and I have forgotten almost everything about it, including the nasty remarks I made at its expense.'

It must be remembered that the Hollywood movie machine was turning out a film a day per studio at this time. Unsurprisingly, not all were of a quality that met with the Knight standard – though some were:

'Fetch all the laurels you can find and run them down here, they're to be laid at the feet of all those involved in *Seven Days' Leave*'

'It's seven days since I saw *Ingagi* and I still feel as though I'd walked through a machine gun barrage.'

By April 1930, *The Town Crier* had become essential reading for Philadelphians. It had apparently done what it set out to do and had had relieved 'the tedium of Philadelphia', the disparaging tag-line having been dropped. The magazine was glossy and classy; it carried hints on couture for both sexes; showcased fashionable places to eat, advertisements for stores selling expensive clothes and for garages selling the latest motor cars. Further syndication in similar publications meant Knight's film criticism was being read further afield, but that did nothing to curb his style: 'If I live to be a hundred, the phenomenon that is Charles Farrell and Janet Gaynor will still be the greatest of mysteries to me.'

A significant change to Knight's weekly feature on cinema offerings came about in May 1930 when his column's heading, *The Movies*, was dropped in favour of *The Talkies*. The first talking pictures had been poor, providing only novelty value. By 1930, however, the sound quality was becoming acceptable, but Eric Knight always preferred the silents. He argued that in them the story had to be told, demonstrated, while the talkies could 'explain' in a few words that which a silent movie actor needed a whole scene to express. 'Conversely,' he offered, 'an entire page of text might be demonstrated by a quality actor or actress in one simple facial expression.' Talking pictures, in Knight's view, could only detract from the artistic nature of a silent movie where the entire concentration of the viewer was on the action. He recognised of course that talking pictures would, if nothing else, 'offer opportunities to actors who could speak', and if the voice and acting ability were matched by excellent cinematography, then the result could be exciting, but he voiced doubts that all three would ever meet on one movie set.

In his view: 'The talkie has done this: it has slowed down the story telling medium. It has limited it by language borders; it has changed the whole damn business around telling the story through the ear instead of the eye.'

These words represent an odd paradox. Here was a man who had been raised on oral story-telling, one who would go on to tell hundreds by word-of-mouth – yet he wanted the movies to tell their story in silence. 'Words or pictures,' he said, 'but not both'. When it became obvious that the talkies were here to stay, he was obliged to formulate new thoughts on the matter. He came to believe that trained theatre actors might maintain the belief of the movie-goer if the right balance was struck between the action and the words, but he had little confidence in the ability of directors to perform this delicate trick.

Behind Knight's conjectures on the merits or otherwise of the talkies lay an idea to which he would devote much of his time, one to which sound reproduction would be put to good use – the documentary. He would come to view the documentary as the perfect vehicle for film, and was quick to see that the genre could be furthered by the introduction of a sound narrative guiding the viewer, while the only other voices to be heard would be those of the subjects under study. The idea became something of an obsession, and some years later he would be able to put his theories to the test.

Talking pictures, however, were the coming thing. It would be Sam Warner, along with his brothers Harry, Albert and Jack, who would perfect the system of voice synchronisation with a device produced by Bell Laboratories – a company jointly owned by those giants of American commercial communications, Western Electric, and the American Telephone and Telegraph Companies. Posters appeared outside cinemas and on hoardings:

> At Last, Pictures that Talk like Living People. Warner Bros
> VITAPHONE Talking Pictures – If it's NOT a WARNER PICTURE it's
> NOT VITAPHONE

'GARBO TALKS' read another film poster, promoting Metro Goldwyn Meyer's *Anna Christie*. It must have brought a smile to Eric Knight's lips. Two years earlier he had had this to say of the Swedish star: "Romance' brings the much-mooted talents of Greta Garbo to the screen. I don't like anaemic looking females. I don't like Garbo's guttural voice. I don't like stories about Italian prima-donnas. I don't think Garbo could give a passable characterization of an Italian opera singer if she lived to be a hundred – even if I did like 'em.'

If that was Knight at his most acerbic, a screen adaptation of a favourite novel had him damning with faint praise: "The Dawn Patrol' is a decent film, which it needs to be, it's no more than 'Journey's End' repeated three times.'

Journey's End marked the first ever collaboration between British and American studios, Gainsborough/Welsh-Pearson/Tiffany-Stahl, and represents Knight's only reference to a British production. That in itself is hardly surprising: in the early days of movie distribution a deal had been struck in Britain which meant ninety percent of their yearly programme would consist of US-made movies, the industry being in its absolute infancy in Britain and unable to satisfy the public's demand for variety. This meant only ten percent of films being shown in America were British, one of them being this adaptation of R. C. Sherriff's autobiographical novel.

Journey's End – first performed on stage in 1929 – studies a relationship under the stress of trench warfare between Captain Stanhope, his second-in-command, Osborne, the newly-arrived lieutenant Raleigh, and the cowardly Hibbert. This understated, restrained work was said by *Punch* to be 'Hollywood's first sex-appeal-less film'. For this reason, and because the film has a distinct documentary style, it met with Knight's approval.

There were of course no explicitly portrayed scenes of a sexual nature in the movies of the time – and what scenes there were would be confined by the so-called Hays Code of 1930, which set out guidelines for morally acceptable productions – but as *Punch* pointed out, there had never been a talkie which did not at least 'hold out the promise of some sexual content'. Movie makers, while constrained by a largely self-imposed moral code were, however, not slow to exploit the sexuality of their stars or to choose movie titles promising more than they were able to deliver, a fact on which Knight was not slow to pounce: '*Unguarded Girls*, if you don't like sex you won't go, and if you do like sex you won't get any.'

The Talkies feature was now taking preference in the *Town Crier* over almost every other element of the magazine, including the short stories of Knight's that it was publishing. Among these was *The Leff Clown* – first published in *Story* magazine – which picks up on the theme of what Eric perceived to be a growing disillusionment with Hollywood. It tells the story of a promising actor who gives up a stage career in order to follow a mundane occupation. 'Most stories,' Knight warned his readers, 'have a happy ending, this one does not.' *The Leff Clown* acted as an antidote to Hollywood's obsession with 'the happy-ever-after'. Knight knew that life was not like that, and while much of his work would involve escapism in its most literal form, he saw no cinematic value in it.

Whether he knew it or not, Knight was developing an enduring style which, in keeping with the teachings of his uncle Richard Hallas on what a story should be and what it should leave to its readers, he would hone and perfect over the coming years in a body of 'fiction' which, with hindsight, may now be seen for what it actually is: social documentary and autobiography. And while he refused throughout his life to write his biography and even deliberately misled biographers, he stated, in a letter to his friend and attorney, Barnie Winkelman, 'If a man writes fiction, he writes his biography'.

These few words to Winkelman are the nearest Knight ever came to admitting in print that the key to the truth about his life was in his fiction. Interestingly, they are contained in a letter of just five two-line paragraphs, yet there exists a draft copy which has been considerably edited and altered, a clear indication that even in brief correspondence with close friends he chose his words very carefully in order to say only what he wanted to say, only what was relevant, only what he wanted people to believe. And it must be remembered that he never intended his private words to escape into the public domain. So he may have given away more in the odd unguarded moment than he intended, like the reference to an Aunt in Lancashire, or the odd sentence about the war, and he may have slipped in moments of depression into confused tenses, into which we may read more than he would have meant to impart. But these slips tell us a great deal about his inner thoughts. At times of great anxiety he also occasionally let slip despairing words on the fate of humanity, but 'the truth', as far as it may be ascertained, lay more in what he omitted or amended or erased, and in the words and actions he gave to his so-called 'fictional' characters that they might act out his own joy and pain.

o0o

The Great Depression may have had America in its grip, but Eric Knight had a good job, plenty of money, a growing readership and regular take-up of his stories and articles. In September, his mother's marriage to

Simon Kahn came to an end, Kahn thereafter lodging with friends Richard and Bertha Broge while Marian Hilda moved in with her sister Nell, and Nell's common-law husband, Elmer Moor. Knight rarely mentioned the break-up, probably because his relationship with his mother had been less close since he returned from the war – and she had never fully recovered from losing her two older sons.

On September 10th 1931, Knight became an American citizen. His passport, stamped that day, shows he had never officially changed his name and that he was still 'Eric Oswald'. This was not the first time he had changed citizenship. And it would not be the last. His final 'conversion' coming in 1942 when close friend Paul Horgan would act as his sponsor. Horgan would later write, 'Eric felt loyalty to both countries, that of his birth, and that which gave him opportunity'. September 10th, however, would live in Knight's memory for a different reason.

His fame was now such that he was recognised in the streets of Philadelphia, his picture accompanying every article he wrote. In some respects, he felt, he was becoming 'public property'. He received telephone calls from irate cinema managers, the occasional incandescent actor's agent, and members of the public, usually over some piece of written work with which they wished to take issue. These calls were expected and dealt with courteously, but the one he received on that pleasant September morning left him speechless. Later, he felt compelled to note its content:

'Is this Mr. Eric Knight?'
'Yes, this is Eric Knight.'
'The Eric Knight who used to live in Fairfield, Connecticut?'
'The same. Who is this?'
'This is Betty.'
'Betty who?'
'Your daughter Betty.'

Betty was in a phone booth in a drug-store around the corner from his office. He raced out to meet her. She was fourteen and had been sent to Philadelphia to begin her working life, having dropped out of school. Eric had written to his daughters, regularly, but his letters were never seen by them. His attorney had sent money to them, but had not disclosed Knight's address. It was by sheer happenstance that Betty arrived in Philadelphia and found her father's picture staring at her from the pages of a newspaper – and now the truth behind the years of silence came out. The girls had been told that their father was dead. Knight knew only too well how this felt. After all, from his mother's stories, he believed his own father to have been killed in the Boer War.

The news of this deception might be an indication of just how deeply

Dorothy had been hurt by the failure of her husband's newspaper business, which dragged the school and their marriage down with it. In many respects it was the least cruel thing to say to the girls and afforded her at least some level of respectability at a time when there were thousands of war widows with young children to support. Divorce was not common in the 1920s and was almost always looked upon as the result of the failure of a wife to please her husband. Widowhood, at least, was without social stigma.

From this moment on, Betty would never be far from her father's side. There exists no record of where she worked, though she gave her father's address as her own and Knight would tell his attorney he was supporting her. The joy of being reunited seems to have been the catalyst for a prolific period of writing with articles featuring in an increasing number of magazines. Betty, however, was not the only woman in Eric Knight's life and he regularly attended the theatre and concerts with a female friend whose name he never mentions in writing. He does say that she left Philadelphia for a job in New York City and that they had one last evening out together before she departed for a new life. They went to hear a concert and afterwards dined at a fashionable restaurant. There, Eric bumped into a friend who introduced him to a woman ten years his junior. She remembered the occasion well.

'We'd been to the Philadelphia Orchestra and dropped in afterwards at the Russian Inn where a mutual friend introduced me to Eric Knight. I was working for the League of Nations Association. Eric and I got into this fantastic argument about wars. He said there would always be wars because wars offered things we can't get in peace.'

Nowhere in Knight's writing does he make any reference to the views he expressed that evening; it may be that he was referring to patriotism and heroism but it is far more likely he was talking of the triumph of good over evil. His words left a lasting impression on Ruth Brylawski, for she recognised him immediately when they met again the following spring:

'Eric came through the door all dressed up. He said: 'There's a newspaper party. I'll introduce you to a world you never knew.' I went to the party with Eric and that was it, just like that. He was multitalented, not only a film critic with a formidable reputation but an artist who had studied at the Boston School of Fine Arts, as well as a born story-teller and a magnetism that could light up a room. He had perfect pitch. Hum a tune and he could play it.'

While Knight's 'stories' captivated everyone, and were entirely believed, Ruth spotted immediately his talent for telling them, but she too fell for their magic. She believed the one about the Boston School of Fine Arts, which was not, strictly speaking, true. He had certainly 'studied' the art works at the Boston School while a student at the Cambridge Latin School, but had never taken a course.

58

As with all good story-tellers do, Knight had mixed the truth with fiction, a trick he employed many times to great effect but a device he knew might, paradoxically, work against him. In that final letter written many years later to his attorney, Winkelman, he provides another small but vital clue as to his motivation for almost always misleading would-be biographers. Winkelman, a biographer in his own right who had written a well-received work on Rockefeller, asked Eric why he had not considered allowing a biographer to write his life story. The answer is worth repeating, because it provides almost the only key to unlocking the door to the complex workings of the Knight philosophy: 'No-one could write it but me because no-one knows anything about me. Ninety percent of what's been written is half-true, which is worse than a total lie because it sounds more credible.'

And the reason 'ninety percent' of what had been written was only half true was because Knight himself had misled its writers, which of course meant that if he ever did write a biography, and tell the truth in it, it would reveal how he had misled almost everyone he ever knew, including his closest friends. Conversely, if he were unable to resist the story-teller's urge to embellish that truth, the result would be a work that would only serve to misinform its readers and would therefore defeat its own object. Half the truth sounded credible, Knight had said, and he knew that to be the case, having earned an income from it since the publication of *The Two-Fifty Hat*, a story that sounded true because it was, but sold only because he labelled it 'fiction'. It was the forerunner of subsequent tales that contained the truth and fiction in equal parts. And now he had a new outlet for his stories – Ruth Brylawski.

Like Eric, Ruth was multi-talented. She spoke German, having learned the language from her mother, her grandmother and the young immigrant servant girls employed by her wealthy parents at their Philadelphia home. She also spoke fluent French and at the age of fifteen had spent a year in Paris before entering college. She found herself the only girl majoring in primordial studies at the University of Pennsylvania and the lone female when taking a Masters degree in political science. She worked as an executive secretary with the League of Nations, later in the movie world, finding and evaluating foreign language film scripts, especially those in French, which she then translated for studio consideration.

As a teenager, Ruth had shown collies and practised her skills at fencing, becoming so proficient in the sport that she had been recruited to the US Olympic Fencing Team at about the same time she became engaged to Robert Archer Pierce, grandson of Franklin Pierce, 14th President of the United States. The relationship, however, had not endured and she was a single woman when she attended the newspaper party with Eric Knight. They would be married eight months later on December 2nd at

Philadelphia's City Hall, Ruth having withdrawn from the Olympic Team to be with her man.

The two were perfectly matched. They both loved dogs and horses, Ruth had had a Quaker upbringing, they shared a love of music and she was possessed of a sense of humour equal to his, a commodity she had needed early in the relationship when, having discovered her German roots, he began calling her 'Jere'. They made an exceptional couple. Eric Knight alone was irresistible company in any circle, but he and Jere together were magnetic and would later number among their friends those at the very top of their literary, artistic and political careers.

Just a few months into the courtship, Eric received news that his mother had died. And it fell to Eric, rather than to his aunt Nell, to go through the family papers. Nell's grief overwhelmed her emotions and led to an outpouring of secrets she had kept from her late sister but could hide no longer. The husband she had lost in 1912, the man who had called himself John Harrison, was, in fact, Eric's father, Frederic Harrison Knight. He had not fought in the Boer War but had sold his share in Frederic H. Knight & Co. Ltd to his brother. Lewis Edwin Knight had taken the business over in 1902 when it became L E Knight – Wholesale Jeweller, whereupon Frederic Harrison Knight changed his name to John Harrison. After a period of separation he had moved in with Nell and his sons. Eric, as we have seen, fell in love with Marjorie Harrison on leaving for the Cambridge Latin School, but through the outpouring of Nell's secrets he now knew that she and her sister Freda were not cousins but his father's daughters, and therefore his half-sisters.

All the time young Eric had imagined his father a hero, lying in some unmarked grave in a far-off land, he was alive and well and living in a rural village with two of his three sons, having fathered offspring by sisters who had produced their children within months of one another under the same roof. Indeed, Nell had been pregnant with Marjorie when Noel Mowbray Knight died early in 1898.

Nell explained that Knight Senior had been deeply disturbed by his son Noel's death and had been unable to cope with the tragedy, but Eric felt cheated, and he felt for his own daughters who had endured the same sense of loss. Nell had not told her sister of the real circumstances behind her marriage to John Harrison so she had died never knowing the truth.

Suddenly, all the disparate pieces of a complex jigsaw fell into place. The uncomfortable relationship between Eric and his brothers was now explained; they had been told not to reveal John Harrison's actual identity and to maintain the deceit no matter what. Knight Senior's final resting place, for which Eric's mother had searched in vain, could not be found because it never existed.

And there was further discomfort: Knight's mother and father, Eric discovered, had never actually been married. There was no marriage certificate, and when its absence was questioned the truth emerged. It also transpired that Knight's Uncle Lewis had left his apparently successful business in the hands of John Joseph Knight at the same time that Nell emigrated to the United States. Lewis had taken his family to Canada, where they lived simply and without the trappings of wealth. The business had continued trading in his name until 1915 when it disappeared without trace.

His mother's death and the truths it uncovered prompted Eric Knight to reveal a family secret of his own. In his criticism of *Fanny Hawthorn*, he had said the film reminded him of his Aunt's home in Lancashire. This is the only mention he ever made in writing of the woman he had found following his visit to Yorkshire immediately after his war service. Her whereabouts had been revealed by Eric's Uncle Percy who had told Eric when he was a boy that Marion and Harriet had 'disappeared' without explanation.

There had, however, been a significant shift in attitudes after the first war when rules governing social etiquette became more relaxed. In this mood of change and under questioning from his nephew, Percy had admitted he knew the whereabouts of one of the girls who had been his 'sisters' but who he now realised were his nieces, their mother being his eldest sister. Upon hearing that news, Eric had cycled out across the Pennines to seek out his cousin. He found a woman in the same mould as their uncles, a jovial and kindly person who worked in the cotton mills and who related tales of her early life, punctuated with joyful laughter. Eric chose not to reveal which of his two cousins she was, using instead the name Molly, but her parentage and that of her sister was clear; they were the illegitimate children of the eldest of the Creasser girls, Ada, and had been taken in by their grandparents to be brought up as their own.

Having pondered all he had learned and the fact that he had been deceived, Eric remembered his mother's distress on returning from France after visiting the last resting places of her lost sons in 1930. The trip had been organised by an American Jewish organisation but embraced mothers from all denominations. On her way back to the United States she had stopped off at Liverpool and journeyed to Yorkshire to search the cemeteries of Leeds for the grave of her first husband, believing he might have shipped home from South Africa as an invalid and later died.

She placed flowers, Eric recalled, at the headstones of her late brother-in-law Richard Hallas and her sister Nell's husband John Harrison, who had expressed a desire to be laid to rest in his home city. She would die apparently still convinced her husband lay in an unmarked grave somewhere in South Africa and never knowing she had accidentally honoured him under his assumed name.

By the autumn of 1932, Eric and Jere Knight were living at 626 West

Chuzden Avenue, Mount Airy, Pennsylvania. They embarked on a honeymoon cruise during which Eric fell ill, Jere favouring some kind of food poisoning as the probable cause. The patient, however, knew better – his drinking had reached a stage where his health was being compromised. He was otherwise fit and not a roaring drunk but he had grown used to taking too much alcohol on a regular basis. He reminded himself of how, as he put it, 'the drink had gotten hold of Hemingway' and determined he would not emulate his friend. He accepted that what he described as 'a collapse' had been a warning, and he was heeding it.

The cruise over, Eric was joyfully reunited with his other two daughters. This was cause for great celebration and he decided to celebrate with a vacation in Mexico later in the year.

Above: Eric Knight with Toots. Below: Eric Knight's drawing of Aunt Kit circa 1912, when Eric was 15 and shortly before he went to the USA.

Above: Eric Knight's brothers, Edmund and Frederic – both killed in action June 28th, 1917. Below: Eric Knight, publicity shot for Princess Patricia's Canadian Light Infantry, 1917.

Above: Sketch for portrait of Eric Knight, by artist Peter Hurd.

Left: Eric Knight, self-portrait California 1935.

Right: Eric and Jere, at the Hurd ranch, San Patricio, New Mexico.

Below: From the left – Jere on Bourbon, Eric on Flying Cloud, Elissa Landi, Hollywood actress – Mary Pickford, and Elissa Landi's brother Toni.

CHAPTER EIGHT

It took place over the following Christmas. What Eric saw down below the border prompted not just written words but drawings of great power. One depicted poverty-stricken Mexicans begging at the feet of a blindfold Uncle Sam. Another showed a Madonna-like woman with a baby at her breast being dragged by her hair into the wilderness. Further drawings captured Indians dancing around a blazing fire on a feast day.

Not wishing to miss an opportunity to sell a story, Knight would combine his honeymoon cruise and the trip to Mexico to sell '*Friendly Smiles are Current Coin in Five Kinds of Mexico*', a short work, published in *Steamship News* in 1933, which explored his impressions of a uniquely diverse society. Knight would visit Mexico several times and always be touched by the warmth of the people, their courage in the face of poverty and their unwavering faith in their religion.

America was already a multi-cultural society when Eric Knight arrived there in 1912, but he perceived 'a need to Americanise its people', a process he had passed through at the hands of his mother and step-father. In Mexico, he saw that the people admired the wealth of America and would take any opportunity to settle there, but he feared that their rich culture might be diluted by mass migration. He formed a view – only reinforced by his further visits – that a multi-cultural society could function peacefully and gainfully while retaining all the diverse religious and cultural traditions of its members, if only an attitude of mutual respect could be embraced.

Indeed, in just the same way Orwell would prescribe socialism for the class-driven ills of Britain, Knight would come to believe that cultural diversity was not counter to the ethos of Americanism but a vital part of its success. He may have been the only writer of any note voicing this opinion at the time, and it would be several years before he would make his feelings publicly known, but this first visit to Mexico set in train a stream of cultural

67

consciousness which would permeate his later and most critically acclaimed works.

One of Knight's first tasks in moving into his new home had been to write a letter to a man in England whom he knew only from reading his 1930 book, *The Film Till Now*, a work which reflected Knight's own thoughts on the film industry and its future role. The two men would strike up an enduring friendship and embark on a body of correspondence, which sheds much light on our subject. The man was Paul Rotha – although at that time he was still known by his original name of Thompson - a twenty-five-year-old English documentary filmmaker living in Berkshire.

Rotha widely condemned the output of movie-makers, seeing the film medium as one that would be better employed in the production of social documentaries. He would expound this theory over a thirty-year period, during which he would make no less than thirteen highly acclaimed documentary films and produce nine books, one of which, *Portrait of a Flying Yorkshireman*, chronicles the Knight/Rotha correspondence.

Rotha had also studied art, in his case at the Slade School where he gained a deep appreciation of German Expressionism. He had won a coveted costume design prize at the Paris International Theatre Exhibition before being taken on by *British International Pictures* at Elstree. There he rose to the position of Assistant Art Director. He lost this job, however, when, like Knight, he criticised the film industry in print. Despite this setback, his interest in documentary films only intensified when he met the legendary John Grierson, then working with the Empire Marketing Board.

Grierson told the younger man that if he wished to succeed in films it was unlikely he would do so with the name Paul Thompson. That he chose the name Rotha is significant. It came from a friend, Rotha Linton-Orman. Linton-Orman had served in the Women's Reserve Ambulance Corps and after the war had been head of the Red Cross Motor School. An ardent Royalist, Imperialist and Nationalist who was alarmed by the rise of the Labour Party in the 1920s, she had been inspired in 1923 to found the quaintly named British Fascisti. How she came to be so closely associated with Thompson, a socialist, is not clear, but the fact that he adopted her name and carried it throughout his life suggests an intimacy. As director of the organisation, Linton-Orman had recruited as head of security a man called Maxwell Knight, who would become a significant player in Eric's life a few years later.

Paul Rotha's mentor, Grierson, was a pioneer of documentary film production and a graduate in Moral Philosophy. He had been in the US in the 1920s as a Rockefeller Research Fellow, the focus of his studies being 'The psychology of propaganda and the impact of the press and film in forming public opinion'. He had film criticism in common with Knight and Rotha and had written for the New York *Sun*. His greatest significance, however, to both his contemporaries and to the film industry, would lie in his coining of the term 'documentary' which appeared on February 8th 1926 in his critique of *Moana*, a film following the life of a Polynesian boy and his family produced by Robert Flaherty, another notable film maker on whose work Knight would later lecture.

Flaherty's theme was always the struggle of humanity against the elements. He had been recruited by Hollywood in its earliest days but rejected when he refused to bend to the required artistic style. He had faced a dilemma while filming his 1921 classic *Nanook of the North* when he realised that he was beginning to 'direct' the action rather than simply record it, telling the Inuit people not to spear a seal, for example, until the cameras, light and conditions were as he wanted them. He grew uneasy with what he described as 'romanticised reality' or what we might call 'docu-drama' today.

When Knight heard this, it resonated with the concept he had in his mind of the character Sam Small: a real, if larger-than-life, character who faced the challenges affecting ordinary people and who should not be 'directed' in his actions. Everything he did should represent 'reality', and this aspiration presented Knight with his greatest literary challenge: how could Sam Small do on paper all he did in the mind of his chronicler and not be too fantastic to believe? Only when this detail was settled would Sam appear to a public who embraced his every word and, regardless of his feats, accepted him as Knight intended him to be: 'just an ord'nary Yorkshire lad'.

Flaherty and Grierson would further shape the Knight mindset through their 1931 collaboration *Industrial Britain*, a sponsored work on which the two, despite their undoubted talents, did not enjoy a happy relationship. Flaherty adopted what Grierson saw as a somewhat cavalier attitude to a limited budget while his own practice involved spending the absolute minimum. Arguments followed, which served to detract from the potency of the finished work. The less-than-perfect result of what should have been a successful collaboration would lead Knight to the view that, 'Those financing documentary should give the film maker a camera and all the time he needs to produce a damn good film.'

He had realised in the early 1920s that film had a role to play as 'witness' to events rather than as a 'participant' by directorial intervention, a ground-breaking theory at a time when a commercial film-maker's first instinct was to take control of every action he recorded. There was clear demarcation in Eric's mind between news, story, and what later filmmakers would call reportage. And though these genres were not yet clearly defined, Knight was sure they were individual disciplines, which required tailored expertise. What he would search for in documentary was objectivity, the reporting of the facts and the facts alone, the emphasis of any work being placed on its subjects and how they lived and worked, such that any audience seeing the work might form their own view on what they had seen. His main interest was in the plight of the oppressed working class and minority groups, but he further realised that the genre might leave itself open to abuse by filmmakers who could use their output to further their own political cause.

It seems clear that, had an opportunity presented itself at this time for Knight to go into documentary filmmaking he might never have embarked on a literary career. Almost his entire future literary output would address real-life issues, which they did with a sense of drama born from his love for story-telling and folklore. This, combined with deep sensitivity and an instinctive expertise in the art of narrative construction, coupled with keen observation and understanding of human nature. Knight's documentary opportunity would not come until 1942 when he and Rotha would work together, but before then the latter would make celebrated films about aircraft production, ship manufacture and, most importantly to Eric Knight, the living and working conditions of ordinary working people.

In his early correspondence with Rotha, Knight gave very little of himself away – even obscuring his English roots: 'I always find the countryside part of this country so damn vital and thrilling. Life is so fast, the roads go on for hundreds of miles and nothing to do but follow them, not roads that make you pause like your English roads, but concrete highways straight as a die.'

He goes on to describe a weekend spent at the home of the legendary Hollywood producer Adolph Zukor, who, impressed by Knight's criticism, had invited him to his house to quiz him on the market in Philadelphia, home to some 200 movie theatres. Reporting on Zukor's house, Knight wrote, 'It's like nothing on earth, except, perhaps, a Hollywood movie come to your doorstep in flesh and blood.'

In the same letter he also spoke of his job in an apparent attempt to contrast his work in the US with that of counterparts in Britain: 'I'm pounding away and giving thanks for this excellent paper which holds no check rein on what I write, allows no-one to edit anything I put through, and backs me up against the almighty advertiser in times of stress.'

He would never have said in what esteem he was held and did not mention Zukor by name, or the fact that the godlike Samuel Goldwyn had also consulted him, by letter, on the subject of Philadelphia's movie theatres. His next letter would be largely in praise of Mexico and the Christmas vacation he had spent there with Jere and his three daughters. And while he had still not encountered the Navajo, he had come into contact with their Mexican cousins: 'Back from Mexico and still fearfully excited about it. The Mexicans are fine people – independent as hell. Much Lenin literature in paperback and Indians who sit unmoving in the sun. The damn Indians with nothing at all and no desire for more. The passionate desire for progress among the new Whites and half-Indians – God, what a country! Sense of death and a fatal acceptance of it.'

It is perhaps easy to see why Knight identified more clearly with the poor Indians than with the Americans among whom he had now lived for twenty years: they were, he said, 'more like the inhabitants of Yorkshire than Mexicans'. And though he had embraced the American way of life to a certain extent, and taken citizenship, he was detached enough to stand apart from what was going on around him and to view it as an outsider: 'Here, now, America seems ghastly pallid and almost indecent – the people, all an indecent white color – rather, strangely unbrown, pale people, overwhelmed with the depression, wildly clutching at clichés they can understand to serve in a Depression they can't fathom.'

The contrast of wealth and poverty in the States was amplified in Knight's mind when he returned from Mexico. Having suffered financially while the rest of America was bracing itself against severe constraints, the Knights were far from impoverished. They were not wealthy but they could afford two servants, a man and wife they had taken off 'local relief', the equivalent of the dole system. The couple presented their new employer with a personal conundrum. He had spoken and written on every man's right to freedom and now had an opportunity to improve the lot of two people by giving them a home and employment; but they were black. Was he simply enslaving them all over again?

Pushing such doubts aside, he did the practical thing and moved them into West Chuzden Avenue to begin work. Rotha had written from South Africa where he was filming; his letter was full of the social injustice and white supremacy he witnessed. Knight replied at length on the matter:

'I have been thinking about your outraged sense of the exploitation of the Negro in Africa. You should be here. The Negro here is supposed to be a jolly sort of childlike entertainer, happily singing all day about 'white boss frowning' and 'someone had to plant the cotton and that's why darkies was born'. The Negro accepts this because he knows if he doesn't the ignorance of white scum rises in mob violence that leads to Negro-burning atrocities. In the south where all men are supposed to be equal, the Negro has not been allowed to vote for years. They have the franchise – but pity the poor Negro who tries to exercise it.'

He went on to talk about the relationship between himself and his employees: 'I have two Negro servants. Even yet I haven't been able to make them understand that, being part of my household, they are part of my life's responsibilities, that they must work honestly and in return expect to get truth, consideration, fairness in every detail. They do work honestly, but seem to expect anger for it. The girl accidentally threw away some papers I had been working on, 'I suppose you just feel like slapping me,' she said. It makes me hopelessly angry to feel we give these people little more to expect than 'slapping'.'

Over the years, Knight and Rotha would exchange views on injustice and oppression, on which topics they unfailingly concurred. Knight, however, made it clear he did not share Rotha's socialist politics. He described himself as a Quaker, but Rotha labelled him a Humanist, 'a man who believes in freedom for all in a tolerant society working for the collective good of its many individuals.'

Knight justified his own most paradoxical dualities – those of pacifist and soldier, agnostic and believer, intellectual scholar and working class labourer, and the anti-bureaucrat who believed that strong political leadership was the only way to true democracy. Most striking, however, was the concept of his own nationality, for if questioned on this subject he described himself, 'English, American, but this above all –Yorkshireman'.

The enduring element of all his pre-World War II letters, however, was always the movies; the critic in him being even more scathing in private than he was in public. He tore apart the cinematic icons of the day and railed against the great directors whose work he likened to tableaux, 'still and lifeless, beautiful but stationary'. And, he repeated his private views in his newspaper and magazine criticism, minus the swear-words he used liberally when angered. Though he was unaware of the fact, he was becoming known two thousand miles away in Hollywood as 'the enemy of the movie industry'. Hollywood would suffer the barrage of criticism for another twelve months before responding as only Hollywood could.

The house in Chuzden Avenue was comfortable but did not live up to Knight's idea of country living, so when an opportunity arose to move to a rambling old farmhouse with ten acres of land, he took it. Pentacres lay just off the Country Club and Valley Park Roads in Chester County, close to both Valley Forge and Phoenixville, and the rent was just $60 a month. Here Knight farmed, kept horses, and took riding lessons from his wife, an experience which led to the publication of 'How Not To Ride A Horse' in the April 1934 issue of Philadelphia's *Merry Go Round* magazine.

Making the most of a new-found riding skill in which he would find unending pleasure, Knight discovered, deep in the Pennsylvania hills, what he called a 'a cock-eyed building in the woods'. The house, which he had taken to be uninhabited, was in fact the studio of Wharton Esherick, a woodworker who would come to be known as 'the Dean of American Craftsmen'. Esherick had been a painter, but turned to carving after finding that his customers were buying his works as much for their superbly carved frames as for the works they contained. He told Knight he felt a deep sense of attachment to his materials and saw ways of expressing images through woodworking, which later commentators have described as impressionist or cubist expressionist. His life had changed when, having read Thoreau's *Walden*, he gave up his teaching job in Alabama to seek what he called 'the simple life based on honest meaningful work'.

Esherick told Knight he had been so poor at one point that he had sold his kitchen table to feed his family, who had to eat off trays on their knees until a replacement could be made. This tale was adopted by Knight who later wrote that he and Jere 'had to sell the family silver' and even 'the family candlesticks' – stories that impressed many but which were blown away when Jere admitted, years later, that they'd never actually owned any silver.

Wharton Esherick was also an excellent teacher and instructed Knight in cabinet-making, a skill he would put to good use in 1939, building his own writing-desk from a fallen walnut tree. Riding home after a visit to Esherick's, Knight met a stranger, a poor farmer and wood-yard owner who invited him to look over the car engine he had adapted to run a saw-bench, and the band-saw he had made from old bicycle wheels. Knight, having laboured in more than one sawmill, was fascinated. Then the man told him how, thirty years earlier, German woodsmen had swept the valley for walnut trees and felled them, using the timber to shape thousands of rifle-butts. These had been shipped back to Germany where they had been attached to barrels, forging guns that would be used against the Pennsylvania Light Infantry. Eric had been as intrigued by the ingenuity of the simple lumberyard owner as he had the artistry of Esherick, but his creative inspiration would be enhanced by the friendship of three other artists living and working in Valley Forge, all of whom would rise to prominence.

Chadds Ford, Pennsylvania was the home of N.C. (Newell Conyers) Wyeth and his family. Wyeth, born in Needham, Massachusetts, had, like Knight, attended school in Boston where he had gained a Drafting Degree from the Mechanic Art School. His love of drawing and his outstanding skill had steered him to illustration. He had received his first commission from Philadelphia's *Saturday Evening Post*, and his work would appear in children's classics, magazines and poetry editions. Knight was fascinated by his ability to complete a masterly canvas in a single morning before moving onto his next project. Wyeth's son, Andrew, the youngest of five children, began studying with his father at an early age. He never attended school because his father felt that the most critical years in an artist's life might be spent pointlessly studying topics that would never be as useful to him as his artistic ability.

Andrew Wyeth was only a teenager when Knight met him. He would hold his first Watercolour Exhibition in 1937 at New York's Macbeth Gallery at the age of twenty, selling every canvas. The eldest of the Wyeth children, Henriette – whom Eric had courted briefly on his return to Philadelphia – had married her father's assistant Peter Hurd in 1929. Hurd would become one of Knight's closest friends and produce the surreal portrait depicting the colours of nature as seen by Knight. Hurd had been at West Point for two years; long enough for the twenty-three-year old to decide it was not a military but an artistic career he sought. He enrolled at the Haverford College in Pennsylvania where he became captivated by NC Wyeth's work, and since Wyeth lived nearby in Chadds Ford, the young man had approached him and became a private pupil. Peter Hurd came from Roswell, New Mexico, and was something of a novelty in Pennsylvania in his denims, cowboy boots and hat.

Wyeth had warned his pupil that artistic study would be much more arduous than anything he might have faced in military training, and after five years Hurd had to agree that was indeed the case. In 1933 Hurd, who longed to capture the exceptional light in his native land, moved to El Sentinel Ranch in San Patricio, New Mexico. He made the move with the help of Eric Knight, who travelled with the Hurds and helped them settle into their new home.

As an army cadet, Hurd had been stationed at the New Mexico Military Institute. There he joined the queue of men waiting for a hand-painted library card produced by Paul Horgan, their librarian officer. Horgan recognised Hurd's talent and the two became friends, Horgan often spending his vacation with the Wyeth family. While Horgan's art would become highly esteemed, it was his writing that brought him his most prized laurels, two Pulitzer Prizes for History.

Back from helping the Hurds move into their ranch, Knight resumed his relentless attack on the movies, motivated in part by Rotha, the only writer of his acquaintance to share his views. But there was praise, unsurprisingly perhaps, for British actor Charles Laughton's portrayal of the King in *The Private Life of Henry VIII*, although Knight's feature in *Merry Go Round* criticised Hollywood for not utilising Laughton's talents more fully. There is a note of resignation in his manner, which suggests he was beginning to feel that his single-handed crusade to reform the filmmaking industry was being lost, and again he refers to Hollywood's 'factory output mentality'. Knight now raised a matter in *The Musical Record* which no other writer had paid attention to: cinema music. His view was that soundtrack music should complement the action in the same way the cinema organ had in the silent movie era.

By the end of 1933 Knight's reputation was leading to commissions from all manner of magazines and newspapers, their readers thoroughly enjoying the forthright views of a man who was seen as the antidote to Hollywood's self-aggrandisement. He himself saw no reason to choose his words carefully, despite being aware now of his reputation in Hollywood where movie moguls found from their latest copy of *Cinema Quarterly* that they were being fired on from both sides of the Atlantic, Paul Rotha having been appointed the magazine's London correspondent. In the autumn edition, Knight's anger leaps off the page: 'After many years of writing on the cinema I have begun to despair…. The would-be filmmaker here and in Britain would do well to bottle up their energy…. [It] would be better expended on good quality films which could be distributed from a central bureau to schools and picture clubs. Thus the public, fed for years on the dope of sex stories, could be made to realize that the screen can give us something far more stirring and vital than *Cocktail Hour* or *Gold Diggers of 1933*.

Knight was promoting here privately funded 'sub-calibre' films of documentary value that could educate and inform. And he spoke from a position of some authority, having been commissioned by RCA Victor to make such a film. The commission came about as the result of pressure from another of Knight's friends, Leopold Stokowski, director of the Philadelphia Orchestra. Stokowski had seen some amateur 16mm films Knight had made, and greatly admired their clarity. The films do not survive and their subject matter is not recorded, but *From Om to Omnibus* was described by Stokowski as 'an avant-garde work of great quality'. In *Theatre Arts Monthly* Knight again instructs Hollywood movie-makers in the art of socially conscious film production: 'To bring sanity and order to itself, a city can clear away its slums and widen its roads… in order to bring health to the other parts. Whether Hollywood can destroy part of itself to bring the cinema to health is a question unanswered. It would need to destroy many of its most beloved creeds… its belief that a film is a thing that lasts a little over an hour and which tells a fictional story in which old faces appear in new costumes.'

Though he knew that Hollywood had read his work, he was not aware that studio bosses had begun to correlate a new movie's poor showing at the box office with evidence that, as one movie executive put it, 'Mr. Knight doesn't like it'.

It is hard to see, given his busy work schedule, how Knight managed to prepare his first novel *Invitation to Life*, which would appear later in 1934, especially since he now had a new innovation against which to revolt – colour pictures: 'Having seen all of Hollywood's latest output I have some advice for you. This is a perfectly swell time to clean out the closet, or go to the park, or write a letter to the Postmaster General, or anything but go to the movies, where Hollywood is determined to ram color down our throats. I warned 'em. I'll puke!'

Of course, being colour-blind, Knight was perhaps not best placed to judge the quality of colour production, but his overriding argument was that colour would do for the talkies what the talkies had done to silents – ruin the plot by forcing the viewer to both listen and see, only now they had to listen, see, and take in the spectacle of colour. Knight feared that plots would grow ever thinner, the acting weaker, and the true craft of movie-making be reduced to nothing more than animated seaside postcards with even less attention being paid to the narrative. Hollywood felt the full force of his anger and frustration and would no doubt have received more had he not become preoccupied with his first novel, a work which, though labelled 'fiction', traces the journey of its author as a young soldier returned from the First World War to find life utterly changed.

Tregan, the hero of *Invitation to Life,* has returned from the War with a bad leg-wound, but learns to hide the injury. Knight reverses the actual events of his own life, allowing Tregan a father but a substitute mother who is distant and foreign. He becomes a newspaper man in the US and falls in love. Though complete with a Shakespearian balcony scene, the plot is modern and addresses the mental anguish and confusion felt by most returning soldiers, even those who started anew in America.

There were other books on the subject of the wounded veteran coming to terms with life after a war, most notably Hemingway's *The Sun Also Rises* and Virginia Woolf's Modernist novel *Mrs. Dalloway*. Woolf's shell-shocked ex-serviceman kills himself when unable to escape the ghosts of his hellish past, but Knight's simply slides into a regime of excessive drinking and affairs with girls, who he cannot love; his ability to do so being the real casualty of his war. Knight's book was and remains very much a work of its time, and as such a valuable social document today. He did not write like any of his contemporaries and rarely looked for guidance from them: 'When I'm writing I don't read anybody else's work. I don't want to write like anybody else, I want to write like me.'

And he stuck rigidly to this regime, though this does not mean he did not discuss his ideas with Horgan and others when the plot was sticking or some technical detail required the advice of an expert, his works always being meticulously researched.

One whose guidance Knight did seek early in his career was Theodore Dreiser. Dreiser had already published twenty novels and plays by the time Eric Knight approached him, having long admired his realism. Dreiser's reply to Knight's first letter seeking advice was: 'I see what you write, but what are you trying to say?'

This simple line prompted Knight to adopt the brevity of his film criticism in his work. The result was a vital and thrilling delivery, which describes a journey but never directs its readers' thoughts, his earliest-learnt rule of never allowing a story to 'die' by having an inescapable conclusion perpetually guiding his authorship. Dreiser was apparently pleased with Knight's output and maintained a brief period of correspondence and a later friendship in which many ideas were exchanged and mutual appreciation expressed, even if Knight considered that Dreiser did not hold him in quite the regard he reserved for Hemingway and Fitzgerald.

Throughout his early writings, Sam Small was never far from Knight's mind. And there is a reference in *Invitation to Life*, which indicates the moment of inspiration that would give him the title of Sam's most famous adventure. The pivotal action takes place on a balcony outside an apartment where a party is in full spate. Tregan is contemplating how easy it would be to jump when a female voice intervenes:

' 'You weren't thinking of jumping were you?'
He laughed. 'If I jumped I wouldn't fall. I've always had the firmest conviction that I would volplane. I feel sure that if I stretched out my arms I could zoom down slowly.' '

Here we see not only a metaphor for freedom in the form of flying but also the birth of the concept that would, three years later, deliver Sam Small as *The Flying Yorkshireman*. Oddly, there exist no 'workings out' for *Invitation to Life* such as there are for the Sam Small adventures. Perhaps this is an indication as to which work required the greater effort. What we do find are typed manuscripts, often corrected in pen, which appear to have flowed from Knight as if planned over many months and finally written down over a period of only a few weeks. And while no planning notes exist, Knight does talk of 'finding other things to do' so he does not have to write, on one memorable occasion 'killing snakes in the spring house' while awaiting the inspiration to apply himself to the job of actual writing. The impetus he required, however, would be furnished by Ernest Hemingway, now his close friend: 'When you stop writing, do it in the middle of a sentence, when you know exactly what's going to happen next, so that when you come back to it after a break you pick up where you left off.'

This method must have worked. While his early manuscripts also acted as sketch books, often displaying pencil outlines of hills and trees and vaguely described distant animals, the sketches cease almost completely after he received Hemingway's advice.

Knight's publisher, impressed with the novel, asked for a screenplay synopsis of the work and the first four chapters of a book to be based on his criticism. Knight told a friend, 'They must be mad. I can't do it. Newspaper work makes me write such a lot that I have to wrack my brains terribly each day.' But this was not the only offer from a publisher clearly excited by his manuscript. Despite his initial reaction, he broke the news of the offer to Rotha with considerable glee: 'Rotha, there is a God and a justice…. Along comes a publisher to take my novel and he wants two more. How it all works out! My second novel is well under way. It's the story of a boy in the English north-country district and the child-labour mills and his escape into a world where people write books and paint pictures and play music. It may have a hard time here in the States because so much of the beginning will be in dialect. But it shall be done as it ought and we'll worry about the readers afterwards.

The work may have been well under way but what Knight does not tell Rotha is which of the fourteen 'beginnings' to the novel he was working on. It is clear from the many manuscripts that survive, Knight sweated more over it than any other work. The response of the American public to *Song On Your Bugles* would, however, be such that his misgivings over the work, particularly its dialect content, would be immediately dispelled, and made up his mind that when Sam Small finally arrived in print, and in dialect, Americans should have no trouble deciphering it.

Meanwhile, America had other concerns. In the four years since the collapse of the New York Stock Exchange in October 1929, share prices had fallen to twenty per cent of their pre-Crash value. Thousands of individual investors were ruined and 11,000 of the 25,000 banks active before the crisis descended into insolvency and liquidation. Industrial production came to a virtual standstill and unemployment stood at close to thirty per cent. Knight, unsurprisingly, had his own opinions on the catastrophe and was ready to voice them to anybody willing to listen. As always when he was addressing matters of what he saw as governmental mismanagement, they were both radical and cynical: 'Me, I call not for a forty-hour week—but for a 25 hour week with intensive education for the workers to show them how to consume luxuries in their spare time.'

This swipe at America's obsession with consumerism was born of Knight's passion for the simple, self-sufficient pre-industrial life. And though he was quick to note a reversal of the trend that saw so many leave their rural homes for the mills and factories of Britain in the early 1800s, he also recognised that the new President, Roosevelt, had the support of the ordinary working people in whom both had great faith: 'One million people have left the cities for the land—as I have done. We eat every day from the land, fresh corn, beans, tomatoes, beets, lettuce, cantaloupes, water melons, carrots, onions—all coming in plenty to the table every day. Everything on the table is raised here, even the chicken or duck we kill.'

Knight was a great supporter during the Depression years of Gifford Pinchot – twice Governor of Pennsylvania – and an even greater supporter of Mrs Pinchot, a woman who gained his lasting admiration when she supported the labour force against the sweat-shops that had proliferated throughout the garment industry:

'Pinchot's wife went around the mill towns carrying banners with pickets addressing the strikers. She had the newsreel men tipped off so she was seen saying: 'This girl is 14 – she gets a dollar for a 52 hour week.' The police were at a loss—you can't go around clubbing the Governor's wife and then arrest her for 'resisting arrest'.'

So Knight was making known his support for the workers, was taking a supportive stance against oppression and what he saw as an abuse of the right to free speech and industrial action. He was not a political activist, but a man whose views were listened to by the public, thanks to his courage in expressing them and the support of a newspaper brave enough to publish. None of this, however, could save his job when the Depression claimed its latest victim – *The Philadelphia Public Ledger*. By now, his half-brother Ed Knight – formerly Adolph Kahn – had been working some time as a junior reporter on the *Ledger*. While Eric was transferred briefly to the sister-paper *The Evening Ledger*, the twenty-four-year-old Ed lost his job. And Eric too was soon in trouble: 'For the first time the paper is knuckling down to advertisers. And in the case of the movies, the advertiser directs his attack at me. Result, I was called in and told my work was 'hyper-critical' and told to end 'petty-fogging and back-biting'. They weren't even honest enough to admit we had to knuckle down to the movie theatres to get their advertising. Where can truth go? I can only write as I feel. This paper is the only one I ever worked on to stand behind its men. I can write 'nice' reviews that mean nothing, but then what have I worked six years for?'

The ticking off merely propelled Knight to perhaps his most violent Hollywood comment to date: 'There isn't a Hollywood film I can speak of that isn't dumbness, stillness, blatherskilting bunkum and mishandling.'

His American readers might not understand such broad Yorkshireisms, but he would not be around to answer their calls. As movie theatres began withdrawing advertising in the face of the critic's tirade, the editor relieved him of his position. He retreated to his farm, determined to make it work. Knight had learned from his hired help and was convinced of a natural rhythm in Nature which he had not until now even partially understood. He told Rotha: 'Henceforth we shall plant at the exact moment the sun dips to the moon. Ploughing shall be done on the sudden appearance of jackdaws, hens shall be set by the colour of the morning sky, mares shall be bred by the chirping of crickets and harvest shall be reckoned by the conduct of caterpillars. And I'll bet it will be at least five per cent better than any scientific method….'

Reflecting upon his writing in this period of unemployment, Eric Knight formulated the view that by writing novels for an adventure-hungry public, by farming in harmony with Nature, and by living off the land, he might just survive financially without a regular job. And given his caustic lashing of the movies, his dislike of the talkies, his hatred of films shot in colour, it seemed unlikely anyway that any other paper would take him on as a critic. Besides, he was heartily sick of the newspaper business and even complained that Pentacres 'smelled of printing ink'.

There was, however, a potential opening in the film industry. He had earlier been promised an interview with Sidney Kent, the President of the Fox Film Corporation, who at that time lived in New York City. Fox had received one of Knight's rare compliments for their 1933 production

Cavalcade, written by Noel Coward. Such was Knight's reputation that this had been seen as a ringing endorsement of their output.

The company's founder, William Fox, had been forced to resign in 1930 and they were in trouble, having lost $21 million in 1931/2, so if they did hire him he could no longer expect a Hollywood style salary. Eric met with Kent on August 6th at a hotel in Manhattan. The job offer was still open, but there was no question of him working at home. He would have to move to Los Angeles. He was reassured that he would only be expected to observe the studio's story activities and, having done so over the period of a year, could decide then as to his future.

Even having chased the job, Knight had serious doubts. Could he leave his farm and throw his servants out of work at such a time? Could he survive in a place and among people and activities he had so volubly castigated? Could he look those stars in the eye whose abilities he had questioned and so damningly criticised? Could he sell up his home and his animals and uproot his wife and move to the other side of the country? Could he, even working from the inside, right all the Hollywood wrongs and single-handedly steer what he saw as a rudderless ship along a safe and artistically rewarding course? There was one question, however, which Knight does not appear to have asked himself: Would he be able to 'observe' yet keep his opinions to himself?

CHAPTER NINE

'After much wrestling with myself and agonised arguments between subjective and objective egos, I write this on the train. I'm on my way to Hollywood. I'm afraid –wishing I'd never started the whole business.'

In a letter to Jere written during the early part of his cross-country journey, Knight had said he was possessed of a 'high heart'. He was confiding more to Rotha about the nature of the job than he had been prepared to tell his wife:

'They want me to write scenarios. I want to make films. This trip will be an attempt to persuade them to let me work it out my way. I'll go in as second assistant director or cameraman's assistant or anything for a year; but I don't want a marble office and senseless punching at vacuums.'

He was set to work in neither of these capacities but as a script editor, working and reworking ideas, always in an attempt to rid them of the 'juvenile love interest, crass comedy, pointless plot and poor dialogue' which had been placed there purposely by the original writer because 'that's what the studio wants' and against which he had spent five years railing.

'Working on other people's scripts is not what I wanted,' he told Jere. What he did want was to write stories for films, or direct, something he realistically saw little chance of, but there appears to have been confusion over what 'writing' actually meant. To Knight, writing was creating his own stories from scratch, but the studio interpretation involved wrestling the scripts of others into a shape that conformed to studio guidelines.

Knight had perhaps expected a stream of editors or producers or writers seeking his collaboration; he saw none. What contact he had with colleagues resulted only in their apparent alienation, either because they saw him as an enemy of the movies or as an outsider with no right to a job in their business. He was, after all, a literary figure with a reputation that preceded him, one whose intellect they neither understood nor trusted. He was provided sumptuous surroundings and given little to do. It cannot have helped when he learned that Jere's letters to him were being returned because nobody in the Fox administration knew he worked there. 'I wonder,' he wrote, 'by what miracle I am receiving my weekly pay cheque'.

For the first time in his life under any kind of organised employment, Knight was directionless. He wrote to the President of Fox to say he was receiving no guidance as to his supposed creative duties. The same letter arrived on the desk of the General Manager. He even wrote expressing his concerns to Will Hays, President of the Motion Picture and Distributors Association:

'All is Showmanship, the sham and indescribable beauty of Hollywood, the fake sincerity, the pointless bowing subservience of hotel staff, the Cadillac limousine that transported me from Pasadena, the over-dressed people and the overdressed food. If you buy a hamburger, you get a roll, toasted, with lettuce in it. Under that there's a slice of pickle, adorned with anchovies. Next is a slice of tomato, flanked with potato chips. Somewhere there's a piece of hamburger – but it's hidden by the Showmanship.'

If Eric Knight had been looking for a metaphor for all he would discover about Hollywood, he found it in the built landscape, the simple task of fuelling his car, and a hamburger diner, all of which forced him back on his observational skills: 'The hideous pinkery of houses not in keeping with the landscape, and the process of filling the car with gas, something which cannot be done without the windscreen washed with the Showmanship of a flourish, and Hollywood's famed eating establishments. You can't go into a restaurant that looks like a restaurant – it must be built in the shape of a derby hat or a gigantic dog – but it can't look like a restaurant.'

What frustrated him was the unexpected grandeur of the country around him, which paradoxically provided the movies with a home but which the movies had never captured. 'California,' he said, 'has never told the truth about California. Was ever there such a land blessed as this? No winter at all. At the eternal beach the children splash in the water. It is a paradise for children who are all suntanned and healthy. They are like gods.'

He was equally frustrated by the unending kindness of the people, 'If only a good city-editorial voice would call me a son-of-a-bitch in lovely harsh tones and tell me for the love of so-and-so get something written in twenty minutes!' He was unaccustomed to being told to take his time, to relax, that there was no hurry, to get used to the climate, to be happy. In truth, he missed the cold Pennsylvania mornings, his farm, his horses, his wife, even his former, hated life as a newspaperman.

Already the resentment had set in; he would not produce any original ideas, he said, until he was given a film of his own and unlimited time in which to shoot it. This had rarely happened, and when it had, studios had found themselves the custodians of artistic and meritorious works that were commercially useless. 'I'll take their money,' he said, 'I'll save most of my salary. I'll make my own movie before I'm through.' Until that time came, he resolved, he would toe the company line.

After two weeks of 'doing nothing', Knight was called to a producer's bungalow on Fox's Western Avenue lot, the home of 'B' movie production. About a dozen men attended. There were cocktails and a meal, after which he was to address the foregathered on the subject of 'New Paths In The Movies'. He spoke about the audience and the fact that film producers underestimated the intelligence of those whose nickels and dimes kept the studios afloat. He told the men their themes were too narrow and their technical treatments lacking in imagination, and he urged them to be more adventurous and more daring, to be ready to 'leave the beaten path and gamble occasionally'. He told them to stop being so reliant on actors who couldn't act and that actors should be chosen to play roles corresponding most closely to their own personality to ensure at least a modicum of realism.

'The rest of the evening,' Knight reported, 'was spent informally with producers talking about roles for Miss Dooh-dah which suited her so she didn't have to act and another not-quite-but-nearly star who might be elevated to actual stardom if only the right script could be worked up'. 'I doubt,' Eric said, 'that the men who matter understood a word of what I said.'

His mailing problems finally resolved, Knight related all this to Jere in letters that were more upbeat and optimistic than those he sent to Rotha. And he sounded particularly pleased when he finally announced that a salary of $200 a week had been arrived at. It would take only another two weeks, however, for Knight to declare himself at his wits' end, the catalyst being a meeting about a script for *Dante's Inferno*, Spencer Tracy's latest vehicle. He had assumed that it would be based on the *Divina Comedia* but was stunned to find that the two were in no way connected. In an effort to conform to his new surroundings and no doubt glad at last to be involved in something constructive, he picked up on the theme of the ruthless, heartless demon at the centre of the action and recommended divine retribution in the form of an accident in which the character would accidentally kill his own son.

The idea was applauded and apparently accepted, but when he returned to the office of the producer in charge of the project, Sol Wurtzel, he found it had been summarily scrapped in favour of one put forward by Wurtzel himself. This was the pattern over the weeks, valid ideas put forward and rejected with no explanation. He continued with the task of dredging through hundreds of hopeless scripts, published and unpublished, from the Fox library, trying to make some sense of their potential. He told Rotha: 'If

I were to furnish an accurate description of Hollywood, you would not believe it. No chances are taken; they work as close to the norm as they can. There are some good men, brilliant men, but none are willing to stand up for their artistic integrity, but I will fight, there's glory in defeat sometimes.'

Before long he was confessing, 'I am lost, I am a lost soul.' His under-employment did, however, mean he had time to take in the Californian scenery, and it became the subject of his writing: 'Down on the shore boulevard watching the Pacific booming in, the sand wetting and drying and people building fires on the beach and running into the warm water. Then later, driving up onto the shore heights and seeing all Los Angeles like fire-diamonds and pearls, all strung on strings, blinking iridescent in the night. That's the stuff they never shoot, what they do shoot are made-up heroes in naval uniforms parading before canvas street scenes of France.... How silly.'

There is no indication at this time that Knight had been warned his job was in danger; he simply felt the impending inevitability of dismissal. He began a new novel 'about the North of England', confessing that, 'Why I should sit in Hollywood and write about Yorkshire I don't know.' He was engaged at this time in finding a new project for Janet Gaynor. All his ideas were turned down as already having been tried, usually in silent movies, or because they lacked excitement. He told Rotha, 'Discussing these silly things is not for me, there are hundreds of people who could do the job, probably for half the pay. Why keep me?'

This question was not addressed by his masters, if indeed it had ever been asked. In any case, there was about to be a change in Knight's attitude prompted by Jere's arrival in Hollywood, a turnaround that he detailed in a letter to Rotha: 'It all happened one evening. Quite suddenly, it didn't matter any more. It was silly to have thought it ever did matter. I knew I should never find a Gaynor vehicle, nor ever make a suggestion of any value to them in finding one. I was merely in their way. Then I began to laugh. I said: 'How silly I have been. I shall never again come home downhearted because I have failed to find Janet a vehicle. I must laugh at myself for ever having not laughed at it.'

His notes on Hollywood would later produce *Rose Without Warning*, a novel, destined to remain unpublished, about a former Vaudeville dancer who, catapulted to Hollywood fame by an ambitious mother, becomes mercilessly manipulated by a system which calls her a star while treating her as a commodity. It was at this time that he formed a view on authorship that had been an integral ingredient of *Invitation to Life*, was all too obvious in *Rose Without Warning*, and would inform all his further writings: 'Why are books not documentaries – documentaries of ourselves? One thing Hollywood has done. It has made me sick of made-up stories, that I never want to have anything to do with another, even characters I made up myself.'

This is not so much a revelation as an endorsement of his practice to date. His stories had always been based in reality. If it had been in his mind to create characters and situations entirely from his imagination, his Hollywood experiences had proved they could never work. Having made the decision to deal only with reality in the future, he and Jere began to enjoy California for all it had to offer. They joined the Riviera Country Club in Pacific Palisades where they rode horses, and formed close friendships with stars like Nelson Eddy, Mary Pickford and Elissa Landi.

Jere had met Landi while the actress was staying in Philadelphia, Jere acting as her guide around the city. An immediate affinity between the two, and Eric, had blossomed into a close friendship. The daughter of an Italian Countess, Landi had worked on the London stage in the 1920s to most favourable reviews. A woman of great beauty and personality who spoke several languages, she had been snapped up by the German film industry and had starred in two important films, *Synd* (1928) and *The Price of Things* (1930). She had come to Eric Knight's attention in 1931 when starring in a New York stage version of Hemingway's *A Farewell to Arms*, at which point her potential had been spotted by Hollywood.

Her first Hollywood film, *Body and Soul*, was not a commercial success but her performance captivated Cecil B. De Mille, who cast her in his 1932 epic *The Sign Of The Cross*. More films followed; most notably *The Warrior's Husband* and *The Count of Monte Cristo*, where her leading man was Robert Donat, the British actor who would later star in *Goodbye Mr Chips* and *The Thirty-Nine Steps*. She received perhaps her greatest accolade, however, when being cast opposite Cary Grant in *Enter Madame*. But despite her success, Landi's passion lay in writing and she would go on to author six novels and several books of poetry.

Their friendship led Landi to offer the Knights a way out of the home Eric called 'the shack'. The Malibu Road house had no heating and an inoperative shower. It looked out over the Pacific ocean and a huge rock encrusted with centuries-old seabird guano. When Knight presented Jere with a wire-haired terrier, on her arrival in Hollywood, they called him White Rock. Landi's offer was that the couple move in with her at 603 11th Street, Santa Monica, a Mexican-style corner plot on a broad street under palm trees.

In early December, White Rock was killed by a car outside Landi's home. Jere was devastated. Her husband, keen to make up for the loss, immediately contacted a collie breeder living nearby. The man came to Knight's attention when he overhead him speaking to a shop assistant. 'When did you leave Oldham?' Knight asked. 'Thirty-five year ago,' the stranger replied, 'An' Ah thought Ah 'ad no accent left.' But he did, and Knight had pinpointed it exactly. Thereafter, the conversation took place in a tongue none of the assistants and customers could understand, and resulted in the breeder making a gift - a runt-of-the-litter cross-collie pup. Eric named her Tootsie after an Eddie Cantor song of the time, *OK Toots*, and carried her home in his coat pocket. Over the next few years her bright eyes and uncanny intelligence would captivate Knight and inspire him to write stories about her adventures. She became a feature of the household and accompanied her master just about everywhere.

Knight made no mention of White Rock's death in his next letter to Rotha, but his mood was even more depressed than it had been of late. He felt no sympathy for his bosses, 'the Hollywoodenheads' as he had lately dubbed them: 'I have compassion for a plucked flower. I truly suffer for a starfish blown up by the tide and dying slow death for lack of water. I suffer immensely for a tree, recently rooted up and towed into the studio for a 'forest scene' shot quickly before the foliage died. But don't be hurt by people who are often hurt less by life than you are by their acquaintance of that life. I am now an authority on torture. I have been railroaded into this magnificent office now more than three months. I have suffered the humiliation of not even being considered or given anything to do.

Rotha, however, was not Knight's only correspondent, though he is one of a handful who preserved their letters from Eric – and as such has become a crucial source. Another was Edward Estlin Cummings, the poet who re-branded himself as e e cummings after a publisher suggested a change of image to improve his career prospects. He was introduced to Knight by Maurice (Moe) Speiser, a Philadelphia lawyer who supported and promoted literature and the arts. Speiser had travelled widely as a young man and, since his years in Paris in the 1920s, had been a friend to Hemingway and Ford Madox Ford, among others. He thought Cummings and Knight might get along and he was right. In one letter, recorded by Cummings' biographer, Richard S. Kennedy, Knight urges his new friend to 'give Hollywood a try'. The poet's reply is typical of his inventive style and incorporates the made up, strung-together, authentically foreign and seemingly foreign words which litter their correspondence:

'Quant a Hollywood cinq mille dollars par semaine pendant un mois (and no effing options) me tempterait peutetre. Mais je crois que les movies, etant sur leur last legs, sont probablement trop far gone pour inviter un specaliste authentique et expensive com moi. Tant pis!'

Cummings had in fact been invited to Hollywood the previous year for a salary three times what Knight was on, but he declined, being 'too busy working on a ballet'. In the interim his fortunes had declined and he later wrote in typically eccentric fashion to his beloved Aunt Jane of his decision to accept his friend's offer:

'I'd had my worst year to date in New York…and our only chance $ seemed to be Hollywood, where 2 of Marion's old friends were highlights in the motionpicpicture industry.'

Cummings and his wife arrived in Los Angeles shortly thereafter and rented a house around the corner from Landi's. Over many years and thousands of items of correspondence, Knight and Cummings would establish a kind of code, which in many cases defies translation. Despite his being 'a curious chap' Cummings enjoyed a special bond with Knight. They shared a certain intellect, a rebellious nature, a capacity for independent and original thought, and the comradeship of having both been through the war. Pivotal to the friendship was Cummings' passion for New Mexico, whence he and his wife Marion travelled to Hollywood early in 1935 to be met by the Knights and transported to their new home.

They arrived with Cummings experiencing the same misgivings Knight had felt on leaving Pennsylvania. Admitting he had 'almost wept' on the plane, Cummings was provided with a limousine and lady chauffer by MGM where a friend of Marion, David Hertz, was a writer. They were shown the sights and introduced to 'the right people'. After only a week, financial constraints forced the Cummings to move into a minute apartment at 849 11th Street.

Knight and many others tried to find Cummings work, petitioning all the major studios and various luminaries, including the legendary Irving Thalberg, head of production at MGM. Knight, a great fan of animation, even introduced Cummings to Walt Disney, another World War I veteran and one of a handful of people Knight regarded as friends in Hollywood. But even here there was nothing to which Cummings might lend his talents. Marion Cummings, a former model, was considered to be a woman of outstanding beauty who should have been a natural for Hollywood, and though screen tests were undertaken they came to nothing, mainly because her exceptional height meant that she towered over most of Hollywood's leading men.

Eric and Cummings often talked deep into the night, mostly on literary topics but regularly reliving the war. The two had a lot in common: a loathing of the 'Hollywoodenheads', a love of Swinburne, Greek tragedy, art and a shared experience of life in the trenches. Cummings had also attended the Cambridge Latin School, arriving just weeks after Knight set out for New York City. Like Knight, he had given up his studies to serve his country. He volunteered as an ambulance driver – an occupation he shared with Hemingway and Walt Disney who, at sixteen, had been too young to enlist in the fighting forces. Cummings, however, had expressed openly his anti-war views and was incarcerated in the Depot de Triage, a French concentration camp. The place became the subject of his best-selling 1922 novel *The Enormous Room*, a work much praised by Knight. Cummings travelled to the Soviet Union in the 1920s, saw Communism in action, and converted to Socialism.

When Cummings expressed misgivings – here he was, living rent-free with the Knights after turning down a large offer for the film rights to his novel – he was quickly reminded that he had made the right decision. 'After all,' Eric told him, 'look what they did to Hemingway.' With Cummings losing even the will to fight what he called 'the regime of pimpdom and arse-kissers', Knight wrote a long and direct letter to Sidney Kent, the man who had head-hunted him, and told him that money was being wasted on flops while good stories which might be cheaply made into worthwhile movies were being overlooked. There was more than a hint of provocation in the letter, Knight hoping Kent would take the bait and offer him the chance to prove his point and make such a film. But the ploy did not work; Kent advised Knight to stick with the story department.

In his discussions with Jere, Knight emphasised that the deal he had been offered was good for only six months and that at the end of that time he needed to escape. He mentioned returning to England for a year but Jere was about to begin work at Paramount as a script editor and felt that, even if Eric was out of work, they would still be able to manage financially. She argued further that if he wanted to get into films, there was but one place to do it, Hollywood. Knight conceded that she was right and decided to 'stick it out as best I may' – outlining to Rotha the almost impossible task he now faced in story editing:

'Yesterday I finished up the hard task of a shooting script on 'Ladies' Money'. It was a hard job because we were told we could not make it if we allowed: 1. the landlady's daughter to be seduced; 2. the gunman to be killed by a young man across the hall in the boarding house; 3. The vaudeville artist's wife to talk like a vaudevillian's wife; 4. The first-floor girl to solve her husband's theft by pilfering the money from a ransom fund hastily jettisoned by a fleeing criminal.'

By Knight's own admission, 'I now did nothing for six weeks.' Nothing for his bosses, that is. He was not idle, however, and worked up no less than four script ideas, presumably to sell in that period of unemployment he now saw as inevitable. One, *The Hypothetical Murderer*, took the form of a country-house whodunit in the style of one of Knight's literary heroes J.B. Priestley. *The Magnificent Liar* was Knight's attempt at a light-hearted London gangster movie. When he did receive orders it was to work on a script, on which he discovered two others were also working without knowledge of his involvement.'This was typical of Hollywood,' he said. 'You put your heart into a script only to find you've been in a race with several others – if they prefer their work over yours, your ideas are dumped without further consultation.'

'So I finally offered my resignation. In typical Hollywood fashion it was rejected. I was fired two days later. The curious thing is that I am now happy. I am beginning to feel honest and can turn to a typewriter once more without apologising to it.'

Out of work, he continued to write. He worked on *Song On Your Bugles* and *Rose Without Warning* and spent much time in the company of Cummings. He declared, 'I feel better than at any time in the past. Me again'. He settled down to what he called 'serious authorship', and a willingness to re-visit his war experiences was perhaps an indication that its ghosts were finally being exorcised.

His hope was that within six months he would have 'scrubbed off the soot of Hollywood'. He rapidly finished *Song On Your Bugles* and his editor, Edward Aswell, also acting as his agent, began the process of approaching publishers. Now he began a further novel. *You Play the Black and the Red Comes Up* follows the misfortunes of a man who finds himself in Hollywood in search of an errant wife who has deserted him in the pursuit of her acting ambitions. The work is no more than a distillation of the author's thoughts on Hollywood dreams turned to dust. A slimmer volume than any of his other works, though none the worse for that, the novel's brevity indicates a recurrence of his inability to concentrate, a difficulty he confided only to Rotha: 'I stare at the paper each day, and not even words come out. I try writing, and when I do get anything down I know it is worthless. I am torn between the desire to lick this place and the knowledge that I must get out. Yet I sit and watch waves, and try to think…'

When the words would not come, Knight returned to art, and it was at this time he produced two telling self-portraits. One shows him as he undoubtedly was, smart, groomed, military-like, the other a bohemian figure, long-haired, with open-neck shirt under his cricket sweater with a handle-bar moustache. He also completed two portraits in ink of Jere, which capture her beauty perfectly. And if the words to a novel deserted him, the same did not apply to their outpouring in letters to Rotha and notes he felt compelled to write to Cummings, the latter exercising his considerable skill in replies which would grow ever more obscure. In July 1935, Knight received the following:

'dear knight,
if i were to zoom from my couch one matutinal appreamidi and (boosting a catch in response to supercollosalhyper prodigious knocks) find H.R.H. the Tennisrackety Monarch of Sweden dancing attendance with all 1 perpendicularsilkenchapeau full of diamanteprizemoney, shouldn't feel more than a 15th as ebloui as now am by your dateless epistle. For money is shit. But in the first place miracles are miracles.'

Punctuation was often missing from the letters which passed between the two, capital letters ignored, names misspelled, words substituted, foreign words used, words stitched together in Germanic fashion, words used out of context, others used as abstractly as the modern artist uses a brush:

'dear captive knight,
since you left here… and much always something happening. there is far more… than there was when you left here. that was conrad cummings speaking. not to be confused with bumwad naval, the movie comet.'

Cummings apparently enjoyed the 'captive knight' title, although it is not clear whether he was thinking of chess or imagining his friend locked away in some ivory tower of his own making, surrounded by beauty but unable to appreciate any of it. In any case, Cummings appreciated Eric's frustration and brought it up in a letter to Jere:
'It was un – of me to not sweet of you to right but if the former wasn't wiping bushes he's been nowing dishes… such, however, shall soon be what futureless people arcanely call past and a pair of airbreathing athletes (from which tridimen signal triumph) are more tan ripe to swoop beaucoup bons boissons with you and your highflying horsefleshing Hollywood hero, assuming, as am, that (1) the latter hasn't yet sold somebodyelse's name for a proverbial mess of garbo (2) has spouse safely ensconced in the vertical vicinity of grateciels.'

We may assume a great deal from this letter, mainly that Cummings felt his attempts at encouragement were making no impact on Knight and was now trying to tackle it through his wife. He recognised Knight's great talent and sympathised with the fact that he was actually earning nothing and living on his wife's earnings.

In an attempt to shuffle the cards, Knight now registered with the H.N. Swanson agency. Swanson also represented Hemingway, F. Scott Fitzgerald, and William Faulkner, whose 1929 novel *The Sound and the Fury* had made a considerable impression on Eric. The new agent tried to find a market for Knight's screen ideas and adaptations but had no success, plunging Knight to a new low, as he told Rotha:
'No longer am I sure of anything. Like all Californians, I have no anger left, and the sunshine and easy air make angers seem silly things instead of the driving powers of life. I watch myself die. A longtime friend of mine is now a success in a studio as producer. He speaks not to me on the telephone nor even answers a note. Then I rage at myself for having been weak enough to write a note to anyone. But I still have my back yard and the shade to sit in with my typewriter on my knees; and my wife still goes out to the office every morning and earns the bread and butter. Horrible, that.'

Knight in his depressed state, however, had Cummings for company and only two days after writing the above took up Walt Disney's invitation of a studio tour. This reinforced his view that what Disney was producing was better than anything being turned out elsewhere. He also, for the first time, endorsed the use of colour, Disney's brighter-than-life depictions appealing to Knight, whose vision was surely impaired by his colour-blindness. Cummings did not share Knight's enthusiasm. He was horrified by the sight of dozens of illustrators working away tirelessly, wasting their great talent in factory conditions

Cummings didn't share Eric's enthusiasm for horses either, but he liked to accompany him on outings to the Riviera Country Club where Jere displayed her considerable riding skill. Present at one outing was Egon Merz, a Hollywood photographer who captured Knight taking fences aboard one of his horses. One picture is captioned 'The Flying Yorkshireman in blue jeans on High Corral', the other 'Eric Knight on Cloud'. Flying Cloud, to give the mare her full name, was one of a pair of matching greys owned by the Knights.

Many movie stars relaxed at the Riviera, including Hollywood 'Royalty' such as Douglas Fairbanks and Mary Pickford, Spencer Tracy and Katherine Hepburn, all of whom would fall under the spell of Knight's Yorkshire charm and the film-star looks of his wife. Jere did not court fame but nonetheless found herself the subject of magazine feature when the *Los Angeles Examiner* put her and her mount, Bourbon, on its front page.

Despite lacking a regular job, Knight found Hollywood society willing to embrace him. Luncheon and party invitations came in regularly, often through Jere. For her part, Jere always felt she did little to further her husband's career, admitting, 'I didn't help Eric much, I never slept with anybody', but she and Landi did at least recruit the aid of the latter's lover, Jean Negulesco who, having been commissioned to make six short films, gave responsibility for four of them to Knight. None would actually be produced but the project did much to restore a flagging spirit. Indeed, Knight told Rotha that what he had written had been 'really very good' and in the same letter registered his growing concern with world affairs: 'I hope to hell the Abyssinians kick what is daily known here as the living shit out of the Italians. It is to be hoped all minor nations who live barefoot kick the shit out of the nations with big populations and machine guns.'

A month later, he had more bad news to impart: 'The latest defeat here was Cummings. He, super-brilliant, creator of one of the most powerful novels of the last twenty years couldn't understand the place at all. Yesterday he called to say goodbye. It makes it lonesome. Cummings was the only friend I found out here, and now he's gone back to New England.'

Lost without his friend, Knight accepted even the most minor commissions, one of which was for a short film script for an independent producer who, being short of money, gave him a horse. Despite a luncheon meeting with Theodore Dreiser, and the regular round of parties and engagements, life without Cummings was almost intolerable and Knight wrote asking Peter Hurd to drive over from his ranch in New Mexico. But Hurd was busy and the trip never materialised.

Even in Hollywood, he concluded, where making friends with stars and directors and producers and having a beautiful wife and sharing a home with a screen goddess, and associating with established luminaries of the arts and literary world was supposed to open doors, he had failed where less able men had succeeded. Lavish parties where stars like Niven and Flynn, Pickford and Fairbanks, Tracy and Hepburn, Astaire, Crosby and Colman applauded his piano-accordion playing and his story-telling, provided only fleeting relief from depression. He had tried his hand at magazine stories and had even offered article ideas to Los Angeles newspapers, but despair was setting in: 'A chap is going to send me a magazine article on 'How To Live in Mexico On Twenty Dollars a Month'. All I need then is a companion article on 'How To Earn Twenty Dollars A Month in Mexico To Live On'.'

In all his letters and notes there had been no mention of Tootsie. He refers regularly to Jere, Landi and her brother, Disney, Cummings, anybody with whom he came into contact even for the briefest moment, but Tootsie, now his ever-present companion, had been absent, except in this reference to his typewriter:

'Meanwhile, I always have the typewriter, who looks at me open-faced each morning and loves me like my dog does. I wear ribbons thin and pound. I cannot be worthless; therefore I must write something that isn't worthless sooner or later. God knows I ask very little of life – and God knows I'm getting it.'

All these words and more on the same theme were written in letters to Rotha in September and early October 1935, but Rotha's replies were returned by the dead letter office. He heard nothing for nine months. Finally, Knight came to the conclusion that escape was the only answer. He bought a four-and-a-half acre plot of land, fit only for growing alfalfa and making hay, in the San Fernando Valley, a little place called Zelzah. Knight now exchanged the pen and typewriter for the shovel and the scythe. He cleared land, dug out footings, mixed and poured concrete and built a fireplace and chimney. Working to his own plans, he erected a timber cabin complete with plumbing, having first excavated enough earth to sink a septic tank. He had for company Tootsie, the horse he'd accepted in payment for the short film script, and a goat. As recently as 2006 some of his former neighbours remembered 'the red haired man' riding to the town's post office each day followed dutifully by the two pets. The shack partly completed, Knight raised alfalfa and retreated from public life.

CHAPTER TEN

Eric Knight's new occupation would define him as a man and act as the springboard to greater things. He admitted that in his labours he had 'completely lost himself' and that he did not recognise himself as the man he had been only a year earlier. He had hoped to change Hollywood but acknowledged that 'better men than I had tried, and had also failed'. When he resumed his correspondence with Cummings, it was from an utterly changed perspective: 'Now I sit in a shack, eight feet by eight, in the middle of an alfalfa field, and am completely happy and never think of films all day long. In our wide valley the mountains reach up, always changing in the light, on three sides cut hay. I irrigate land and make a living alone.'

The house stood close enough to the railway track and the passing trains for him to see the passengers clearly; he remembered how he had looked out from trains at shacks where a single oil lamp shone on a lone resident. 'I often wondered who that man was,' he said. 'He was me. And he didn't envy my superior luxury.' Finally, Tootsie began to feature in Knight's letters. 'She was once a house dog,' he wrote, 'but now she barks if other human beings come near; in a flash she becomes a country dog.' He cursed himself for the errors he made in his joinery and his plumbing but learned quickly. 'I make mistakes and call myself a dumb bastard, but plumbers have one brain and ten fingers, as have I; maybe I am a plumber and just never called myself one.' While Knight owned his property and everything that went into it, others around him were not so lucky. He was moved to write to Rotha of their plight: 'Even here there is unhappiness. The Swedes and the Mexicans who live about me live under the rule of the banks. They have sweated for years on the land, and now the banks begin taking it away when their money fails, year by year grabbing a stronger and stronger hold on the farms. Poor people, reaching old age, seeing a lifetime's work slipping away from under them like wet sand.'

He rose at three in the morning and retired at dusk, learning quickly that hay becomes brittle in the sun and that alfalfa leaves fall off if the plants are handled in the heat of the day. In a land where there is no rain at all for nine months of the year, water was piped five hundred miles to irrigate the land, something Mr Smith would later point out to regulars in a Yorkshire pub in a Sam Small adventure. The water was turned on by Water Company officials who raised floodgates and opened valves at a pre-determined time, obliging the farmer to be ready to work frantically to ensure all the crops received a dowsing and that no water was wasted.

Eric applied 'Yorkshire logic' to his husbandry methods. While his neighbours spent much of their time plugging gopher holes in an effort retain water on the land, he decided he would allow his land to resemble 'the Paris metro system' because the water would not evaporate deep in the ground and would therefore serve alfalfa roots which can reach down five or six feet. 'Already, he said, 'I can see my crop growing considerably taller than that of my neighbours.'

With no bank loan to service and no trouble paying his water bills, Knight began to trade with his neighbours, accepting a bullock in exchange for two tons of hay, three tons of barley straw for a new bridle, five pounds of walnuts for a new bit, and – from a woman clearly making a play for him - hour-long riding lessons for a token payment of 'one tiny walnut'.

He farmed steadfastly, determinedly, but the day came when the beckoning of the typewriter could no longer be ignored. His fingers had grown thick and battered and he found himself unable to press any one key without depressing the one next to it, until he realised he had splinters in his fingers, which had become embedded with labour. 'My hands,' he said, 'are not my own'. They would, however, be persuaded into action and would finish a work that had been in progress for some time. 'Song On Your Bugles is better than anything else I've written,' he told Rotha. Isolated he may have been, but a regular supply of newspapers arrived at Zelzah post office from Yorkshire, all of which spoke of the desperation of near-starving colliers in the face of pit closures.

Between 1935 and 1937, Eric Knight worked harder than at any time before, and with less success. Fearing his friend would abandon writing completely, Cummings persuaded him that *Story Magazine* might provide an outlet for some of his works. They did. In December 1935 they published *Meet Me in The Shadows*, the Great War story about the destruction of the detested pianola. Encouraged, he submitted his latest story, which was also bought.

The Ten Gallon Hat follows the story of Yorkshire lad, Davie Manly, a single man who lives alone and works as a shop assistant for shirt manufacturer Josiah Dobley Bros. & Sons. When they send a rep to the US he returns with a ten-gallon hat for each of his colleagues. All of the hats behave perfectly, except Davie's, which begins talking to him. Josiah has decided to open a shop in New York City to sell his British shirts, and Davie's boss has been earmarked to run the American side of the business, a job for which Davie feels he would be better equipped. The hat persuades him to fight his corner, get drunk and insult his boss. Davie throws the hat away but it returns; he sells it, but the buyer gives it back. Finally, he gives it to the son of his landlady who is thrilled with the gift – until it gives the boy ideas above his station, whereupon she returns it. Unable to resist the hat's insistent demands, Davie puts himself forward, and though he is acting out of character, his boss notices him and finally hands him the job of running the business in America, which is a huge success, but only because Davie has realised that the brash bombastic side which the hat brought to the fore is as much the real him as the mouse of a man he used to be. Having once recognised his true self, Davie finds that the hat no longer speaks; it is forever silent.

Whit Burnett, editor and co-founder of *Story*, loved Knight's work and was thrilled to receive next, not a story, but the manuscript of *Song On Your Bugles*, which he decided immediately to publish in partnership with Harpers, always assuming Knight would make some dialect amendments for the US market. Simultaneously with Burnett's enthusiastic response, the author received word from England that Boriswood were equally taken, and ready to publish.

In the face of this success, Knight was suddenly more excited about his writing than he had been for three years, during which he had started to fear that *Invitation to Life* might be his sole published novel. He now farmed during the day and re-wrote *Song On Your Bugles* for the American market by the light of his oil lamp in the evenings, a process during which he came to a decision: if and when the Sam Small stories were published, the reading public on his side of the Atlantic would negotiate the Yorkshire dialect, having been largely introduced to it from this current work. He put in epic sessions at his typewriter, sometimes surviving on two or three hours' sleep.

The ideas were now coming so fast that Knight began to experience difficulty in keeping them in check. In the American version of *Song On Your Bugles*, a man is described going about the streets with a 'fishing pole' rattling on windows to wake the workers, a practice that had originated in the mill towns of England where a 'knocker-up' used a wire trident at the end of a bamboo pole for the same purpose. Eric would soon incorporate this in a Sam Small story, the plot for which was unfolding in his mind.

The life of the author was suddenly happening; he was earning a living, being published on both sides of the Atlantic and finding himself included in *O'Brien's Best Short Stories* for *Meet Me in The Shadows*. His Sam Small stories were now flowing from deep in his sub-consciousness, where they had resided for decades and where the characters had developed personalities of their own. Each was multi-dimensional, even the simplest of them being open to varied interpretation. And the duality present in Sam could now be found in his dog, which looked and acted like any other dog, but turned out to have the personality of a sheep.

Strong In the Arms would be the first story in the novella, the one that would introduce Sam to the world. It was one of Knight's favourite 'telling stories', often being recited by popular request at Hollywood parties. It is introduced by the unflattering rhyme – A Yorkshireman born and a Yorkshireman bred, strong in the arm but weak in the head – or *'yead'* as it appears in the work. The saying inspires the story of the Malton lad who wanders out of Wada's Keep, the moorland bastion of the last giant in Yorkshire, to take on Black Cawper in a fight, which Black wins in an almighty show of strength after a titanic battle. The next day, Black and Sam are working in the mine when a cave-in occurs. Sam tells later how Black saves the lives of his fellow-colliers by arching his great back against a roof beam, thereby preventing a dreadful tragedy, but at the cost of his own life.

The slaying of the last giant in Yorkshire has been variously credited to both Black Cawper and his son, Ian, and though the legend predates Sam by many centuries, he and his mates have become inexorably entangled with it. Black Cawper, 'the strongest man in Yorkshire – and therefore the world' proved his right to the title by chasing the giant across the dales, the moors and the Wolds, before finally hurling him into the sea off Filey, on Yorkshire's east coast, where he lies to this day. His bones have become encrusted with rocks and barnacles, which form the Brig – a popular tourist site, which has attracted generations of children who have no idea that they are climbing over the bones of a tyrannical oppressor. They fish innocently in rock pools, which have formed in the cavities of an ogre whose demise 'freed all Yorkshireman for all time'. And the story carries with it even greater significance, for it is said the concession handed down to all Yorkshiremen as a reward for the slaying decrees that all their children, regardless of where they are born, will be Yorkshire folk – a privilege granted to the natives of no other county in England.

The almost metaphysical *Sam Small's Better Half* is perhaps the literal manifestation of its author, dealing as it does with duality, a subject that had fascinated Eric since his first encounters with the 'theatricals' lodging with his aunts and uncles in Halifax. Sam's homeward staggering after too many pints of ale is reminiscent of Hobson's exit from the Moonrakers pub in Harold Brighouse's Lancashire drama, *Hobson's Choice*. While Hobson encounters what he sees as a terrifying image of the moon reflected in a puddle, Sam is similarly afraid when he bumps into a man who looks and acts exactly as he does. The two come to blows but are equal in strength; indeed, they are equal in every way, except one: the 'other' Sam is sober.

Mully, Sam's wife, is called upon to arbitrate as to which of the two she prefers – and, much to the disappointment of the bleary-eyed one, it is not him. Sam must reform; an internal struggle ensues against alcohol, into which we may read a truth about Eric Knight's own battle with drink. While Hobson is defeated by his addiction, Sam sees that the love of a good woman is worth the cost of moderation.

Sam is both an amalgam of men and the crystallization of years of deep thought and introspection; Sam Small is Yorkshire, Yorkshire is Sam Small. He is a working class lad who was born and raised in Polkin'thorpe Brigg, but he has done that 'varry remarkable thing' of making himself rich by brain power alone, for Sam is the inventor of the 'self-doffling spindle', a device that has revolutionised the spinning industry and made him a millionaire at a time when a mill-hand earned twelve pounds a year. Is Sam changed by his success? Yes, immeasurably. Is he still the same man? Yes, absolutely. He continues to live in the house he has always occupied and follow the pursuits of his mates, namely, the game of 'knur and spell' – best described as a very early, and crude, form of golf – and the sport of whippet racing. And though Sam stands his round in the lounge bar of the Spread Eagle pub, he never allows his mates the embarrassment of not standing theirs.

Far from being ostracised or even envied for his wealth, Sam is elevated to the position of oracle; the voice of reason on all matters. All this, plus more than a smattering of what we might today call 'Harry Potter magic', is what made Sam Small an international hero. He is not a man whose fortune takes him to new and wild adventures outside the normal sphere of understanding, although he does travel widely; neither is he carried away with his wealth. In short, the enchantment of Sam is this: while he keeps both feet firmly on the ground, he discovers that, by the power of his mind alone, he is able to fly.

The revelation comes after a visit to the Temple in Los Angeles where he and Mully are visiting their daughter Vinnie, a would-be starlet in the movies. The theory of unaided flight was always in Knight's mind and he even planted a love of aircraft in the mind of Vinnie's boyfriend, a man modelled on real-life aviator Howard Hughes. But the inspiration for the method by which Sam's revelation might be sparked came from Knight's visit to the imposing Angelus Temple in Los Angeles' Echo Park.

Knight had been as much moved by the faith invested in the preacher, Sister Aimee Semple McPherson – one of the most theatrical and powerful evangelists of the age – as he was with the words spoken. Sister Aimee believed that the arts belonged to God and that God would therefore be in favour of any story that endorsed acts of great faith. Eric had already decided Sam would fly and he now had the inspiration to endow him with the means so to do.

In *The Flying Yorkshireman,* Sam and Mully hear, not Sister Aimee but Eric's own creation, the inspirational Sister Minnie Tekel Upharsin Smith. Congregation members are asked to state where they had travelled from, at which point Sam 'came over all bashful', but not Mully. She rose to her feet to announce in a thin Yorkshire voice, 'Mister and Missus Sammywell Small, Polki'thorpe Brigg, 'Uddersfield, Yorksha.' Sister Minnie proclaims that faith can move mountains, and that she'd be willing to prove it – if it wouldn't 'adversely affect real-estate prices in the San Fernando Valley'. Sam becomes so convinced by the lady and all those who had travelled across many states and continents to hear her that on returning to his hotel, and after many false starts, he finally takes a literal leap of faith and in no time is swooping low over the bay with the seabirds.

The adventure, however, comes to an end when Sam realises that his feet belong, literally and metaphorically, on the ground. On returning to Yorkshire, he cleverly distances himself from all his flying feats by telling one enquirer, 'that flyin' Sam was another Sam Small, the lad what wouldn't pick up 'is musket', a reference to the famed monologue, 'Sam, Sam, Pick up thy Musket', delivered by British music-hall star Stanley Holloway.

Knight said of his heroic creation, 'I could have made him Superman, but I didn't, he is an ordinary man who can simply do extraordinary things, just like any man.' 'Godlike', however, was always employed when referring to Sam's flying abilities, and also in reference to stage actors and even when talking of jumping hurdles on horseback. 'We felt like gods,' he said when remembering the fences he and Jere had taken while riding across the Pennsylvania farmland, and in his foreword to *Sam Small The Flying Yorkshireman*:

'You may notice that Sam's character is quite flexible. Sometimes he is just an ordinary mortal, limited by human abilities – and then suddenly sometimes he seems godlike, like a dream come true. Don't let this worry you. Fiction is just dreaming out loud, that's all.'

Here Knight distances himself from any readerly assumption of autobiography, claiming that his fiction was merely 'dreaming out loud', and that Sam's adventures are 'dream-like', the implication being that they have no basis in either truth or traditional fiction. But there is an honesty in the stories that endears them to the child in every reader, and a truth that appeals to the adult in every child – the whole being tied together with a sincerity born of their autobiographical content, all of which propelled the Sam Small stories to international success.

Asked who the Sam Small stories were aimed at, Knight replied 'The world, or wherever there's a Yorkshire lad feeling homesick.' Interestingly, in *Sam Small The Flying Yorkshireman*, the eponymous tale does not feature first, the author allowing the reader to build up their expectations before taking them on a flight of inventive fantasy from which they are allowed to recover in the safety of more 'grounded' adventures like *Sam Small And The Ugly Tyke*. In this story Sam finds himself the owner of yet another dog, on this occasion a cursed terrier, which assumes human form – and with it, the human failing of argumentativeness.

While he may never have appeared on the big screen – despite the film rights having changed hands a dozen times – Sam's exploits were broadcast in the form of plays adapted by Stephen Fox. These were heard in the United States, Canada and South Africa in the late 1930s and early 1940s and, most pleasingly to their author, on the BBC's Northern and Regional Broadcasting Network from Leeds. Sir Cedric Hardwick took the part of Capper Wambley in *Never Come Monday*, Lady Hardwick portraying Capper's wife Mary, who, in a role written especially for broadcast, narrates the action. The programme, put out at 9:30 p.m. on 9th May 1939, was produced by Olive Shapley, a pioneer of women's broadcasting, schools programmes and the live interview. Shapley would later be responsible for BBC's *Woman's Hour*, still a staple of British radio seventy years later. She had been the first producer to put northern voices before the microphone, something of which Eric Knight wholly approved but which received a mixed reception, particularly in London where listeners claimed to have understood very little of what was said.

In a groundbreaking departure from the norm, Shapley had been brave enough to deviate from the BBC's ethos of 'Received Pronunciation', a standardisation of speech designed to improve the verbal dexterity of the working class while being acceptable to the middle class, and in so doing initiated a move toward the regional broadcasting which is an industry standard today.

The radio, or 'wireless' as it was then known, was part of everyday life for millions but was still not universally accepted. While Socialists like Rotha saw any broadcast medium as a tool worth employing to bring the plight of the working class and the unemployed to wider attention, there were others, like George Orwell, who believed the BBC's output to be 'patronising to the working class'. Neither did he see the value of broadcasting the words and opinions of the working class whom he saw as being exploited by the new medium, a curious reaction from a man who spent the greater part of his socio-political career crying out for a platform from which the poor might be heard. Shapley and Knight took a completely different view and embraced what would come to be known as the documentary, a form in which an unmediated representation of the subject is presented, leaving listeners to form their own view.

If Knight's sudden inspiration to document his Sam Small stories was fired by publishing success, there was another motivation, the death in Halifax of his beloved Uncle Percy, the man who inspired his nephew to an American adventure, which was now beginning to fulfil its promise. With his Sam Small stories, a body of work a lifetime in the creating, now making the transition from 'telling stories' to manuscript, Knight was invited to return to Hollywood. Moe Speiser, the Philadelphia lawyer who had introduced Knight and Cummings, suggested to his brother-in-law, Barnie Glazer, sometime Fox script-writer, ex-Philadelphia newspaperman and executive producer at Paramount, that Knight would be useful in his story department at his old salary of $200 a week. The deal done, Knight approached his new post with a different attitude. This time he did what he was asked to do and did not try to change the system. The result was utter boredom. It could not last, and it did not.

Knight had lately enjoyed a brief break in New Mexico with Peter Hurd, during which he had made a decision on his future, and it did not include California. The beckoning of the fertile land in the east could not be ignored; the farmer in Eric Knight had prompted the writer in him into action. They spoke together in a summing up of their lives to date:

'Pennsylvania land is like a wife to a man, Mexico like a big horse that kicks the shit out of men, and California land is a whore who drops her pants for the first man with a watering pot.'

Knight enjoyed this analogy. The words would appear in *You Play the Black and The Red Comes Up*, also in letters to Rotha, among others. So once again he was leaving Hollywood, and was about to repeat a mistake he had made when he and his family left Connecticut for the Bronx. The result, however, would be very different, for Knight had found new optimism in his abilities, and he knew who to thank for his present state of mind and his success:

'All I am – all I ever hoped to be, I am because of Cummings.'

CHAPTER ELEVEN

With Jere working out her month's notice, Eric journeyed to New York City where his wife would shortly take up a new contract as story editor for Selznik's *International Pictures* in their east coast office. He and Tootsie met her at Grand Central Station where she alighted 'resplendent in orchids, from the luxurious Super-Chief, looking more like a star than most of the stars left behind in Hollywood'. She carried with her the good wishes of Tracy and Hepburn, Landi and Eddy, and a gaggle of others. Several sent photographs, including 'Queen of Hollywood' Mary Pickford, who signed hers: 'With much love to Eric & Jerry, from Mary.' Being in many respects an archetypal Englishman, it seems odd Knight never moved in the ex-pat circle revolving around the likes of Niven, Portman, Colman, and honorary Englishmen like Flynn and Fairbanks, despite the fact that he and Jere frequented the same sparkling 'Pickfair' parties where stars of musicals played, danced and sang the night away. Just about all of his friends out on the west coast were Americans.

Eric had turned his back on Hollywood, but he was in good company. Neither F. Scott Fitzgerald nor William Faulkner had found anything in the town or its people to sustain them. Eric's frustration with the place was plain to see and his reasons for leaving manifold, but not being 'popular' cannot be offered up as one of the excuses. He and Jere were considered excellent hosts and often flung open their door, or Landi's, to the most glittering stars in Hollywood. He told his stories, played his guitar, made the people laugh, and performed his favourite party-pieces. As Jere said, Eric had perfect pitch and could play any tune on the piano having heard it only once. And while this talent does not appear to have extended to classical music, it did not stop the Knights working out a practical joke that involved Eric sitting down at the piano to begin Chopin's Fantasy Impromptu in C Minor. Halfway through the introduction Jere would sweep in to announce dinner. Eric and his guests would look suitably disappointed as they made their way to the dining room – and would never know that those few bars represented his entire classical repertoire.

The Knights had funded their return east through an auction of their possessions and the farm, from which proceeds Eric had taken a hundred dollars for his train ticket and expenses, travelling most of the cross-continental journey in the baggage car with a pregnant Tootsie. On his arrival in New York, he and Jere took an apartment at 307 East 4th Street. The couple lived on Jere's salary while Eric worked on the Sam Small stories. Jere soon fitted into her new position and as always received many invitations to film and literary gatherings, all of which were taken up in the hope of furthering Eric's career, but as he told Rotha, things did not always go smoothly:

'We go to big literary parties and meet big literary people. Thus far… I have achieved:

1. One slanging match with an Irish Fascist in a literary-art cocktail party….

2. One beautifully bloody battle with a Jew-baiter….

3. Getting into a swinging match at a cocktail party at which I punched (a) the nose of the editor of a publishing house, (b) accidentally hit the editor of a magazine, breaking his pince-nez glasses and cutting his cheek.

4. I have a cut cheek, a bump on my forehead, and a broken finger, which as an admiring pugilist pointed out, all came from my tendency to lead with a right swing instead of a jab, and lack of knowledge of how to make a fist.

So… life is not dull. There are so many persons who need a smack in the snoot in New York. I'm damned if I can keep quiet before the smug bastards when I think of Almeria and Guernica and Bilbao, and I just feel it's time all us guys just stopped being peace-makers and did a little retaliation ourselves.'

Knight had told friends that he felt his career would 'take off' in New York and that it was the best place to be for an up-and-coming writer. Privately he liked it no more than Hollywood. The apartment, though far superior to the one he had occupied in the Bronx ten years earlier, was stifling and claustrophobic to the writer and farmer within him. He soon slipped back into depression, a fact he confides to lawyer Barnie Winkelman:

'I do not wish to write much today, as I am in the deep moods. I find they overcome me more and more as I get older, and I have no way to combat them. So I do nothing but just wait until they are over. When I'm in them I despair of humanity, of ever sense coming from Germany, Italy and the welter of Spain; I see no hope in Communism nor more than in Fascism, and I see little hope for myself as one of those things called men.'

He goes on to say 'I still have confidence in my work' and that he feels New York might offer more opportunities than he has found elsewhere, but it is clear that his initial optimism is fading. 'I might try to find a Pennsylvania farm,' he says, but then goes on to bemoan a lack of income and his former wife's demands for money. 'She has a damn sight more than us and knows how to spend it'. This was the first, last, and only reference to Dorothy in any of his writings since the break-up of their marriage.

Knight's depression was relieved on seeing the advance notices for *Song On Your Bugles*, which stimulated a new burst of creativity. What he called 'fiction' now poured from him, and over the next few weeks he wrote *The Lad Who Made His Fortune*, which follows the life of a Yorkshireman who enjoys financial success in America before returning home to find that his wealth has alienated him from his own community. The short work has the feel of a Sam Small story – hardly surprising, since Sam was occupying every corner of his mind as interest grew from *Story Magazine* on the heels of *Meet Me In The Shadows* and *Song On Your Bugles*

On June 18th 1938, *Story* published *Sam Small The Flying Yorkshireman* in novella form – a collection of adventures that won the American Book Society Book of the Month Award – and on July 12th Knight's typewriter was packed into its box and loaded into the Buick ready for his escape from the city.

The editor of *Story*, Whit Burnett, must be credited with furthering the Sam Small cause, for it was he who persuaded Knight to produce more of the stories. In his view, America had not since Mark Twain produced a 'social satirist of any calibre'. He saw a similarity between Twain's Huck Finn and Knight's Sam Small. Both were proud of their origins, both exercised a considerable intelligence in pursuit of adventures, both encountered injustice and ignorance as they overcame daunting obstacles to achieve legendary status. Huck, it may be said, has achieved enduring fame because, unlike Sam, he has been portrayed on film and television. But in all other respects, it seems, Burnett considered Knight's talent as a writer equal to that of Twain.

Sam, of course, is not just a man who can fly. There have been many of those, and Knight's decision to have his hero achieve flight only in the third of eight stories is intended to show the reader that he had to endure many hardships, and grow as a character, before performing the ultimate feat of willpower. Later, Sam would prove that his real strength lay in deciding not to fly, despite having the ability to do so.

Approaching a publisher with an unlikely hero from an unusual background, one who faces life's injustices with no weapons but common sense, willpower, and the assistance of a select group of unlikely mates, a hero who embarks on adventures of mythical proportions and manages to fly unaided as the plots spiral into the magical, might sound like a recipe for instant rejection. The same probably applied to publishers who were approached with JK Rowling's *Harry Potter* adventures, but if the character is 'real' – and Sam, like Huck Finn and Harry Potter, is as real as a written character can be – he may embark on all manner of adventures and still remain 'grounded' in the spiritual sense of the word.

Knight knew that Sam carried with him a strong moral message, and claimed that he had captivated generations of Yorkshire people because, despite his powers, he never became too fantastic to be unbelievable. The word 'magic' is never used to describe Sam the character, but as so often happens in literature, magic occurs when it is being pursued. It should be noted that there is actually no evidence of Sam's existence prior to his appearance in Eric's work; but to him, having heard about Sam as a toddler, the character was ageless.

Knight was now in an interesting position. On the one hand, he believed that a story was 'dead' once it was written; on the other, by writing each one down after a lifetime of allowing Sam's tales to 'make themselves up', he had finally ensured that they were being *read* for the first time. And since Sam was a country-man whose hope for the future was once all he had, it was fitting that his chronicler should now be moving back to the countryside and to a new chapter in his life.

It is unclear whether Jere had already set out for the Knight's new home or if she remained for a short time in New York City, but we do know that Knight travelled, not to Pennsylvania as he had hoped, but north from the city, deep into the Hudson Valley to a spot where that great river is at its widest and where the distant wooded hills beyond its shores shine blue in its reflected light. A dozen small towns like Yonkers, Hastings-on-Hudson, Scarborough and Ossining dot the map between New York City and the Knight's new home, all of which the author passed through before finally arriving in Croton-on-Hudson, a quiet, picturesque, tree-lined village which might trick the traveller into believing they had arrived in an English market town – although behind the façade was a structure that spoke of great industrial endeavour.

The Croton Dam has been compared to the Pyramids as one of the great man-made edifices. A remarkable feat of late nineteenth-century engineering, the twenty-mile long structure holds back the thirty-two billion gallons needed to satisfy New York's demand for fresh water. It provides Croton with breathtaking vistas, which have attracted artists and writers for over a century – two of whom, Isadora Duncan and the photographer Man Ray, were Croton residents in the 1930s. There were two others, however, whose influence on literature had been considerable, and both had lived at different times in the Knights' new home.

Cherry House, part of Croton's Finney Farm estate, stands on the side of a wooded hill at the end of an unpaved country lane. It looks out over a sunlit, grass-covered courtyard dominated by a huge concrete barn, the first of its kind to have been built in America. It was erected by Horace Greeley, founder of the *New York Tribune*, who occupied the great house in the 1840s. Born in New Hampshire in 1811, he became an apprentice printer and worked in New York before starting his own weekly, *The New Yorker*, in 1834. Four years later and having made a name for himself through his pro-Whig journalism, he was asked to edit the campaigning *Jeffersonian*. The two papers would come together three years later to form the *Tribune*.

Knight was well aware that he was now the occupier of a house once the property of a man who lived in rebellion against the establishment and the standard practices of the newspaper business, and not least one who had contributed hugely to literature through his support of Mark Twain's early career and the aspirations of the working class, famously urging their sons to 'Go west, young man!'. Not surprisingly, Knight set about his new life in Croton inspired by the countryside, relishing the isolation and the history of the house, and doubtless intrigued to find that it had been home to a second literary figure of note, one with connections to his beloved New Mexico.

Mabel Dodge Sterne Luhan was an internationally celebrated patron of the arts for over sixty years. She was a key player in the life of Greenwich Village in the early 1900s, later in the artists' colony in Taos, New Mexico, a place Eric Knight and Peter Hurd knew well. Luhan had lived in Florence with one husband and in Paris with another where she mixed in an elite circle including Hemingway, Ford, Pound, Picasso and Gertrude Stein. On her return to New York in 1916 she moved out of her 5th Avenue apartment and into Cherry House with husband number three, Maurice Sterne, a painter. It was in 1919 that she decamped to Taos, marrying Native American Tony Luhan four years later.

Knight came to the Hudson River town to concentrate on the completion of a project to which he alluded in a letter to his attorney dated the very day of his arrival in Croton, and in which he admitted to the abandonment of *Rose Without Warning*. The novel had attracted no interest from publishers. He was, he wrote, thrilled to be out of the city and receiving literary praise for *Song On Your Bugles* on both sides of the Atlantic:

'Myself, I am in a heavenly beautiful spot, in a rather damp but pretty cottage, where I am now deeply concentrated in my next book – which looks like being the life story of an American town – a one-factory town. I want to have it all roughed out by the end of summer, and all completed by Christmas. I am trying to keep a schedule of six pages a day. *Song On Your Bugles* seems to be getting the same terrific critical reception here that it got in England. Story Magazine is building big publicity. (Get the current issue of Story, July. I have a small novella in it called *The Flying Yorkshireman*, which is also going in a Harper collection book.)'

Knight was justified in his hopes for *Song On Your Bugles* in the US –
even if he had been obliged to include a glossary of terms to guide the
American reader through Yorkshire dialect words from 'Addle' (earn) to
'Yead' (head) – and received a great boost to his confidence when he read a
review by Elliot Paul, an American journalist based in Europe:

'Song On Your Bugles is the reawakening of British literature. It means
a farewell to the Freudian miasma of the late D. H. Lawrence, and adios to
Aldington and Huxley and their passel of clever and intellectual nitwits. Too
bad you are not with us in person, old man Hardy. You would have liked
this book.'

Paul's words were more significant at the time than they may appear
today. Huxley and Lawrence had been friends and part of that 'passel' the
critic mentioned; the world was still captivated by Huxley's vision of
dystopia as depicted in *Brave New World*, published five years earlier.
Aldington – the husband of Hilda Doolittle, better known as the poet H.D.
– was also a member of Huxley's set, a highly respected critic and poet,
whose imagist work *A Fool I' the Forest* (1925), was said to have captured the
desperation and hopelessness of war and its consequences.

Knight, though thrilled to find himself in the literary company of those
mentioned by Paul, wrote to Winkelman: 'Geesis! If it's good as that I
ought to read it again myself,' adding that he had 'put all the guts and
strength and beauty and tragedy I had into it' and that if he never produced
another novel, *Song On Your Bugles* would 'stand about 10,000 times higher
than *Invitation to Life*' which, he said, had been an 'eye-tooth-cutter'.

Outstanding endorsements from Britain – and more importantly,
Yorkshire – were also finding their way to Knight in the form of cuttings
posted by his aunts and uncles at home. *The Evening Standard* in London
called *Song On Your Bugles* 'a magnificent story, a model of how a novel
should be written', with the *Yorkshire Post* adding praise for the hero of
Knight's plot: 'Perhaps Mr. Knight's greatest feat is that he has succeeded,
where so many great writers have failed, in presenting a convincing portrait
of a genius in Herrie Champion'. The London *Times* said: 'Song on Your
Bugles is both moving and impressive…Mr. Knight's story moves fast. He
writes in a forthright way which compels your admiration.' But when one
British critic proclaimed the work to be 'A Sophoclean Tragedy' and Knight
as 'the finest writer on proletarian life now alive in England', his prose 'pure
music', all the author could add was 'what the hell'.

It is worth noting here that Orwell's *Road to Wigan Pier* – a work entirely
concerned with 'proletarian life' and now held up as an outstanding
example of English descriptive prose – would appear in 1937 to nothing
like the critical acclaim that greeted *Song On Your Bugles* and to questions
about the validity of the narrative, and its author's qualifications to
represent the working class – objections never levelled at Knight's novel.

Orwell's was, of course, never 'a story', rather a social documentary and as such open to doubts as to its reliability. Knight got across an equally strong message and avoided the critical questioning by doing what he had learned to do many years earlier, dressing the truth and biography in the clothing of fiction, something Orwell could not and would not have done.

There is no doubt that *The Road to Wigan Pier* would 'illustrate a theory' as one London critic would put it, or that Knight's works allowed the reader to witness the events portrayed and use their intelligence to see a solution if that is what they felt inclined to do. But when we take in isolation Orwell's outstanding descriptive and observational talent – as portrayed in *The Road to Wigan Pier's* brief, single-paragraph account of a girl unblocking a drain with a stick – there can be no doubt he too was an immensely talented writer.

Not until many years later did Orwell hear praise such as Knight received for *Song On Your Bugle*. In fairness, Orwell, like his contemporary P.G. Wodehouse, was happiest, at least in the early part of his career, in what he described as 'lower-upper middle-class prose', chronicling the lives of those he knew so well and from whose class rules, teachings and distinctions he could not escape. And the same is true of Knight at this time: he wrote about what he knew.

Had Knight actually been living in England, his literary abilities might have been recognised earlier, and seen as equal to those of the author of *Animal Farm* and *Nineteen Eighty-four*, for he would have been more in the public eye and more easily accessible than he was as the Englishman living in America. There was, however, one element missing from Knight's work, which was ever-present in Orwell's – controversy. Unlike Orwell, Knight offered no political solutions to the hardships facing the working class about whom he wrote, nor did he make any reference to the multi-layered class system so painstakingly defined by Orwell. Indeed, his work does not concern itself with class comparisons, and the reason Knight gave for this approach says much about him. 'Nothing is worth fighting against,' he said, 'but some things are worth fighting for,' and the 'fight' to which he was referring was not for class equality but for a society that embraced all classes and cultures, and recognised their rich diversity as a societal asset. Of course he believed in a fairer distribution of wealth and an end to exploitation, but at no time did he advocate a classless society, believing it neither desirable nor possible.

For Knight, battling against the class divide diverted energy from the struggle to improve the lot of those on the receiving end of social injustice. Perhaps if he had been more controversial he might have enjoyed greater or earlier success, but this would have meant being committed to a political cause or veering from his chosen path of story-telling. In any case, he was possessed of a natural propensity for contradicting any political diatribe on the basis that, by its very nature, it must be insincere. When one politician campaigned with the slogan 'America needs men of action, not dreamers', Knight countered with: 'I say we need more dreamers and less action; dreamers don't start wars.'

Because it is less controversial, Eric Knight's work on the miners of the north of England has never enjoyed comparison with that of Orwell. 'Wigan Pier' is held up as being unique to its time, but if we accept both as social documentary we must remember that Knight's is written by a man who had lived with the kind of poverty from which the miners had no escape. Orwell made much of his vagrant life and destitution in his earlier *Down and Out in Paris and London,* but while he made every effort to live the life of the tramp he could never forget that he might, at any time, call upon friends and family for a lifeline.

It is therefore interesting to note that while Orwell, a firmly middle-class author, promotes a political solution to the social injustices affecting the working class, Knight tells his story in the hope it will inspire those whose plight he had at one time shared and from which he had escaped, by virtue of his own efforts. As one critic wrote of *Song On Your Bugles*:

'This is no proletarian novel written to illustrate a theory. It is a story about flesh-and-blood human beings in which love and hate, success and defeat, comedy and tragedy, light and shadow, alternate and merge as in life itself. Not since Dickens has any author created a more convincing set of characters.'

This writer clearly has in mind the socio-political content of works being published at the same time. The same writer also points out that the first British publisher to see the work, Boriswood, had immediately taken up an option to publish despite the author's protestations that the work required some editing. Even the thirteen discarded openings to the work and the years spent in writing it had not convinced Knight that *Song On Your Bugles* was truly a 'finished' work. Notes scribbled on a date-stamped envelope suggest that the work had in fact begun its journey as far back as 1931 when Knight was still in Philadelphia and that it had therefore been a work-in-progress for several years before its author gained enough confidence to mention its existence to friends.

In spite of the literary praise the novel was receiving and the comparison drawn between its author, Twain, and Dickens, Knight confessed that all he wished for was that it would bring in enough money to pay the rent for two years and allow Jere to stop working. In any case – and despite what he had told Winkelman about the novel's quality – Knight still privately felt *The Flying Yorkshireman* was his best work and only hoped, as he told Winkelman, that he could sustain work 'nine tenths' as good. But with his old insecurity never far from the surface, Knight promised his attorney a copy of his next book with the words, 'that way it will at least have one reader'.

Knight had spent some time at Cherry House prior to moving there permanently. In a letter to Rotha dated July 8th he described the place in great detail and told of another resident of the Finney Farm estate, namely his hero in the sphere of documentary film, Robert Flaherty. It seems Flaherty had lived at Cherry House in the early 1920s before moving to larger premises on the estate. He had produced *Man of Aran* that year, as accomplished a work in Knight's view as the much celebrated *Nanook of the North*, and streets ahead of the Flaherty-Grierson collaboration, *Industrial Britain*, from which Flaherty had learned his lesson about working alone. In his later lectures on the subject, however, Knight would call on all three of these works to instruct his students, holding up 'Aran' and 'Nanook' as masterpieces of the genre.

In his letters, his description of his new surroundings is lyrical but there is no mention now of Sam, only a renewed concentration upon Tootsie:

'The cottage is beside the great stone walls of a barn whose roof tumbled in years ago. Now the space within the barn is lawn. Only here, of all places, can one find that feeling of quiet age that is so common in England. The collie, with us once again, lives in a riotous new world. Gophers, jacks, she knows. But not these strange animals: cottontails, who sit in the quiet of the evening on the cloistered lawn, pheasants and quail that rush up from the fields around; even a deer with great white rump and tail that went springing on India-rubber stiff legs across a swamp. Flowers I do not know, smells I had forgotten in the dryness of California and the dust of New York – they are too much at present. Soon I shall become used to them and work better.'

Knight further tells Rotha, 'I have started a new novel' – but at the same time voices his insecurity:

'I write with an awareness of knowing so little, and good writing often is that which avoids what the writer does not know. I would want to know all things and write on them. Every word written is an index of a man's capacity and every sentence he writes indelibly his autobiography.'

More profound words perhaps than Knight knew, for here in the excitement of his new surroundings he expresses what he would repeat to Winkelman later – that his fiction was always, unavoidably autobiographical. His desire to produce 'good writing' would not allow him to write about anything of which he had no experience.

Unfortunately for scholars, *The One Factory Town* died forever for reasons on which we may only ponder, and would have been forgotten had its author not briefly mapped out its plot to Rotha. The autobiographical content of the work would have filled a gap in Knight's life about which he wrote almost nothing – or more likely destroyed all he had written – namely, the period of his marriage to Dorothy. We might have learned first hand from the work an admission that Knight had not been 'at Yale' but had merely been a part-time machine operator at the lock manufacturers. We might have discovered more of his exploits as a Captain of the National Guard and artillery instructor down in Oklahoma. What else might have been revealed cannot be known.

It was, however, not all work at this time. Knight continued his horse-riding, and he found a keen tennis partner in the shape of another man whose work he admired, Max Eastman. A Croton resident since 1929, Eastman lived at Sheepbarn Cottage on Mount Airy Road where he had built a tennis court he described as 'too short for professionals, but with plenty of room for enthusiastic amateurs'.

Eastman, his wife Eliena Krycenko and Knight became instant friends. Max Forrester Eastman was born in Canandaigua, New York, the son of parents who were both members of the clergy. He had studied for a PhD in philosophy at Columbia University, then settled in Greenwich Village with his sister, Crystal, a writer. There he involved himself in politics and became a founder member of the Men's League for Women's Suffrage in 1910. Eastman was essentially a social reformer whose natural left-leaning politics were entirely in keeping with the Greenwich Village community to which he belonged. Deeply interested in what he called 'the psychology of poetry' he published *Enjoyment of Poetry*, which established him as a literary authority. But poetry could not satisfy his political aspirations and in 1913 he became editor of *The Masses* – a publication strongly opposed to America's involvement in World War I.

The editorship introduced Eastman to contributors like Amy Lowell and Upton Sinclair, whose 1906 novel *The Jungle* had created a public outcry in its chronicling of conditions in the meat-packing business. Lowell was yet another whose European travels had led her to friendships with Lawrence, Doolittle and Pound, and their influence had guided her to the Imagist style of which Eastman was an avid supporter. A shortage of money closed *The Masses* down in 1918, Eastman and others having twice stood trial under the 1917 Sedition Act. They were acquitted on both occasions.

Eastman was not above criticising the world's most respected writers and questioned widely-held Freudian concepts. His new tennis partner, equally outspoken, was apparently seen as being above reproach. In finding they held similar views on the role the movies should be playing in raising awareness of social issues, Eastman encouraged Knight to consider lecturing on the topic of film production. Eastman, it is worth noting, would reverse his views on Communism by 1940 and eventually become a supporter of Joe McCarthy and his anti-Communist 'witch hunts'. He would go on to become a *Reader's Digest* editor.

Knight and Eastman found they shared an admiration for the work of Isadora Duncan and F. Scott Fitzgerald – and for Mexico, where Eastman had toured with Hemingway before leaving for Russia in 1922, and on several occasions since. Movie director Sergei Eisenstein also enjoyed the respect of both men and would later feature in Knight's lectures on movie makers, principally for his original story and subsequent direction of *The Battleship Potemkin*. Russian films in general and Russian directors in particular were greatly respected in America in the 1920s and '30s and one of their number, Anatole Litvak, would direct the film adaptation of Knight's *This Above All* in 1942. The common ground in the friendship, however, was not mutual associations and admirations, nor even common dislikes, rather the concern the two shared for humanity. Eastman's words 'I was fanatical in my zeal for human equality' applied equally to both men.

So it is easy to imagine Croton days spent in mutual admiration, with artistic and erudite friends who shared a concern for humanity and the validity of the written word and the movies. Settled and happy in their company, Knight began to plan his future in discussions with his closest friends. Letters addressed to Cummings – now living in Culver City, California – attest to Knight's friendship with Eastman, his plans, and the fact that *Esquire* magazine were considering his work, principally *The Lad Who Made His Fortune*. They did not take it but would, in December, publish *Mary Ann and the Duke*, a Sam Small adventure.

It is worth noting that the Sam Small stories and their author, while unique, bear a resemblance to another Anglo-American literary figure of the period. P.G. Wodehouse, an English middle class émigré to America, was sixteen years older than Knight and had already established himself as a successful writer. Like Knight, he wrote about that which he knew best, the machinations of his own class, most notably portrayed in the adventures of his creations Jeeves and Wooster. Jeeves, like Sam, is the master-negotiator, able to extricate his employer, a hopeless hooray, from any situation by the application of simple common sense. Although a similarity exists, there is no evidence to suggest that Eric Knight had ever read Wodehouse or vice versa; indeed the opposite may be the case, for Knight noted the names of almost all those whose work he had read, and there is no mention of the creator of Bertie Wooster.

So much of popular opinion is informed and mediated by others, and while Knight was receiving high literary praise during his life he has never, since his death, come to the attention of the 'literary' critics. Evelyn Waugh famously called Wodehouse 'one of the finest writers of the century'. He may well have been, but Waugh shared his social class and, most importantly, had not, as far as we may ascertain, read Sam Small's adventures. And it is worth remembering that by the time Wodehouse, Isherwood and Huxley were settling in America and creating their Anglo-American identities, Eric Knight had already been there twenty years or more. That they have endured longer is because their stories, unlike

Knight's, have been repeatedly told and studied in university English departments, while Knight – if he has been noticed – has been taken for a foreign writer whose work belongs in American Studies.

Unlike the characters created by Wodehouse, of course, Sam Small was possessed of a fantastic gift, the power of unaided flight, an attribute which would in the end be taken from him in favour of one that is available to us all – common sense. If Knight was ever afraid his readership would desert him once Sam could no longer fly, he never expressed this concern. When Knight called Sam 'sometimes godlike' he was not referring to his flying ability, rather to his skill in rising above any situation, including those involving magic spells and mythical giants brought to life, and dealing with them in a manner that can only be described as omnipotent – and all this while his author retains a sense of absolute belief in the character.

This is undoubtedly where Knight's greatest skill lay, not in promoting belief in his 'godlike' character but in the suspension of disbelief. Given this expert handling of a complex set of dynamics, it is no surprise that Sam was about to take the reading public by storm.

America read Sam's adventures first, but London publishers Hamish Hamilton would introduce them to the rest of the English-speaking world in 1938, just as their author was about to embark on one of the busiest periods of his professional and personal life. It is clear therefore that all Sam's adventures in that first volume had been laid down well in advance of the Knights' move to Croton where they were once again told and retold, now to a new audience including the Eastmans, Litvak, and others.

In these early days in the new home, Tootsie was Knight's main literary preoccupation as he began a series of what he called 'juvenile adventures' based on her outgoing personality and intelligence. The work might have progressed more quickly into print had Knight not received an important commission – although he even shoved that aside to complete a slim volume inspired by Hollywood and published under the name of his late uncle Richard Hallas. The rapidly written amalgam of one-dimensional stereotypes and transparent plots would bear Knight's longest title. Although nothing more than a backhanded swipe at Tinsel Town, *You Play The Black and The Red Comes Up* may still be found on library shelves and is studied in American universities under the heading 'Cult Classics', a genre not even conceived of at the time of its publication.

The commission that delayed the work on Sam Small came about after a visit – at last – from Eric's long-time correspondent Paul Rotha. Many scholars have said in defence of Orwell's *Road to Wigan Pier* that while it was in some respects flawed, and may not have adhered to the remit dictated by the charity commissioning the work, the author was at least willing to travel to those areas depressed by mine closures and enter a thoroughly alien world. Such scholars overlooked Paul Rotha, there in early 1937 shooting documentary footage. Rotha was a dedicated Socialist who would have been the first to join any action aimed at political change, one who truly conveyed a deep-seated empathy for the hardships suffered by the miners. As for Eric Knight, here was a man who talked the way they talked, one willing to scramble up slag heaps to riddle out the few lumps of coal that could be used or sold, just as he had in his boyhood, a man who could spit and curse and smoke the way they did, a man who knew the true worth of money and, more importantly, one who knew what life was like when you were obliged to live in poverty.

In September 1937, fresh from the coalfields, Rotha finally came face to face with his correspondent of many years when the Museum of Modern Art Film Library and the Rockefeller Foundation invited him to give a series of lectures on documentary filmmaking. Here was a chance to meet Eric, and to enlist his help in preparing his presentations for an American audience. He was met in New York City by Jere, who escorted him up-state by train. Rotha later wrote of his arrival: 'There on a dark evening, Knight came to greet me at Harmon railroad station; he was red-haired, in a white sweater and jeans, with a smile you could never forget.'

The two joined forces, Knight being contracted to speak on his Hollywood script-editing work and his film criticism. Among those present would be Alfred Hitchcock and Alistair Cooke. Rotha's part in the programme – held at New York City's Grand Central Building – comprised the showing of films made recently in the UK by the *Strand Film Company*, one of which, *Today We Live*, dealt with the problems of unemployed miners in South Wales and a rural community in Gloucestershire. Inspired by the film, Knight began pitching the idea of a similar written piece to several newspapers and magazines. He envisaged a series of articles on the plight of the coalminers of Yorkshire for the *Saturday Evening Post*. Once he'd sold the idea, he planned his trip and mapped out his ideas. He would visit not only Yorkshire, but also Lancashire, Wales and Scotland, and his articles would inform the American people of the desperate conditions under which the colliers were living following the pit closures, as industrialists abandoned coal for more profitable enterprises. He could not know that Orwell was already covering similar ground but it would not have mattered even if he had, for his stories were destined for an American readership and would be told by one utterly familiar with poverty and hardship. He was ideally suited for the work, far more so than Orwell. It was no problem for Eric to cast off his adopted in favour of his childhood accent, throw on a pair of pit boots and mingle unobtrusively with British working men and women. Orwell, on the other hand, probably never saw real life in the mining communities. People he met were unlikely to act naturally in the presence of a man whose accent cast him as one of the employer class.

Knight would set sail for Britain on December 31st 1937. Before leaving, there was time for tennis matches, horse-riding, and adventures in the woods with Tootsie – where a group of grown men of letters would play cowboys and Indians like so many children. The legendary director of *The Big Parade* and *Hallelujah*, King Vidor, joined in the game in the reeds around a lake with Knight disguised, not as a Navajo but a Comanche, Eastman as an Apache, and Rotha in the garb of the Blackfoot, all of which was captured and labelled a 'Western' by Eastman's son, Dan, on a 16mm movie camera.

Following the western adventure, Knight suggested a new game – darts. Having no board on which to play, Jere telephoned Macy's in New York City to enquire after a 'British dartboard'. They had one in stock, freshly imported from Fortnum and Mason's in London. The cost, however, was fifty dollars. Knight pointed to a fallen elm behind the house and declared, 'We could take a slice off that for a board', at which point he and Rotha began work. Having cut what they needed, the two travelled to nearby Peekshill to buy copper wire and nails to complete the task. There was, though, a flaw in the plan: neither had any darts. They would drive into New York City and call at Macy's.

On the way they realised that neither could remember in which order a dartboard should be numbered. No matter, they would scrutinise one in the store. Rotha faithfully noted what followed:

'A suave young assistant in the Sports Department produced a splendid hogsbristle dartboard and a set of flights. Idly I threw a dart at the board. 'Eric,' I said in my most English accent, 'this is not a regular board.' Eric was busy noting down the numbers of the beds in their locations. 'The distance from the centre of the bull to the double's ring should be seven and a half inches,' I said soberly, 'this one is only six and a half.' The assistant called for the manager of Sports Department. Knight confided in him. 'See, my friend here's from England. He was the runner-up in the Kent county darts Championship last year.' I threw another dart. 'These measurement aren't right,' I declaimed. 'I'll fetch a rule and you can measure them, sir,' said the manager. He did. I measured them all right. Knight wrote it all down. 'I'll send in a complaint to London, sir,' said the manager. You do just that,' said Knight, 'in the meantime we'll take this set of arrows.' All evening we marked off the with nails and wire and played our first game around midnight.'

As autumn turned to winter, the lake that had provided Dan Eastman with his Western backdrop froze over, and Rotha watched as 'Jere and Eric skated in the moonlight with dazzling grace, as they do so many things together.'

CHAPTER TWELVE

On his arrival in England, Knight travelled first to London and from there to South Wales to conduct his research. Later he went to Tyneside and Scotland's Lanark Valley, before finally arriving in his native Yorkshire. While working there he found time to visit his Aunt Kit in Leeds where he also found Aunt Emily. She had moved from Halifax to live with her sister-in-law on the death of her husband Edwin two years earlier. The meeting was timely, Aunt Emily taking the opportunity to hand her nephew the papers on family history she had researched in Paris in the 1920s. This was Eric's last meeting with Kit, who would die later that year aged 57.

The material he gathered in the coalfields would appear in newspapers, in later novels, and documentary film. The extended articles in the *Saturday Evening Post* first appeared on March 24th 1938 under the heading 'Britain's Black Ghosts' and 'The Stricken Arenas', and were supported by stark photographs of miners 'grubbing' on the slag heaps for coal, resting in Salvation Army canteens over coal-stained teacups. There were pictures too of shops with windows displaying 'Going out of Business' notices and, most poignantly, of pallid, unkempt, filthy children hungrily devouring the sugarless biscuits handed out by charitable relief organisations.

Articles, however, could not convey the full reality of their desperate situation, but a novel could, and the one Knight later produced, *Now Pray We For Our Country*, captures the utter misery of the time. Published in Britain in 1940, it took its title from a popular school song, *Medal For A Hero*, which Eric had sung in his Bewerley Street days over thirty years previously:

Now pray we for our country
That England long may be
The Holy, and the happy,
And the gloriously free.

The novel would be renamed for the American market, probably to avoid confusion over whose country was being prayed for. Its U.S. title, *The Happy Land*, came from another rhyme remembered by Knight, this time from F.W. Faber's poem *Paradise*, which he had read at the Boston Latin School:

O Paradise, O Paradise,
Who doth not crave for rest,
Who would not seek the happy land
Where they that lov'd are blest?

And while Knight avoided any obvious socio-political message, he could not resist the urge to deliver a social history lesson in the picture he painted:

'Once they were fair, those valleys of Britain, and the order of life in them seemed unchangeable. The church was the cultural center; the village about it, where the distinctive communal crafts flourished, was the social and economical nucleus; but the true richness came from the land in the valley. The land was a hard taskmaster, but the peasant farmers served it well, giving most when it demanded most – during the plantings and the harvests.

But if there were harvests, there were spring rains too. Burns, becks and afons came down in spate and freshet, tearing at the soil. And they laid bare a new fount of richness for Britain – minerals beneath the earth. The men who owned the land leased it to other men, who supplied capital and machinery. Shafts went down into the earth. The era of a new sort of fullness for Britain had begun.

The peasant farmers left plow and pastures, and streamed to the collieries and ironworks. They forsook the land gladly, for the new kind of work promised more hours of leisure and its higher wages held promise of a fuller life.

Thus it was that the fair face of Britain began to change. From the pits and the ironworks the regimented rows of bleak houses thrust themselves out into the green valleys. Slag tips spawned on the hillsides. Grime began showering the soil.

The people did not mind, for the grime was the rich dirt of industry. Coal was power. Factories had to be near power. Potteries, brickyards, cotton mills rushed to the new towns. They needed more men. The Scots came over the heather and the Yorkshiremen over the moors; The Welsh shepherd left his hills and the Irish peasant came across the sea. They jammed themselves into the new areas to share in the wealth. For it was wealth. If the houses were ugly and grim, the life inside them was warm and full and compact. Men worked in the heavy industries; the women and children were needed in the weaving and spinning mills. Children were now an asset. A big family could have eight, nine, ten wage earners. They ate lustily and their bodies were strong. British ships were carrying the British goods they made out to an eager world. More people were needed to make even more goods. The towns grew larger and larger; under the pall of soot they roared louder and louder.'

Through his short, illustrative sentences Knight painted a poetic picture of Britain for American readers who then saw it torn down before their eyes by greedy mine owners, whose first response to an economic depression was to abandon the very colliers who had clawed out their wealth. Little wonder that those with whom Knight scrambled on the slagheaps were willing to share their deepest thoughts, for he was one of their own, a man brought up in those same little houses while labouring in those same mills. If Orwell in his research for *The Road to Wigan Pier* had hoped to gain the same level of confidence while carefully keeping his hands clean and living in pleasant hotels, he was seriously mistaken. He did not speak the tongue, and though he genuinely had their interest at heart, this alone alienated him from the very people he wished to know.

In his second newspaper article, Knight calls upon his own boyhood for descriptive narrative:

'Since coal was power, the growing industries moved nearer the source of that power, for it was heavy to transport. Mills grew beside the one-time market villages. This meant more fullness for the people, for mills needed deft fingers to spin the weave. The men were working in the ironworks and the mines; the women and children worked in the mills. Children were an asset. Out of a family of ten, eight or nine – or perhaps even all ten – were working, earning. Although living quarters were poor, unsanitary, in general the people were well-fed, grew sturdy. It seemed the cycle of fullness from coal would never end.'

But as the author pointed out, it did end, and the old industrial 'centers' offering hope for the future died in almost every respect of the word, elbowing its people into the dole queue:

'Once families scaled down their living to the pitiful survival of dole existence, it was the end of hope. Thus the dole aided in creating that strange anomaly of the stricken arenas – strange islands in the middle of a modern social system in which all basic laws of the system seem paralyzed, centers where children grow to maturity without ever having known the law that the right to live entails the right to work.

In the villages of the stricken areas, the crumbling houses sink as the land subsides in the disused mines. In those houses women struggle to make ends meet. Their husbands stand all day on the street corners in defeated idleness. Their sons roam the streets in a constant but lifeless

Knight was careful in his dealings with the miners and mill workers not to do what his 'Mr. Smith' had done when visiting the inns of Yorkshire, extolling the virtues of America. He knew he would not have been believed.

The first draft of his novel was far too long. It had to be cut. He would bemoan the fact in a letter to Barnie Winkelman after working on it at Peter Hurd's ranch in New Mexico.

'Dear Barnie:
Back in the East – and your letter. I've read little – only Steinbeck's. It is damn strong. It's the book he's been pointing to all his life, I think. Me – I'll never write the book I'm pointing to. I've come back from N.M. with the 300,000 cut to 160,000 and Harpers have it. Seem to like it – but I must cut more. I go to Colorado for the summer soon.

So, I am busy, well, working hard. Manage to live. What more does man ask? The [coming] war – it will not touch me this time. I have proven to myself once that I can do things I am afraid of without showing I'm afraid, I'm afraid. So I'm afraid I don't have to do it again.'

The thought process of the author seems disjointed here; he is clearly frustrated with having to cut so much from his manuscript, but the last paragraph represents a declaration with which he was as uncomfortable as he had been as a boy when he promised a dying Richard Hallas that he would spend the rest of his days caring for his Aunt Kit. Back then he had never had any intention of remaining in Yorkshire all his life. Now, despite his protestations in the letter, he had already committed himself to playing a part in the war if it came.

In January 1938, in London at the beginning of that fact-finding trip, Knight had offered his services to the Army 'in any role'. Later he would claim he had been turned down, 'due to my age'. It was not strictly true. The letter made no mention of a meeting of some significance. Paul Rotha had arrived back in England just a few days prior to Knight's departure for the States, and invited Eric to a formal dinner at The English Speaking Union where he, Rotha, was to deliver a lecture on his American assignment. Eric Knight was to be seated at a table with Rotha, Alistair Cooke, and a man whom Knight viewed as a literary giant and an inspiration in his own work, J.B. Priestley. The two got along famously according to Rotha.

Back in the States, Knight began an intensive period of work, riding the wave which accompanied the success of *Song On Your Bugles* and his Sam Small novella – a work dedicated to *Bronx Home News* editor Sam Schwab, 'and ten other newspapermen who encouraged me to write 'understandable English'.

The *Saturday Evening Post* had published *The Flying Yorkshireman* in February, and in March *Esquire* magazine took up Sam's most famous adventure *Never Come Monday*, which was also broadcast on the Columbia Broadcasting System on March 23rd at 7:30 in the evening – and within days by the South African Broadcasting Corporation. Its success prompted the *Post* to print *Strong in The Arms* in their April issue.

The June issue of *Town & Country* magazine, a glossy publication full of advertisements for fine houses, expensive cars, jewellery, furs, pedigree dogs, golfing holidays, diamonds and horses, carried Knight's *In A Small Way*, based on the cruise he and Jere had taken after their wedding. The tale concentrates on the fact that it was not necessary to occupy a lavish cabin and that even in the cheapest accommodation it was possible to feel royally treated.

Esquire renewed their association with Knight when the June issue carried *Time For The Pie Boy*, the autobiographical story of the duties of the youngest employer in the bottle plant who had to sneak out on shopping errands:

'Mostly they were useless and silly things the men sent out for: a plug of chewing tobacco, or coughdrops, or licorice, or, in summer, a bottle of pop or Coca-Cola. But mostly they were pies that the old store woman baked and sold for a nickel. So Danny got the orders and went out through the fence and ever after that it was the same way every afternoon, with the pie-boy going out and breaking the afternoon and helping the men forget that the hours were long and the work hard and dreary.'

It seems that Knight had decided by this time to use American English in stories he thought might only be published in America, even though the story had its roots in Yorkshire where Cornish pasties and Scotch pies were the staple workday diet of labourers.

MacLean's – Canada's National Magazine, introduced Knight's Flying Yorkshireman to readers on June 15th. As a follow-up, it would publish both *Sam Small's Better Half* and *The Ten Gallon Hat* in October. Knight was in Albuquerque, New Mexico, with Paul Horgan and Peter Hurd when the entertainment magazine *The Passing Show* began serialising *The Flying Yorkshireman*. Now embarking upon a new project, the three friends were staying at the home of Lewis J. Korns of the US Soil Conservation Service. Not having written to Rotha since his return to America, Knight penned a three-page letter in which he makes no mention of his writing success, his latest book or his impending lecture tour. Instead his concentration is firmly on the people he sees around him:

'Here I sit far away and the mountains have shut out the rest of the world. Now I am here I understand how these people are not concerned with Hitler, Spain and the world and its problems. They are concerned with their own life about them, and life here means a land-changing range eaten away and turning into desert, lumber robbed from the hills so that rainfall loses its kindness and becomes infrequent and savage cloudbursts.

Here we are in a great basin, which is just as much a story of man and his doings and misdoings as the stricken coalfields of England. The only thing is, the Government is proceeding so vigorously here, which it is not in England.

This is the basin of the Rio Grande River – where stand the small mud houses of the mild Pueblo Indians who traditionally worshipped only rain and corn and led their communal life in protection against the Apache and other plains Indians who were warriors. They spoke of themselves as The People and of the other Indians simply as The Enemy. They sang and danced to the corn and the rain. The sun was no worry; it was always there and didn't have to be worshipped. The rain did.

They had no gold. You know the rest. The murder of the Indians, the sporadic revolts of the Indians, the way the Spaniards drove them from their beautiful adobe apartment-house cities to the hilltops and starved them. How women and children jumped from the cliffs and men slew themselves when there was no food – how the remains were sold as slaves.

Now slowly begins the new story of wise Government. Already they have brought back grass roots to the meadows. Private enterprise, of course, fights the building of dams to hold back water and petitions to graze more cattle than the land can take, but unfortunately the Indians are here, and the Indians are Government wards. Their land is nominally under Government control. And most fortunately, the Indian looks at life correctly.'

The Indians of the area spoke their own language and Spanish, in which Knight questioned them about religion and ritual. The men would speak only about their crops, their corn, their squash, and would not enter into any discussion on spiritual beliefs:

'Thus their only combat against the White man is the secrecy which preserves their religion. The superior White man scorns soil conservation while the Indian accepts it knowing that a man may have bonds and stocks and photographs and not live, but a man must have water to go on corn and land to plant it to live. When you work on these things you are doing something sensible.'

Knight and his party were invited into the home of one Indian woman where three older ones made pottery, a scene he describes in detail:

'The place was spotlessly clean with a picture of – guess who – Nelson Eddy pinned to the wall, I must write him about that. We bought a pot for fifty cents. The traders buy them for ten and sell them to tourists for several dollars. The Government wants the Indians to drive out the bullying White take-it-or-leave-it traders and sell direct to the tourists.

So I have seen Indians, pueblos, ruins, watched the dance to the corn in the mesas, where they dance all day, men and women together, dancing in this fierce sun till sundown, with a drum working out rhythm patterns that no White man can understand, but without one of the dancers ever missing by a single beat or a single change all day. And in the center the elders face together and sing to the corn, and pantomime, and the drum goes on, and the koshari, who are clowns, shout jokes to the dancers to encourage them, and call out insults at the statue of the Virgin that has been carried from the church to watch the older dances for fertility. And the tip-off is this. When we wish to be slapstick, we black up. But the Indian – the koshari – are painted half white. And they say the Indian has no sense of humor.

There it is, the whole story of an entire valley unfolding before me, and it needs writing.'

Knight spent the rest of his vacation living around the Indians and learning about the many injustices under which they laboured and lived. And the story he said needed writing was hammered out on the portable typewriter, which had accompanied him now through the greater part of his adult life. In it he explores his deepest and perhaps most honest feelings, the place and its inhabitants reminding him so strongly of Yorkshire and its people that he felt unable to write anything but the truth.

Early in September he, Jere and Tootsie journeyed to Boulder, Colorado, where Knight had been contracted to give a series of literary lectures. Here he would meet a significant contact, Erik Barnouw, lecturer, broadcaster and writer on documentary filmmaking who would become head of the US Army's Educational Unit and, in the post-war years, chronicle the work in that genre of Knight's heroes, Grierson, Flaherty, Rotha, and Frank Capra. From Boulder, the Knights went to the University of Iowa where Eric was to be the first creative writing lecturer at the Iowa Writers Workshop.

If Eric Knight was now something of a star, he was about to be eclipsed, not for the first time, by his dog. One morning Tootsie let herself out of the house the Knights were renting, found her way first to the University and then to the lecture hall in which her master was teaching, to general amazement. Two days later, on returning to their car one afternoon, Eric and Jere were met by a stranger who had found Tootsie sitting by it and assumed she was lost. 'That's a hell of a dog you got there, mister,' the man said, 'I thought she was a stray, I've been trying to take her in but she won't budge an inch'. Tootsie had in fact been locked in the car with a window left open far enough to keep the air cool, but, having worked out how to open the door, got out and sat against the running board.

Tootsie, Eric realised, was a creature of high intelligence, and so, at the end of each day's writing, he would read his output to her. 'I read what I had written to Tootsie,' Knight said later 'Those parts that went well I kept in, and those that didn't I left out.' Further inspired by her intelligence, Knight continued his earlier exercise of writing adventures with Tootsie at their centre, but his efforts were curtailed by further lecturing, this time as the guest of the Department of Fine Arts at the University of Columbia where, on October 25th he was introduced as 'An author of considerable note and the 20th Century Fox story editor'. Knight would speak on Flaherty and Grierson and discuss the work of Eisenstein, but the focus of his 'History of Motion Pictures' would be five directors: Vsevolod Pudovkin, a contemporary of Eisenstein, and particularly admired by Knight for his 1926 movie *Mother;* the German Georg Wilhelm Pabst, the man who launched Garbo's career, and French director Rene Clair, who wrote and directed *Sous Les Toits De Paris*. The only American was D.W. Griffith, whose *Lady of the Pavements* was held up by Knight to be a work of outstanding direction. Last to be presented was Josef Von Sternberg, who made such an impact with *The Blue Angel* – as indeed did its leading lady, Marlene Dietrich.

Immersed as he was in the movie world, Eric was still alert to developments elsewhere – particularly when he received news from Rotha about the growing threat of war in Europe. Prime Minister Chamberlain had returned from talks with Hitler in Munich waving his infamous slip of paper and uttering the words 'peace in our time'. Knight's response suggests a depth of feeling in the States not chronicled by any contemporary commentator:

'You wrote on the blackest day. Now peace of a sort is with us, and the alarm seems far away. Today in the papers there are pictures of men digging trenches in the London parks, with captions mourning the tearing up of London's age-old sod. Somehow the only feeling I got from staring at the pictures is a sort of glad feeling that the men in their shirt-sleeves in all probability got a few days' work, and possibly hadn't had any job for a long time…. Feeling over here mingled, but, I think, very clear-sighted. There is a general, broad feeling that Czechoslovakia was needlessly betrayed by Britain. Most of the people are not near enough to say 'betrayed by Chamberlain….' But they feel scornfully that democracy in Europe is gone. Open diplomacy is gone. The day of the secret alliance has returned. Civilization as we know it – the right of common man to seek fullness of material and spiritual life – has been set back as far as all the work that we have done in our lives. It is all undone.

The only thing that saves this from open and vehement expression here is a sense of fair play – a real and understandable feeling that it would be foolish to rant at Britain for lack of courage from her location two hours away from bombs that might blast cities, when the criticism comes from a land safely on the other side of a few thousand miles of ocean.

But believe me there is clarity of viewpoint and indications that that view is more open than in Britain. Our radio brings burning denunciation of the peace-makers. It brings open assertion that the money-cliques organised in Switzerland took huge sums to buy up both British and French securities at the darkest moment, showing that someone knew there would be no war. It is strongly hinted that the whole affair was known in detail, set and staged, long before the 'events happened'. In other words, there's still a stinking polecat in the woodpile that is further hidden, rather than revealed, by the issue of White Papers.'

As always, Knight's mind was occupied by the good fortune of Americans who firmly believed that they would never be drawn into another foreign war: 'At least we have peace. It is not that we don't want peace. But rather that we do not want the real threats of war to be used as just one more screen for the further robbing of human rights by those who find it convenient to usurp those rights.'

His anxiety, however, was short-lived. Nobody in America believed war would come to Europe. Indeed, most in Britain believed the same. And Knight goes on to talk about the ripeness of the apples, the harvest, a recent hurricane that passed close by, his new cross-cut saw that made woodcutting 'a pleasure', closing in the apparent belief that conflict has been avoided, despite his dislike of Chamberlain's reported plans. Letters between Knight and Rotha were now more frequent as they exchanged views on the reporting of events in Britain and across Europe.

For himself, Knight had reason to be feeling positive. *You Play the Black and the Red Comes Up* had appeared and been well-received, and as the year drew to a close his recent successes lifted his spirits. In response to Rotha's conviction in another letter that war would be avoided he wrote:

'Your letter did me good. I know very plainly what I want to do. I want, if I can speak of ideals, to hammer, hammer, hammer, until I think I have helped make this place a bit more sweet for man to live in. If that goal lies through writing, films, speaking, Democrats, Republicans, Left, Right, Center, or whatever, then I'll take advantage of whatever tide goes in my direction and hammer at it best way I can.

Your letter, too, comforts me about Chamberlain. It seems incredible to me that he can stay in power, or that the British nation can be so short-sighted as not to see his determined, edging, incessant drift to reaction – working always without courage but with no let up toward conscription and mass regimentation of unemployed labour. The subversive press is outrageous, and books being issued here are slamming England as hard as possible, saying it has had one policy in the last 20 years – the undermining of Socialism or anything that will lift labor proud and strong and unsubservient to the shopkeepers and pound-ponderers who will bow, scrape, take indignities from abroad. Let the British Empire crawl in the dust, ignore insult abroad, as long as they have a cheap source of labor.

Perhaps we see more clearly from here. The British are too close to see the havoc and ruin to their country that is being produced on their own hearths.'

He moves on to the social issues he had encountered in Britain and arrives at the same conclusions as Orwell: the need for slum clearance. And Knight's proposed 'clearing', like Orwell's, included the system of Government:

'England needs the most sweeping house-clearing it ever had in its history. Out with the blockbusters – a recognition from the bottom to the top, bringing in a true England, an England worth those hundreds of thousands of damned, good, starving men I talked to in Durham, Wales, Yorkshire, Lanark. They are lowly men; but lowly as they are, they are worthy of a country such as Chamberlain could never even envision in his weak mind, let alone create – or operate if it were created for him.'

Most importantly, Knight also told Rotha, 'Here too we are changed. America is responding to news of the rise of Fascism.' The belief that American attitudes had changed and that it was not, as he felt it had lately been, detached from Britain, would provide the impetus for what might have been, had not *Lassie Come-Home* eclipsed it, his greatest and most influential work. Still two years away, his novel *This Above All* was merely an idea he was thinking about, albeit one that kept pace with America's changing opinions:

'The weakening of Britain as a bulwark against Fascism, if it has done any good at all, it has worked the miracle of making America see that it is OUR concern, now. We trust England less than we did, but we are nearer to her because we trust Nazi Germany even less. We are not so moved by methods of ruling, as we have been shocked by what happened to Austria and Czechoslovakia. And, most of all, what happened to the Jews.'

Knight registers America's disapproval of Chamberlain and his Cabinet, even to the point of suggesting that any Government would do, provided it was not the present one. Most importantly, his perception is that American people were beginning to sympathise more strongly by the day with the plight of those opposed to Fascism.

On November 11th 1938, after the German annexation of Czechoslovakia, Knight spoke at a New York Armistice Day gathering. Only a draft of his address survives, but his developing feelings on the subject of war were clearly stated to Rotha:

'Roosevelt has always edged towards world participation – more of it than America would take without protest. And now, Hitler has given him the cards to play, and he finds the nation unprotesting – rather cheering him on – toward a firm international stand that he wants to take anyhow. His arch-foes are all behind him for once. So, we have moved far more toward international influence than when you were here. The old 'We fought one war over there, and what the hell did it get us' is now no longer heard. Everywhere instead there is a deep anger at Germany which wasn't there before…. The British Sovereign's visit to Canada is not so much for Canada half as much as for the United States. Four days in Washington – tremendous publicity to the American nation to get them over their history-old antipathy to British Kings. In other words, to sell the British to the American public – and to make us realise they couldn't hold back Germany alone.'

Reading between the lines, it seems that Eric was taking the opportunity to hint that he was privy to information not in the public domain. In so doing he indicates he was already being consulted at the highest level upon matters Anglo-American. Indeed, photographs would emerge decades later to show that he and Jere had been guests of the President on several occasions, as far back as November 1938. An increasingly inquisitive press would reveal Knight's presence at the President's New York Hyde Park residence as war speculation grew, at which time he and the First Lady were photographed playing tennis together.

Rotha later commented, 'All that winter letters came thick and fast; about American reaction to events in England and Europe, all typical of Knight's ever-increasing preoccupation with the threat of war and its implications for Britain.'

As soon as the break was over, Knight returned to work. So successful had his 1938 Boulder and Iowa lectures been that he was invited to be principal lecturer at the University of Colorado Writers' Conference in July and August of 1939. Magazine editors were now asking him to write articles based on the very successful and well publicised Boulder engagement, and with a regular income assured by the string of magazines to which he was now contributing, Knight was free to concentrate on his own projects. In March he was back in New Mexico with Peter Hurd, who was working on the frescos for the Post Office in Dallas, Texas. 'I have come here to get it done,' he wrote, 'in isolation.' He was referring to *The Happy Land*, but he was still uncertain as to its fate:

'Whether or not anyone ever will want to read the kind of fiction that I have regurgitated from the emotions of seeing Yorkshire on the dole, is far away. I cannot know; I do not know if the novel is good as art or as writing or anything else. I only know I want it to be as good and honest as I can make it within my limitations.'

Knight would remain with Hurd until March 22nd and would spend more time with the Indians. 'We play polo on Saturday mornings when the cowboys come over', he told Rotha, 'and make coffee and biscuits but they cannot understand why a painter who paints pictures cannot paint his ranch or how a writer just writes, but since he does – oh well.' In the past, Knight had enjoyed isolating himself from the world. Not now:

'It is escapism and I know it, so I shall not stay in it. I want to be back east. Life hurries past and I have done so little – and I know I shall not have another life in which to do all the things I meant to in this and didn't.'

Having reduced *The Happy Land*'s first draft to the 120,000 words required by his publisher, he returned to Croton. It was in his letter of early May that he voiced doubts about ever writing the book to which his life was pointing, and about the coming war, which would not involve him:

'I shall hunt a farm East of our own. I think I shall find a place in Pennsylvania, and settle there until I have grown old under the weight of mortgages and responsibilities that owning anything incurs.'

With this new plan in mind, Knight asked his publishers to make haste with proof-reading *The Happy Land* so that he could get it 'smoothed as soon as possible'. He filled the waiting with thoughts of a move to a place of their own in the Pennsylvania farmland which so reminded him of his boyhood surroundings. 'They wonder,' he said, 'how a man can write of England and Yorkshire when he is so far removed from it. Good God, it is just the contrast that allows us to see it, don't they get that? I only know how lush and green England is when I am in the aridness of New Mexico, or how English towns always smell of coal smoke until I am in a Mexican village where it always smells of wood smoke. I can only see how bad is the poverty of a Yorkshire town when I am in the far more blessed poverty of the New Mexican land.'

Such thoughts were shoved aside when his publishers, finally, declared themselves satisfied with the novel. They planned to publish the following year, provided he could deliver the final adjustments within three months. While awaiting his publisher's decision, Knight had been thinking about Steinbeck's latest novel, *The Grapes of Wrath*. 'I did not like the way he pushed his characters round to make them say what he, as the author, wanted to say. The Oklahomans discussing banking in abstract terms seemed to me to be the old dodge of having a character speak not for himself but for the author. I don't need to hope he'll write better stuff, for I feel he has a greater novel than this in him.'

It is interesting to remind ourselves, in the light of his comments, that Knight saw his own creations as individuals who should remain in the character provided for them by the author, that they should stick to the parameters of their character and class if their credibility was to be sustained. He admitted that, as a critic, he was given to the kind of nitpicking analysis alien to the average reader, but since his own characters captivated readers' imaginations so thoroughly, we are compelled to the conclusion that his own rigid rules were adhered to at all times, and this may also be why he refused credit for creating Sam Small, his thinking being that since Sam was in his head at birth, the character only ever followed his own personality traits and operated outside his authorial direction.

Final amendments to *The Happy Land* now took his attention. He declared himself 'busier than hell' but so encouraging were his publisher's words that he told Rotha:

'It's funny, we are getting older… but we are both bound to succeed simply because we have an insatiable and incurable itch. We think that our kind of power is a nobler ambition than politics and wanting to earn millions or dominating the minds of other men, true; but we can't pretend that we were responsible for the things in us that make us think it is a nobler ambition. To hell with it – I am getting suspended on slender cobwebs of my own reasoning.'

In this optimistic mood, it is hard to believe that Knight was ever downhearted about his own abilities. There was a new urgency, an excitement, surely fired by his meetings in London in January 1938. For now, though, he worked feverishly on the book before him, admitting that while the background and theme of his novel were right, his characters needed 'flesh and blood'. It was in his ruminations on this point that he voiced his formula for credible characterisation:

'I think the vital forces of a book flow through a character, to the characters, to general life, to the particular aspect of life you want to show. If the first link in the chain isn't strong enough to make people play make-believe with you, then you never progress through the fictional game to the point you want to make. Through the actor, to the play, to the truth. Through make-believe to reality.'

In strengthening the characters in his novel, Knight now realised that he had to re-write the plot; the simple 'adjustments' had become a major task. He had returned to Croton but could not concentrate fully on the work, so set off to the Hurd ranch once more, working feverishly to meet his publisher's deadline. Once there he had set himself up as usual on the veranda with his portable typewriter while Hurd painted in his studio. When he returned to Croton-on-Hudson his finished manuscript was posted off to his publishers. After only a few days of rest, he, Jere and Tootsie set out on the long journey to Boulder.

The conference was scheduled for the last week in July and the first in August. Knight was to lead the students in the study of the novel, but was determined to take a few days' break after the period of intense work just completed. They rented the same house they had occupied the previous year, frequented the same coffee shops, restaurants, and booksellers. Once again, the whole campus was captivated by Tootsie, who now accompanied her master to all his lectures. She was not the only one to crave his company. On one well-documented occasion, students realised moments after taking their seats for a lecture to be given by Robert Frost that a scheduling error had occurred and that Knight's lecture was taking place at the same time in another lecture theatre, at which point they left en masse, leaving the celebrated poet and Amherst College Professor of English in an empty classroom.

CHAPTER THIRTEEN

'We want men of action, not dreamers, is what they're always telling us.' So Knight had told Rotha, and he returned to the theme in a short story he wrote in New Mexico: 'I say we need a damn sight less action and more people who'll let their dreams get a little peace and quiet in which to flourish. When I was kid I used to dream. My God, how I used to dream. And what, if you're polite, you'll ask me, was your dream?'

We have already discovered that much of Eric's dream involved living with the 'Nava – Nava – Navajo'. He had certainly lived around Native Americans at San Patricio, and his waking dreams were of a liberal world in which tolerance was key, a world where the oppressed found freedom to practise their religious and social rituals unhindered and unexploited, a world where the wise were recognised for their wisdom regardless of their financial status or class, and where the wealthy were equally welcome – provided they were decent citizens. In short, he dreamed of a world where, politically, internationally, any association with the United States would be enough to deter any oppressor from declaring a war on either them or their allies. But by September, Germany and Britain would be at war, and all Knight's dreams subject to revision.

He had, he said, always been a liberal. And many Americans were liberal too, in Knight's view. He saw those of the far west as inhabiting a country of their own, and the farmers of the mid-west as self-sufficient and comfortable – now that crop prices were on the rise again. He told friends that the time had come to 'define liberalism' because 'it is now time for men to rely on their own convictions and not political party tenets.' But the fact remained that there was deep apprehension in most quarters, and a determination at the highest political level that America would under no circumstances become involved in a foreign war.

Indeed, the President himself was saying as much publicly. In private, however, Roosevelt was formulating plans for pro-war propaganda and discussing those plans with Churchill. It is likely that even Roosevelt's closest aides were unaware of his true intentions. Having kept Rotha apprised of his Hyde Park meetings, Knight now appears to indicate he has become even closer to the President. He refers to him by his first name and, in a simple, off-hand statement – always indicative of a Knightian 'truth' – says that he feels confident enough to disagree with the President and predict 'a good war', something which could only happen if America were involved:

'Franklin said there wasn't a good war or a bad peace. He is wrong. The last war was a good one, and it was the peace that was bad. May they both be good this time.'

The public stance of the U.S. Government led Knight to the view that Britain's need for support would need 'selling' in order to sway popular opinion in its favour, a task to which he was more than ready to turn his hand. An administrative complication over his American passport prior to his 1938 visit to Britain had resulted in him reverting to British citizenship, and this would work to his advantage. Being British meant he could legitimately espouse the British cause while equally legitimately abusing the British government:

'There is a great difference between Chamberlain and the manhood of Britain. The men of England and the heritage of England is something any good salesman can sell to America. And we shall sell it.'

Knight had previously told Winkelman with considerable conviction that he would be 'taking no part' in war if it came. Now he sang a different tune:

'I have no right to talk about it [the war] one way or the other. Last war old men were determined to fight to the finish if it took every drop of blood – from the youthful men. Now I am over the age limit. If I don't get in, at least I shan't fight with other men's blood. Let them use it themselves. When I am in, then I can be bloodthirsty.'

And indeed it was the 'age limit' that would officially disqualify him from the British army, a matter that had been settled, ostensibly in early 1938. In June, Knight had said the war 'will not get me this time', but by September that had become 'when I'm in', although he closes his last letter to Winkelman for over two years with:

'I don't know what I shall do, probably the hardest thing – go on living as normally as I can and try not to write anything foolish during the next few years.'

It is almost as if he were trying to send out a confused message to those few friends he trusted with the truth at all other times. He was a meticulous letter-writer who made several draft copies of even the simplest note and often referred to much earlier correspondence in order to continue a theme, so to contradict himself so obviously is quite possibly contrived. We have discovered that at times of great mental stress, however, he was less careful with his correspondence and occasionally allowed the odd word to appear, which he would normally not have used. But in his next letters to Rotha he contradicts himself so completely that his friend was still drawing attention to the fact thirty years later. Knight had said that the 'shocking' news emanating from Germany, combined with a Royal visit to North America and the positive publicity from England, had swung American popular public opinion in favour of the British cause, but only a week later he was saying the opposite:

'I thought and wrote, after the war started, there might be a swing back to England, but due to the appalling errors of the British censorship, it has gone the other way. And, despite Germany's reputation for blundering propaganda, she has succeeded here just where England has failed.'

Rotha came to the conclusion that his friend, unable to say publicly on American soil what he could say privately in a letter to an Englishman, was in fact sending a message he hoped might filter through to a higher authority. Rotha was an ideal conduit, because he was now working for the British propaganda machine, albeit in an advisory role, as a consultant on public information films. And here we are forced to ask how Knight knew this, for nowhere in his letters to Knight does Rotha mention his new position. We can only conclude that Knight was privy to information far from the public domain and that originated in the highest offices of government. Rotha does not say whether he passed on any message on this occasion, but it is clear from his tone that he understood what was being said to him and what he was expected to do with the information he received. And there was plenty, as Knight warmed to his theme:

'Hitler! His speeches come through direct. We hear his voice. We hear the throated roar of thousands in Danzig hailing at the proper moments. We hear softly a voice giving an interpretation in English. Now let us not consider the rights and wrongs of anything, let's only consider dramatics.

The British broadcast is so silly that no station wants to repeat such a thing here. The German one is so dramatic, that although scheduled for only one hour, it was still being carried after an hour and a half by the great chains.

I would not report any of this to you if my hopes and my heart were not, as they truly are, for the men of Britain who must fight this war. But, if the British expect any sort of understanding and sympathy here – which I suppose they do, if they are truly desirous of standing on the democratic front... then their tactics must change.'

Eric Knight would say four years later that Hollywood had 'created the Yorkshire they imagined in their minds' when filming *Lassie Come-Home*. That image, however, was acceptable to Americans because most had never been to Yorkshire, and British film-goers would accept it because they understood everything emanating from Hollywood was make-believe. Despite Knight's efforts to persuade Hollywood to inject more realism into their pictures, movie-goers had been conditioned to accept a stylised view of everything. Now, however, Knight was arguing for precisely that – stylised propaganda designed to sway American public opinion. 'The Americans are not British,' he writes. 'If you want to keep American interest, you must give it to them in terms they understand.' And once again this message was transmitted to Rotha, who began incorporating the information into his work and, as one former colleague remembered, mentioning Eric Knight's opinion to anyone willing to listen.

Rotha was inundated now with letters from his friend, many of which ran to a dozen pages, all commending British bravery and ingenuity, and all telling those in any position to affect policy that the publicity arriving in America via the British press and radio was losing the battle for American sympathy:

'The Germans are telling of great acts of heroism which impress Americans; their publicity machine stresses the righteousness of their cause and, despite the fact that most of it is publicity with no basis in truth, the American public are believing what they hear.

He told Rotha that if the War Department did not like this idea, somebody should tell them 'Eric Knight, as a newspaperman in America for twenty years, knew what an editor wanted to see, knew what would make a front page, knows what will be reached for by the American public… and draw them toward us'. If Rotha had not already gathered that he was expected to pass on all he heard from Knight, it had now been made quite clear.

There is at all times now a note of desperation in Knight's voice; he is far away from Britain and unable to influence matters personally, but he makes it clear that he is closer to Washington and closer still to the President:

'Roosevelt sees the issue clearly, knows that Britain and France are fighting for our democracy as clearly as they are fighting for their own.'

A change to the American Neutrality Law was now 'essential', Knight said. It would soon go before the legislature and, after revision, would at least allow America to send Britain essential goods. His constant concern, however, was that while Americans disliked Hitler, they distrusted Chamberlain. He told Rotha that Anthony Eden was far more popular in the US than Chamberlain and recommended the latter's 'quick resignation', which would 'do wonders to swing American public opinion'.

Rotha now sent copies of Knight's letters to both the Ministry of Information and the BBC, although he was sceptical about what effect they might have. A Knight postscript drives home the strength of American anti-British feeling:

'Well, there it is. If press and radio have been almost solely the arena of German victory here, let us hope that the screen may give a British victory.

I am calling my latest book *Now Pray We For Our Country*. I do pray for Britain – pray the sins of the last ten years of the Government will not recoil upon the heads of the governed.'

Now Pray We For Our Country, the British title for *The Happy Land*, had of course been worked out well in advance, but Knight never missed an opportunity to reinforce his point. In this case with a little of the socio-political comment never seen in his novels, but always present in his correspondence. Between his letter to Rotha on September 18th and his next on November 16th 1939, Jere left her job with the Selznik organization, and the Knights left Cherry House and moved to Pennsylvania. In Britain, it was the time of the phoney war. Dunkirk, the Battle of Britain and the Blitz were still several months away as the Knights settled into their new home.

Springhouse Farm, near Quakertown in Pleasant Valley, Bucks County, is green, leafy and alive with birdsong. It is easy to see, even today, why Knight was attracted to it. The property was surrounded by Pennsylvania-Dutch farmers of whom Knight told a friend, 'They farm well and are thrifty, poor, good neighbours. They send over fresh vegetables as gifts.'

The generosity of their neighbours and the joy of having achieved his dream of becoming a farmer would inspire Knight in many ways, but his immediate attention was only upon agriculture. He told the same friend, 'The land is red and rich and fertile, and there is all the room necessary for industrious farming.'

Among their new neighbours, the Freehs would prove to be the most generous of friends, welcoming Eric and Jere into their home and introducing them to those whose land surrounded Springhouse Farm, men like Titus Cressman who, with his sons Linford and Wilmer, farmed to the west, and Marvin Kunsman, a farmer but also a foreman at the nearby Bethlehem Steel Company. Harry Weierbach, the storekeeper in Pleasant Valley, became well known to the Knights as the postmaster who delivered the many letters and newspapers that arrived from England. Riding his horse to Weierbach's store on sunny Pleasant Valley mornings, Knight would call on the Fluck family and their neighbour, Balley Rogalavitch.

Springhouse stands on a shallow hillside, which means that on entering the front doors you are on the first floor, from which a kitchen and dining room – a cellar when the Knights moved in – may be accessed via a steep, twisting staircase. The house is surrounded by woodland but has a large stone and timber barn, which became both workshop and study to Knight. A few strides along the lane from the house stands a timber-built wagon shed, which was used as a garage. The hills opposite are full of white oak, hickory, red cedar, beech and maple. While in the flat, green, sunny pasture behind the house, the stream is lined by elms, sycamores, poplars and osiers.

Though Springhouse Farm was beautiful, it was little more than a wreck when the Knights moved in. It required repairs, mainly to the roof. Installing electricity and plumbing in the house was tackled by contractor Joe Reibman, assisted by John Freeh. For the second time in four years Knight had to excavate a cistern, though on this occasion an electrically operated pump was installed. Another job was to build a broad stone wall in front of the house, a project in which Eric and Jere were helped by the Freehs' teenaged son, Joe.

In all Eric's correspondence at this time there is an unparallelled tranquility. For once he was not concerned about money. 'We do not worry. We can live on $10 a week easily,' he told Rotha, 'and there is more money in the offing', by which he meant his invitation to be visiting lecturer at the University of Iowa in the spring semester. His new home, though demanding much of his time, inspired Knight, and for a time he put all thoughts of war aside. He was much encouraged by *The Happy Land* which, he told Rotha, 'Harpers are calling The Grapes of Wrath of England – which it is not.' He said he was 'busy doing the illustrations for the juvenile which Winstons like very much'.

One of the reasons why *Lassie* has been assumed to be an American adventure – albeit one set in Yorkshire – is that it is tailored almost exclusively to an American readership, its author never being sure it would 'go' in Britain. Had Knight been writing exclusively for a British market, much of the descriptive detail would have been superfluous. Paradoxically, however, it is his exceptional awareness of mood, time, place and character that captivated and still captivates British readers. He might also have been freer with dialect and colloquialisms, but in making the work universally accessible he created a novel which endeared its American character to the British and its 'Yorkshireness' to Americans, Canadians, South Africans, Australians, New Zealanders, and readers of the twenty-seven non-English tongues into which it has been translated.

That the story hides its metaphoric meaning so well reflects the duality within its author and his expertise in suspending disbelief. That he discussed only its 'juvenile' nature with Rotha suggests he wanted any deeper meaning to be visible only to those who chose to find it. His original title for the work, *A Dog Returned*, was dropped just prior to publication in favour of *Lassie Come-Home*, which is universally mispronounced as a plea, calling the dog to return, rather than as a statement of the fact that she has already done so. As he was completing the work, he had a visitor at Springhouse Farm. Ernest Hemingway arrived bearing an advance copy of his Spanish Civil War novel *For Whom the Bell Tolls*, which he had inscribed,

'To Eric Knight, Go for the money, Eric, just go for the money.'

Meanwhile, what would become *This Above All* was taking shape in Eric's mind as distressing reports came in from Europe about the treatment of people in countries occupied by the Germans. Knight's Pennsylvania-Dutch (i.e. German) neighbours were largely sympathetic to their old homeland but anti-Hitler and anti-Nazi. That their new neighbour was English was no problem to them. 'They do not hurt my feelings,' he said 'and like country-people the world over, are good, honest, close to realities.' He added that the people, the land, and the news from Europe made him think more of England than he had at any time in the past. He was living near Quakertown and revisiting his Quaker beliefs while justifying what he already knew would be his military participation with words that would one day crystallize themselves into the simple phrase, *Nothing is worth fighting against, but there are a few things worth fighting for.*

'Hitler, damn him, is utterly bad. Yet war is bad also. I should like to think that war is being fought to remove, not Hitler, but the things and conditions that make it possible for Hitler to rise. The war can only be good if it reveals… to what low estate the terrible mismanagement of the Baldwin-Chamberlain Government have brought England. If the people of Britain win this war for Chamberlain, they also win for themselves the perpetuation of the Chamberlain spirit of internal Government. All people must be led. It is always a question as to whether the leader takes them along the path alive, fighting, contradicting, agreeing, but always human and vital; or whether he takes them as a band of drab, unspeaking, tired, defeated people. I think Roosevelt takes this country after him in the first manner. In Europe, too many go in the second manner. They march in better order; but their hearts are never singing.'

His frustration is evident; he is far away, and though more in touch with the mood of America than Britain, equally patriotic to both and deeply concerned for those who might find themselves unwillingly dragged to their destruction.

In the spring of 1940, having set the farm to rights and entertained in succession Cummings, Hemingway, Hurd and the Wyeths, the Knights left their house keys with Joe Freeh and set off with Tootsie on an extended tour, which would end in Iowa where Eric was to take up his lectureship. Iowa's tree-lined streets and stone-built university reminded him of the Boston he had known in his youth. Remnants of winter remained, however, with snow piled into blackened banks by the side of the city's roads while the sky, heavy with coal smoke, was reminiscent of winters in industrial Leeds. He described the university as 'liberal, a kind of Renaissance for the farm lands' and would applaud its attitude to the arts and the modern world. The students were mainly from agricultural backgrounds and struck him as 'very raw, very alive, very naïve and un-culchawed'.

Established in the small office provided for him, he wrote to Rotha, 'the Juvenile is finally finished. It's a neat job of bread and butter workmanship.' In Iowa, the war in Europe seemed far away, newspapers consigning it to page two. Knight read reports of Finnish victories over the Russians but knew the cost in lives of their triumph. He related to friends a story about an ancient war between the Chinese and Japanese and a battle in which 350 Japanese were killed at a cost to the Chinese of 350,000, 'Pretty soon,' one Chinese soldier said, 'no more Japanese'. 'I think with a few more months of staggering victories,' Knight concluded, ' there will be no more Finns'.

With the semester well under way, Knight continued to do well. *Story* published *A Bit of a Do*, the tale of a mine disaster, as did *The Listener*. His tutoring duties now left little time even for writing letters, but such was the continued success of the Sam Small stories that he was being bombarded with requests to write on the subject of humorous prose, all but one of which he turned down. *Humor in Writing* appeared in *The Writer*, published in June, Knight characteristically approaching the subject from a novel viewpoint:

'It is my belief that few writers, when they are writing, are intellectually unaware of their attributes and traits concerning writing – and praise the Lord for it.'

Knight implores writers to recognise and accept their own abilities and failings, to stick to their own style and delivery rather than embrace what might be described as the 'established formula'. He was drawing from his own experiences and in particular his belief that Sam's stories would not have been so successful had he not established himself first in other genres. The impetus of the article was, however, not just his own work in isolation but comic prose in general, of which he considered there was too little in wide circulation.

With a steady income from his articles, the university stipend, and excitement growing about his latest novels, the Knights were able to enjoy their surroundings and the artistic community around them. The invitation to return to Iowa had come from Paul Hamilton Engle, a graduate of the University and, from 1941 until 1969, Director of its Writers' Workshop. Iowa's most distinguished man of letters, Engle was a gifted poet and writer and prodigious talent scout who inspired a host of writers through his great enthusiasm for the written word. He had read Knight's published works and recommended him for the post on the strength of his descriptive, narrative and observational abilities. Moreover, he had invited the Knights to stay with him until suitable rented accommodation could be found, but so well did they get along that they remained with him for the entire spring term. Engle was not the only attraction; there was also his friend, the artist, Grant Wood.

Wood, best known today for his startling painting *'American Gothic'*, was a former University of Iowa student, a graduate of the Art Institute of Chicago and the Minneapolis School of Design. He had lived and studied in Paris, Germany and Holland in the 1920s, having served his country during World War I. The German and Dutch primitive painters had captured his imagination in the late '20s at which point he gave up on design, returned to Cedar Rapids and became an art lecturer at his old university. By the time of his friendship with the Knights he had been Director of the Works Progress Administration's Federal Arts Project for five years. He had a great passion for the land and the farmers who worked it, their pioneering spirit and 'toil without profit attitude' as Knight described it.

With *The Happy Land* doing well in America, news arrived from Britain that its publication there would be delayed. The reason? A wartime paper shortage. The Knights returned to Pennsylvania in early June, and if any doubts remained in Knight's mind with regard to his 'juvenile adventure', they must surely have been dispelled when *Lassie Come-Home* appeared to immediate and international acclaim. Originally, it had been no more than a short story, completed at Croton in November 1938, and published in the *Saturday Evening Post* on December 17th. And it was here that Tootsie assumed the identity of the canine heroine whose story still captures the imagination of filmmakers and audiences the world over – *Lassie*.

Myth always accompanies legend, and it has been said by those unaware of the part Tootsie played in Knight's life that *Lassie* came from his imagination. Others have attributed to Knight the words, 'It's a story that will bring home the bacon'; or have claimed that he was inspired by his observation of farm dogs at work in his boyhood. Imagination undoubtedly played its part, as did memories of childhood, and he certainly earned some money from the adventure, but that is as far as those particular myths may be respected.

Firstly, Knight never demonstrated any propensity for the great imaginative leap required to create an entirely new character. Everything he wrote, every character, came from life. Indeed, he denied any responsibility for imagination even in the Sam Small stories – adventures peopled with some of the most extraordinary characters and situations in English literature. All his fiction was an amalgam of biography, autobiography and observational documentary. Secondly, he was never certain anything he wrote would ever bring anything 'home' but disappointment. He lacked confidence – not in his writing, but in the ability of publishers to see its worth. He had only recently destroyed a work on which he had expended an entire year, *The One Factory Town*.

Thirdly, Knight never wrote anything possessed of a single meaning or solitary narrative strand – and with the exception of *You Play the Black and The Red Comes Up* never produced a one- or even two-dimensional character. If his early efforts had completely failed he might well have tried a different approach, but they did not, and he was now beginning to enjoy the kind of fame he had seen his friends enjoy, largely due to works characterised by multiple narrative strands and multi-dimensional characters.

Lastly, the sheep on the hills and dales of Knight's boyhood were free-roaming. They even lambed out among the wild hills where shepherds were sent to tend them at the appropriate time with a dog trained to guard them. It is unlikely that he ever observed any kind of sheep-herding. Anything he did see as a child and later as a man in the coalfields, and upon which he may have based any *Lassie* theme, would relate to freedom of spirit and not to manipulation by a man of his dog. Indeed, his canine heroine was utterly resistant to any kind of coercion. She belonged to no-one.

However, there is a true story that makes a far more convincing myth, and that is how the longer, book-length version came about. Some time over the Christmas and New Year period of 1938-9 Knight had had a surprise visitor at his door. It was Jack Fraser of the John C. Winston publishing company. His daughter Betty had seen the *Lassie* story, had fallen in love with its heroine and asked her father whether she might 'have the book for Christmas'. Winston, reading the story for himself, saw the potential, and drove out to Pleasant Valley to talk turkey, convincing Eric that a full-length book would work.

Lassie Come-Home not only exhibits the vital elements of adventure, social documentary and autobiography present in almost all Knight's writings, but for the first time a message in metaphor outside the author's usual domain. Far more subtle than Orwell's political drum-beating in *The Road to Wigan Pier*, *Lassie Come-Home* exhibits a new kind of duality. It may of course be read simply as an adventure, or as symbolic of American society and Government. Knight had removed Sam Small's apparently greatest power – that of unaided flight – and left him with a more valuable ability, common sense; but his reasoning in presenting a canine heroine went one step further:

Sam could have been Superman, but he wasn't. Any superman or superwoman needs possessions, a home, money, a job, but a dog has need of none.

In Knight's original work, *Lassie* barks only once when in all subsequent movies barring the last, and in the TV series, she barks unceasingly, usually being 'understood' by humans who apparently recognise every 'word'. The most recent version, directed by Charles Sturridge in 2005, is the only one to be shot in the UK. It captures the intent of the author and portrays the dog as one who uses her canine powers only as a threat, and only when necessary. She employs her intelligence to overcome obstacles, her stamina and speed to escape threatening situations, her considerable charm and guile to find friends and shelter – in return for which she offers only friendship. Most importantly, she recognises those who love her and crave her company for that reason alone – and those who would 'possess' her simply because she is a fine example of her breed and beautiful to look at.

When she is sold to the Duke of Rudling by her impoverished family – something which actually happened a great deal in mining communities where fine dogs were reared as a hedge against poverty – she treks hundreds of miles from the Duke's estate in Scotland to be with those she loves. The obstacles she encounters along the way, and the good deeds she performs for all members of society, are part of her 'journey' through life and send a message to her readers for humankind.

When the Duke realises she has outfoxed him and all his men, he too learns about something his wealth has not taught him – loyalty. And Knight saw America's might in his creation, a country powerful enough to deter all aggressors, one with a wealth of intelligence and ingenuity capable of overcoming any obstacle, one easily able to embrace all members of society, especially the wealthy – always provided they recognised that money is not everything; in short, a society in which love, tolerance, loyalty, understanding and kindness would ensure its furtherance and prosperity.

Few read the message, probably because Hollywood did to *Lassie* what Knight said it did to everything. It 'screwed it up'. But in contrast to his other works, Knight, in *Lassie*, takes the 'sneaking through humour to the truth' ethos a step further and applies it to drama, adventure and pathos, and in so doing creates what must be Hollywood's most enduring heroine, one who, having made her debut in 1943, is still filling cinema seats some seventy years later. Jere Knight would later say of the film treatment of *Lassie Come-Home*, 'We loved it' but then, she was always a great deal more diplomatic than her husband.

Lassie's adventure would elicit a great response from readers and a great many cartoons and stories. Over the next five years, 'collie-dog' would all but disappear from the language to be replaced by 'Lassie-dog'. As the novel's popularity spread, the irony of owning an immediately recognisable dog when her internationally acclaimed creator was still largely anonymous was not lost on Knight. To those who stopped him in the streets in order to pet her, he never admitted to being the man responsible for a literary icon, and when asked, 'Is this *Lassie*, Mister?' he would reply 'No, this is Tootsie'. The two, however, were well known in Pleasant Valley and would visit schools and colleges where Tootsie would soak up the attention while Knight talked of her adventures and assumed the identity with which he was always most comfortable – that of story-teller.

The success of the stories over the next year convinced Knight that his heroine might succeed where Sam Small had failed and find her way into the movies. Back on the farm, he began work in earnest on *This Above All*.

Pleasant Valley was and is just that, a rural haven far from the troubles of the outside world. Foremost of those farmers around him whose values and spirit he so admired were his neighbours the Freehs, and on a blank page of a copy of *Lassie Come-Home* which he dedicated to them on June 10ᵗʰ 1940, the fourteen names of the family members are listed, against each of which he has drawn a cartoon. Joe Freeh was fifteen years old when the Knights moved into Pleasant Valley but his memory of those days could not be stronger. Having no children of their own, the Knights often took the Freeh youngsters ice-skating at the public rink, piling as many as they could into their 1938 Chevrolet convertible.

In recalling their early days there, Jere said later, 'Eric had a propensity for childlike goofing off and daydreaming. I found it necessary to counter this by refusing to prepare his evening meal until a certain number of pages of whatever work he was engaged in had been completed.' She effectively managed his time, allowing him to take off in his convertible in the afternoons with the portable typewriter on which the bulk of his work was produced, with a set quota of work, usually ten pages. He would drive only a few miles to a favourite spot, slide over to the passenger seat and dutifully complete the work before returning it for scrutiny.

Jere, however, had no control over her husband's fascination with the new Oliver 60 Row Crop tractor he had purchased. Unable to find him one evening when running late for a formal dinner, she discovered him driving it around their hayfield bedecked in his pristine evening suit and patent leather shoes.

Until the Knights arrived, Joe remembers, there was little musical interest within the Freeh family, but the Knights would have them around to play and sing, encouraging them to pick up an instrument and try it out. Several subsequently became proficient on various musical instruments. In quiet moments, perhaps when stepping outside to take the night air, Eric passed on to the men the odd lewd joke he had heard in the trenches. Indeed, he once remarked, a propos the prostitutes he had met in wartime France, 'As far as sex is concerned, back in Yorkshire they're still living in the Dark Ages.'

Joe Freeh was interested in literature and asked Eric about *You Play the Black and the Red Comes Up,* a copy of which was resting on a bookshelf. 'Oh, it's just something I wrote,' was the reply. 'Pay no attention to it'. Joe Freeh finished High School at seventeen but could not take full-time employment until his eighteenth birthday. Knight met him in the lane one day while heading for his afternoon writing session and asked what he wanted to do. The young man said he'd probably have to go to the steel works in Bethlehem. Knight thought the lad was worth more than that, as Joe recalled, decades later:

'Eric pushed himself back in the seat, away from the steering wheel, grasped the loose end of his belt, pulled it back several notches and said,

'I'd go hungry to see you go to college.' I haven't the slightest doubt he meant every word of it.'

The impression Eric Knight left upon Joe Freeh was huge:

'When I sit and recall, I relive those good years when I was between 15 and 18 and the Knights were our neighbours. Eric opened lots of doors for me. He showed me that there was a great, wide, wonderful world out there, full of interesting people and wonderful things. My life was not going to be limited to bending over under a hot sun to pick tomatoes and forking unpleasant cow manure that was sometimes frozen solid. I could sense that Eric liked me and that he had a good opinion of me.'

It is apparent from Joe Freeh's account that Eric was in a more relaxed frame of mind than he had been for some time. Gone were the 'deep moods' and the anxiety over his work. Here he was, the farmer he had always wanted to be, enjoying the success of his latest novel. With the British version due to be published shortly, Knight, somewhat surprisingly, played down its prospects in a letter to Rotha:

'I cannot imagine that it will mean much when it comes out in England, for its dreary song is of a cause, and now the effect is here to occupy all attention.'

His interesting use of the word 'song' is not just a reference to his earlier novel but the fact that early 'story tellers', as he had discovered and discussed, had been strolling players who 'sang the news' from one town to the next. And in a brief comment on the subject which later led some commentators to link him to the legendary outlaw of Sherwood Forest, he said 'all Yorkshiremen are descended from Robin Hood and all story tellers from the strolling players of old.' Rotha, it is worth noting, was of the opinion that the novel would have been a greater success in Britain had not Richard Llewellyn's *How Green Was My Valley* – also set in a mining community and already in its second printing – been topping the best seller list.

While the novel might have been on his mind, it was the war situation that preoccupied him, and his letters to Rotha contained more than just his reflections. The purpose, it now seems clear, was to oblige Rotha to pass on their content to his superiors. In case that message was not getting through, Knight, alarmed by the withdrawal of a defeated British army from Dunkirk, tells him, 'Perhaps now you need letters from a far perspective more than ever.' And to reinforce his ethos that while 'nothing is worth fighting against, but there are a few things worth fighting for', he tells Rotha,

'When slugged by a maniac, you no longer spend time wondering what made him a criminal. You fight back and leave consideration of causes until the time that he is either caged or caught. People ask me here if the war news isn't bad. I do not feel it is bad because Germany has conquered land.

I feel it is merely bad because it means millions of young men are dying, and a system and form of Government that I personally loathe seems to be in the ascendant.'

He further hints that he was privy to high-level information, telling Rotha that public sentiment has swung wildly in favour of Britain while Congress, previously supportive of the Allied cause, is blocking progress. 'I cannot tell how or why all this reverse has taken place,' he says, 'I just report that it has. Churchill is acceptable in every way to the American mind.' Thereafter, Knight voices the view that if Europe were to fall to Hitler, it would not automatically mean defeat for Britain, who could 're-arm, build planes, re-house workers, train her young men, build National unity,' in other words, protect her own shores even at the expense of the rest of Europe. These were radical, unthinkable ideas at the time, but they would come to fruition after the man now in charge, Churchill, expedited the same plan in bringing the British army back from Dunkirk to do just that, even leaving the wounded until last in order that all those able to were in place to defend the homeland while the rest of her European allies lay in the hands of the Germans.

Having used all the tact and diplomacy at his disposal to impress upon Rotha the need for action, Knight closes with a re-assessment of British history:

'Wellington was wrong; the battle of Waterloo wasn't won on the playing fields of Eton half so much as the playing fields of Eton were won upon the battlefield of Waterloo. It is time that was known. I believe in Britain. I believe that in the top brackets and lower mass there is a race that is worthy of honest and equal government. I also believe that in the middle class, Britain has some of the smuggest dumbest bastards on the face of the earth. Give me a British Duke or a British collier, and I can talk to him and understand him – by God, more than that, I believe they can talk to each other deeply and truly and well. But give me the British middle-class and I'll show you the most stupid, blind, contented, smug individuals on the face of the earth. He's worse that the Long Island social set – and that's the absolute.'

Through the summer of 1940, Eric wrote in the mornings under Jere's strict regime, then tended the ten acres of corn, the five of peach trees, the sweet-corn, cantaloupes, egg-plants, wax beans, string beans, lima beans, potatoes, carrots, spinach, beets, lettuce and onions. Then there was the planting of the new orchard with the five varieties of apples he looked forward to see growing to maturity. Remarkably, there was still time for trips out in the convertible with Jere and the Freeh children, and visiting colleges to give lectures with Tootsie. He also found time to write the only cowboy story of his career – *Bison Bill and Jonnie Bull*, published in *Esquire* in November.

Knight had achieved a great deal in 1940: the continued publication of his short stories, his professorship at Iowa, the cultivation of his farm, the securing of a regular income from his latest novels. Copies of *The Happy Land* were selling in increasing numbers to high critical acclaim. In Britain his publisher had finally gathered enough paper to put out the British version, and it too was selling well.

The story is set in the ginnel of Knight's boyhood. The head of the family might be described as a 'poetic Communist', driven to adopt radical views by long periods on the dole, his ear bent by a fiercely Communist friend. The mother having died, it is the daughter, Ada, who effectively runs the family, though she does so subtly, so as to avoid undermining her unemployed father and her younger brother, the only family member bringing in a wage. Ada is pursued by the ruggedly handsome neighbour she knows will marry her only to take her from one hovel to another and burden her with children. There is another suitor, the wealthy pit owner's son whom Ada admires, although not for his wealth. The fact is, he is her equal, a strong young person willing to stand up to the older generation and propose better housing conditions for pit workers. The two are further united by their dislike of an interfering Quaker whose 'charity' they both suspect and resent. Then there is the mystery man of the ginnel, the one whose wealth is apparently substantial but who lives modestly and charitably, running a soup kitchen for the unemployed. He is newly returned from America, but nobody knows where he acquired his wealth.

There is no doubt that many characters are mirror-images of those present in the author's life. He of course represents himself, but his father, brothers, and the many employers he knew as a boy are all represented. Many of the scenes are reminiscent of those painted by Orwell, a fact that Rotha spotted immediately. 'It stands,' he wrote, 'shoulder to shoulder with Wigan Pier'.

Knight of course allows us to be escorted through his story as witnesses and participants; we are not sold any socio-political message and there is no happy ending, only a story which offers a graphic portrayal of a place and its people, believable because it was, for the greater part, true. His author's notes reveal the inner workings of the novelist's mind and the fact that he allowed his characters the freedom to direct the action and maintain a considerable level of self-determination:

'If the novel has no form, it is because their lives have no form. If their prejudice provides what little driving force they have, it is because prejudice provides most of the driving force in life everywhere. The system that organizes their lives seems above them. If some of them are meek, it is because they have learned that the meek are left to inherit nothing in peace, whereas the rebellious inherit nothing without peace. The fight is over if you drop down, and the pain stops... better to be a live coward than a dead hero because dead heroes don't even get one glass of beer on Saturday night, nor walk in the sunshine on Sunday; and only the most stubborn man can throw off this thought occasionally.'

The tone of the finished work leaves the reader in no doubt as to the anger and frustration being worked out by an author who felt passionately about his subject. He was acutely aware of the times in which he lived, and the novel charts that period in British history when the country moved from peace to war. *The Happy Land*, Knight told Rotha, was not a 'Grapes of Wrath of England' as it had been called in the press. But he wasn't quoting the critic in full. What the reviewer actually wrote was the book was, 'the Grapes of Wrath of England, done with a warmer, more loving touch than Steinbeck's.'

Even before the work was published in Britain it attracted the praise of both critics and readers who had managed to secure US copies. And while Knight retained very few copies of newspaper and magazine reviews, he did preserve letters from the public, all of which he answered, but always after the passage of exactly one month, by which time he had read them several times. One came for a Mr John W. Coleman of Surrey who said, 'Nobody has ever so graphically or movingly written about England and Yorkshire since Dickens', to which the author's reply was only of thanks and gratitude that a reader had taken the time to put pen to paper 'at such a devastatingly difficult time as this'.

His next work was being eagerly awaited. Invitations flooded in for personal appearances and lectures. *This Above All* had been written in record time with the minimum of fuss. Its goal was simple, to persuade any wavering Americans to get behind the British war effort as quickly as possible. Keen to get ever closer to those in the American Government whose job it was to monitor affairs in Europe, he now gave the door of circumstance a mighty shove. On September 5th 1940, Knight wrote a letter that set in train the series of events that would shape the rest of his life:

'TO:
War Department, Militia Bureau:

1. The undersigned, formerly Captain Field Artillery, of the National Guard of Connecticut, respectfully request appointment in the Army of the United States in any capacity for which he is fitted.

2. The applicant was, for five years, adjutant 3d bn., 192d F.A., CIIG., realigning on moving to this State. Status was terminated as of December 21st 1926, on Militia Bureau records; by 50. 141, go., Conn., 1926.

3. Applicant also attended NG & RO course at Fort Sill, Okla., in Spring of 1925.

4. Applicant asks appointment in any capacity or rank on training course or with troops wherever deemed fitting.

5. He considers his fitness to serve as of following: He is 40 years of age and in perfect health[1]; he is five feet 11 inches in height, and 155 pounds in weight exactly the same as on recruitment; he is married but has no dependents of a minor age; beyond operation of his farm he is engaged in no employment which contributes to national well-being. The latter would continue to operate perfectly well without his presence.

6. He asks immediate appointment.

7. Medical certificate accompanies.'

The Quaker pacifist Yorkshireman was now only months away from donning a uniform once more. This time it would bear a row of highly polished pips on its epaulettes.

---

[1] Eric was actually 43 years of age.

CHAPTER FOURTEEN

What remains of Knight's *This Above All* files contain only his corrected manuscripts and a single letter from a reader. There are no references, as there are with many of his other works, to alternative beginnings or endings, no plot ideas like those behind *The Happy Land*. The work was produced quickly, and like his Sam Small stories, appears to have assumed its finished form in his mind before being transcribed to paper. In his correspondence it is mentioned only in passing, and must qualify as his most rapidly produced work. The urgency was necessary. American support was swinging in favour of Britain as Knight had said it would, but a catalyst was needed to drive home the message that she was in desperate need of help. Knight knew by now that what he did best was to portray the sufferings and triumphs of ordinary people, who always bore the brunt of any conflict.

He called first upon his recollections of noise, from the bottle works of his childhood to the First World War. He knew from his own experiences of war that 'only those who have been bombed can know that terror'. He knew what it meant to be a serving soldier and had seen many stricken with shellshock – although he never admitted to being a sufferer himself. He loved the 'Old General' character who had appeared in many of his works and he loathed, as he had recently said, the middle class. Representatives from all of these would be included in a work that would once again contain explicit sex scenes. Long-held taboos were broken in order to emphasize that 'war changed the world and everybody in it'. He also knew that the American reader loved a tale of heroism, and that British morale was in need of bolstering.

He chose the title *This Above All* from Shakespeare, fully aware that most readers would be able to complete the quotation from *Hamlet* - 'to thine own self be true'. This was Knight's way of telling Britain that she might indeed have to stand alone against the rest of Europe. The book's cover would depict searchlight beams fingering the night sky in search of bombers, and leave no reader in any doubt as to its content.

Harper & Brothers released the book in April 1941 while the author was in New York City for the official launch, stateside, of what would become his first international bestseller.

Echoes of Hemingway's *A Farewell to Arms* and Cummings' *The Enormous Room* may be found in the love affair involving the absent-without-leave Clive and his middle class lover Prudence who, against her family's wishes, joins the Women's Auxiliary Air Force (WAAF). Otherwise, the novel reflects the author's frustration with the British Government, his loathing of war, the class system and oppression of the masses, and his concern for the ordinary people unwittingly caught up in the hell of it. Not for nothing did Hemingway later call *This Above All* 'the most influential work of World War Two'. He knew it had achieved the desired effect of bringing the attention of not just the American but also the worldwide community to Britain's plight.

Many works of art have captured conflict in all its horror, but few have influenced so many so quickly and so far across the world. The first fan mail to be filed away at Springhouse Farm was dated April 11th. It came from Ruth Hutchison of Allentown, Pennsylvania, and simply read:

'It's a magnificent book. I will certainly be taking it to my desert island. I felt that in FOR WHOM THE BELL TOLLS we had a book of our day, but that was before I read your book.'

Harry Graham, a lecturer at Holyoke College, South Hadley, Massachusetts, wrote on April 20th to say he was already teaching *This Above All* to his literature class. Another lecturer, this time from Houston, Texas, wrote, 'You see the truth, and boy, how you write it'. Ethel Jackson, the actress, refused to believe that the author lived in America, commenting, 'Mr. Knight could never have left England to write as he does'.

That July, Knight noted the four top-sellers in the U.S. were, 'Churchill's book, a book about Churchill, Hilton's *Random Harvest* and mine'. Fan-mail continued to pour in, but the letter that pleased the author most came from Elias E. Sugarman. He had worked with Knight on both *The Eagle* and the *Bronx Home News* in the mid-'20s as a theatrical news reporter, and had now risen to the editorship of *Billboard*:

'Dear Eric,
It's been many years but I remember you very well. You probably remember me as one of the cubs on The Home News in the sweet days of long ago. I remember you as a swell guy and it makes me feel awfully good to see you established as one of our top-rank authors.
Funny thing, I read and enjoyed immensely *The Flying Yorkshireman* and

did not connect the name of the author with my newspaper boyhood at all. But when 'This Above All' was published, the photo that appeared with the reviews hit me like a charge of TNT.

This is not a request for help, nor am I soliciting funds for the homeless ladies of Singapore. There is nothing I want except to have you receive this little memento of days that are no more and to have you know that I wish you everything good.

Sincerely yours,

Elias E. Sugarman.'

Knight's work was not only highly praised by his public. *The Sunday Review* critic noted, in an extended review:

This Above All is a far better book, as a novel, than we have any reason to expect, coming as it does so early in the war. It is difficult to judge it as a work of art, yet it is not propaganda. It seems to me to be a sincere, but heartfelt piece of work by an admirable writer, and a British patriot.'

If the press were not seeing his novel as 'propaganda', Knight's plan had worked; he had produced something that would transmit its message without any audible tub-thumping. By September, the *Readers' Digest* was reprinting it in condensed form as 'The Number 1 Best-Seller' while editor George Kent was describing its author as 'the mill town miracle'.

A review followed by another former colleague. Oswald Quinlan had known Eric as a newspaperman in Connecticut. 'A week ago I was in Stamford, and Grant Cunliffe told me you had disposed of the movie rights to *This Above All* for a substantial sum, and, that you were, that very day, guest of Mrs. Roosevelt at a lunch, in Hyde Park, what a man!'

Cunliffe had been a friend in the early '20s, but Knight must have kept up correspondence with him as he appears to have known of the author's movements. What he could not know was that the Hyde Park meeting, where Knight reportedly addressed the First Lady's circle of associates, was far more than a simple luncheon.

Knight had actually been there to talk with journalists who had been interned in prison camps in France, about the nature of their incarceration and release, after which secret meetings had taken place with the President's 'kitchen Cabinet', followed by the luncheon and a game of tennis with Mrs Roosevelt. As a celebrated author, Knight could now go anywhere he pleased and mix in any company, the perfect cover for a man now moving around the corridors of power. Indeed, he even told Rotha of the Hyde Park invitation, knowing very well that the content of his letters would be shared with people of influence on the other side of the Atlantic.

Now, for the first time, hard cash came on the heels of success. MGM, allegedly acting on behalf of Katherine Hepburn who saw herself in the lead role, put in a bid for the film rights. They were outgunned by Twentieth

Century Fox, who secured their prize for $35,000, part of which was soon spent on the new study at Springhouse Farm. So smoothly had the transition been made from work-in-progress to finished manuscript that Knight had found the time for several more articles. One, *War News – Secret*, was published in *The New Yorker* on March 24th. It dealt with the censorship of wartime correspondence and the heartache it caused to families who were not allowed to know where their loved ones were stationed. Knight saw the practice as paranoid, just another hardship for the embattled British.

New Mexico Magazine published *The Funny Men* in June, the story being derived from his as yet unpublished tale about the 'Nava-Nava-Navajo'. Meanwhile the author was busy touring American cities, promoting *This Above All* and signing copies for the queues of buyers forming lines around the block. It was at one such event in Boulder, Colorado, that Knight was photographed with a man he now knew well, and whose influence upon his life was to be considerable.

The face is not familiar to most, but the smartly dressed man in the cream summer suit was Harry Hopkins, architect-in-chief of America's New Deal. Almost a decade earlier, Hopkins had been appointed director of the Federal Emergency Relief Administration (FERA) by Roosevelt and had helped usher in ground-breaking work and youth employment programmes paid for by Government funds. He would later play a vital part in the wartime Lend-Lease initiative, which would bring essential military hardware to Britain, in his capacity as unofficial emissary dealing directly with Winston Churchill, Lord Halifax and Anthony Eden. Indeed, on one occasion he dined with all three as the guest of His Majesty King George VI. Since meeting Knight at Hyde Park, Hopkins had become a close friend.

Knight's introduction to Hopkins was engineered by the writer Martha Gellhorn. She had travelled widely in Europe in the early 1930s and, as one of the first female war correspondents, had covered the Spanish Civil War, an assignment that led to her professional and romantic association with Ernest Hemingway. Knight admired her novel *The Trouble I've Seen*, a work inspired by her experiences in depressed industrial areas while working for Hopkins at FERA. She and Knight had similar views on the plight of the poor and the apparent inability of the US Government to address their problems. Gellhorn recognised in Knight a man who might prove a valuable asset to Hopkins, perhaps the President's most trusted aid.

As Knight continued on his promotional tour his publishers mounted large boards in bookshops which trumpeted:

'Eric Knight has written the first great story of the war, more intense and moving than *For Whom the Bell Tolls*. This is a love story as powerful and moving and as much a part of its time as *A Farewell To Arms*. He has written a novel also of England at war, an England in which all sorts of people, in spite of bombs and blackouts and invasion threats and food rationing still fall in love and hate and fear and laugh and fight for their beliefs. It is a sensitive rendering of an intangible atmosphere. In its feeling of mourning, unbearable suspense, its complete timelessness and inevitability, it is as dramatic, swiftly moving and unforgettable as *Escape* [a 1930 British movie based on a play by John Galsworthy].'

So Knight found himself in exalted literary company and rejoiced that his message – that it was not a matter of if Britain were to be invaded, but when – had come through.

Even on the road Knight found time to write, producing an article that was published in November's *Soviet Russia Today*, for whom he had earlier reviewed Sholokhov's *And Quiet Flows the Don*. This, however, was less a critique, more a plea for post-war unification:

'Let us now consider, in these days of war, the comradeship of the three great powers, whose common people are dedicated to the destruction of Fascism wherever it shall be found. Let us remember, and carry on into peacetime, the war-found brotherhood between Russian, British and American men.'

On December 20th, the *Saturday Evening Post*, in publishing yet another Sam Small story, devoted its front page to 'the highly acclaimed author of America's best selling novel', referring to him as 'An American Institution'. This caused him great delight. Here he was, publishing Yorkshire stories in dialect, which could only have been written by a Yorkshireman, being fêted as an American. Knight read so many articles beginning with the words 'This Above All' and going on to talk about him without any mention of his English upbringing that he wrote a one-line letter to his publishers, which he hoped they would transmit to publicists and reviewers:

'They say nice things about This Above All, but This Above All… I am a Yorkshireman.'

The novel was an unqualified success, and a movie version starring Robert Donat and Greer Garson was already being filmed. The man brought in to write the screenplay, R.C. Sherriff, had scored a huge success with MGM's *Goodbye, Mr. Chips* – and would repeat that triumph in 1954 with *The Dam Busters*.

The novel had been written quickly and with the same self-confidence that imbued the Sam Small stories, yet *This Above All* registers a departure from his usual pattern of autobiography dressed in the story-teller's carefully tailored garments. He had not been in London when the bombs started to fall; neither had he visited the south-east coast of England, where the story was set. He had not written from the viewpoint of the soldier at the centre of the plot and certainly not from that of the middle class family also involved. The story is a social documentary, a Modernist narrative that invites the reader to witness the terror, against which their defence is to 'stick it out as best they may' and go about their lives with stoic resolve.

Knight had been largely absent from Britain since 1912 and still remembered the class divisions and oppression he had known as a child. He carried all these impressions into *This Above All*. It is, perhaps, his one truly 'fictional' story insofar as the majority of his material lacks autobiographical content. Indeed, when writing the book, Knight had to ask Rotha to help him out:

'Because of the probable youth-conscription here, there will be great interest in the British work with women's services. I want a character in the WAAF, and I know nothing of it. Can you tell me – everything? What the uniform is, how they enlist, for how long, whether they go into camps as do men, what they learn, what the ranks and controls are, what the girls like about it, what the girls don't like about it, what the discipline is, how much leave they get to go home, who instructs them as drivers of motor vehicles, do they have cooking schools for the service of army camps, are the girls allowed to walk with soldiers, do they do land services with crops also, is there any handling of firearms, that and a hundred other things?'

Dutifully, Rotha had answered all the questions, seemingly with no regard to the fact that, had all this information fallen into the wrong hands, a serious breach of security would have been committed. Rotha had simply complied without question and in so doing had registered his absolute trust in Knight's integrity. Everything, therefore, that Knight wrote about the women's service into which he recruited his heroine, Prudence, was second-hand, but so accurate was his portrayal that neither he nor his publishers received any complaints.

Knight was probably the only writer in America who could have written *This Above All*, and its contribution to morale and the greater war effort was not overlooked at the time of its publication. Perhaps the reason it is not now as widely appreciated as war novels by Cummings and Hemingway is that it was written in and of the moment rather than as a chronicle of events published later and having all the benefits of hindsight.

Having acted as the oracle on all matters WAAF, Rotha heard nothing from Knight for almost a year – by which time *This Above All* was a huge success. He later recorded the content of their last conversation on the matter:

'American critics hailed Knight's *This Above All* as the first novel to come out of World War II, but Knight said it was the last book to come out of World War I.'

The book's success, however, did little to alleviate Knight's deep unrest about the war in Europe. If Jere knew nothing of her husband's letter volunteering himself for military service, or the arrangements he had entered into in London in 1938, she was not fooled into believing he could remain out of the war. Having read Rotha's letters from London during the Blitz, she wrote to him:

'We are deeply impressed and moved by your accounts of what you have seen and been through. One of the things that is hardest for Eric is to be convinced that he can do more good by staying out of the front line. I think, after reading your letters, there is no choice. Do you think Eric should return to England? Is there a real job there for him to do? If you have any advice for him, don't spare it.'

Knight was itching to cross the Atlantic. 'I feel useless in America,' he wrote. 'I want to be in England where I might be of some use to the war effort.' No response to his letter of application to the US Army had been received and he assumed he had been passed over. He acknowledged that in America he had been accused of 'anti-Semitism, anti-laborism, anti-Britishism, and anti-democracy', all as a result of the publication of a book that was fiercely patriotic from the British viewpoint but which those opposed to America's involvement in the war chose to read differently.

He was incensed by the attitude of some Americans to his novel, and wrote a twelve-page letter to Rotha to say so. In it he praises everything that is good about Britain and rails against everything he sees as bad, mainly the style of Government, which he finds ineffective and pandering. He talks of the wastage in America when food is so scarce in Britain, the reality of the living conditions of the working class, the arrogance of those above them on the social scale, the need for education, industrial reform and, overwhelmingly, his hope that loss of life on the scale of that suffered in World War I might be avoided. In all his correspondence with Rotha he had given away little about his origins and upbringing and regularly used the collective 'we' to refer to both the British and the Americans, but here, for the first time, he puts his early life in perspective:

'Look, I am a product of England, and poor England, and was born knowing wealth, and soon dropped into slums – not an unusual story. But I know what food and diet in a slum district of a British industrial town is. I know what an orange is. I got one every Christmas morning. I know what fruit is; I know going into restaurants in England and paying God knows what for a peach. I know the glut of peaches here. I can drive by the roadside and get a bushel for twenty or thirty cents. The only reason I don't is that my own trees load with them and they fall to the ground, and after we've eaten all we can and given away all we can and preserved all we can, we're licked.'

In the midst of all this, Hollywood came calling. Given his troubled history on the west coast, Knight must have thought he was finished with 'Hollow-Weird' forever. Now he learned that Twentieth Century-Fox was having considerable difficulty with *This Above All*. Darryl Zanuck had decided that in the interests of decency, the sex scenes should be toned down or cut completely. In his view it was 'still a beautiful love story', one that deserved to be as big as *How Green Was My Valley*, which would win five Academy Awards in 1941. Knight, however, had handed the rights to the movie-makers, banked the money, and had no desire to be further involved. He knew in his heart that Hollywood would 'screw it up as always' and insisted that he didn't care.

In most regards he was correct. The film, and in particular its conclusion, bore little resemblance to the novel, but the message was still clear – and that was all he cared about. He concluded that the American movie-goers would recognise the danger facing Britain and act accordingly. They did, but by the time the movie was released in 1942, America had been catapulted into the war by the Japanese attack on Pearl Harbor.

The movie starred Joan Fontaine, whose English accent and demeanour were faultless. The sets offered a credible portrayal of the Blitz and Knight's message of the proximity of war, symbolised by the sound of cannon fire from across the English Channel, came over loud and clear. The snobbishness of the upper class was well portrayed and while some of the accents were less than perfect, they would have passed for Eton and Oxford to the America ear. The film today is lost in a plethora of oft-repeated war movies, but when compared to others of the period it does display an immediacy not present in some; and though those who have read the novel will find the end result unsatisfactory, it is interesting to observe the attitudes of those facing the greatest threat to their country since the Spanish Armada.

After the Japanese attack on Pearl Harbor, followed four days later by the Germans declaring war on the U.S., America had no choice but to fight. Eric could now more easily justify his application to join the armed forces, and one of his last acts of the year would be to assign his power of attorney to Jere in anticipation of his involvement and – he presumed once more – his 'inevitable annihilation'. Late that year, the Knights left the farm and Tootsie in the hands of Eric's daughter Betty and set out for England on a trip that would last over four months. It seems strange that Knight would take his wife with him, given that the German U-boats were knocking out a huge percentage of Allied shipping in the Atlantic, but there is no record of Jere having queried what does seem an odd decision.

oOo

On the face of it, Knight was to be in London for the *Saturday Evening Post*, to report on food rationing, also on the progress of the Lend-Lease programme, and he soon came up with the idea of making a documentary film on the same subjects. What started out with the working title *The Strategy of Food* would become *World of Plenty*, a vehicle in which Knight, who would write the script, could re-visit his earlier-stated belief that food, plentiful in America and often wasted, could be redistributed in order to sustain those whose very existence was being threatened. Rotha had enlisted the help of British novelist Arthur Calder-Marshall, recently appointed script editor at the Ministry of Information Film Division, and an official proposal, supported by Calder-Marshall, was drawn up. The film was to be scripted by Knight and Rotha in collaboration with Sir John Boyd Orr, a specialist in nutrition. On his return to the U.S. in the spring of '42, Knight would draw on the British Information Service's facilities there to gather stock footage and shoot new material, which would be edited by Rotha in England together with newly recorded and existing film.

Shortly before Christmas 1941 Knight delivered a BBC address to the nation under the title *The British Eat To Win*. The broadcast provided him the opportunity to speak on behalf of both the British and the Americans, beating the drum for Lend-Lease and sending a clear message: that although the Americans' attitude had changed considerably since Pearl Harbor, they were still not, in his view, fully behind the British cause.

The idea was that British morale would be lifted by the promise of food, and that Anglo-American relations would be further cemented as a result. 'Nutrition and nourishment,' Knight said, were 'vital to the war effort and will be forthcoming when the scheme is working to full capacity.' The extent to which he had access to privileged information was not evident in his broadcast, but in an American newspaper article he wrote some months later, on May 16th 1942, it was: 'Britain's distribution network today is highly effective and the food reserves are in good shape. But until this war is over, no spokesman will admit how close Britain came to going on hunger rations. Actually, on a certain day Britain's food chiefs looked at the bottom of the basket. There was less than the peacetime two-weeks supply of vital proteins left. The kingdom faced the beginning of national hunger with its inevitable decreasing production, rising incidence of disease and slow-climbing death rates among mothers and children. At that moment, dramatically, came the announcement of Lend- Lease food. The food chiefs, with that announcement, dared scrape the bottom.'

Knight goes on to make it clear that while in London he had been allowed to question high-ranking officials like the Surgeon General, Parliamentary officials and even Lord Woolton, the head of the Ministry of Food. 'Secret stores of health-giving foods have been built up,' he said. 'Britain is sustained not so much by rationing as by direction of food to proper places.'

It seems that Knight had had access to restricted areas, like industrial facilities closely guarded against enemy spies. 'I have seen workers in heavy industries,' he wrote, 'shift as much protein in one meal as a ration-book calls for in a week,' and he goes on to describe the mechanism of rationing and its failings in some detail. Knight describes a scene he and his guide, Sir John Boyd Orr, witnessed in 'a gloomier-than-usual British teashop'.

'We were pretending that we didn't like much sugar in our tea anyhow. 'Look at 'em all,' Orr said. 'All eating. Every man jack of them a human body, but a human soul too. Sometimes I want to take each one and say, '*You poor devil! Go out and get your nasty, greasy fish and chips. Go on out and buy your pint of beer instead of good sound food. For I still don't know whether it wouldn't be better for you to be happy awhile than to feed properly.*' I can measure a vitamin, but none of us yet know how to measure human happiness. But there's one thing sure. Whether food will win the war or not, I don't know. But only food can build a peace. There can't be too much food. Only too many bad ways of directing it. America, Canada – none of 'em can really grow too much food for the universal human need.'

Given this attitude, it is little wonder Eric and his companion got on so well. Food was vital, and Knight's drum-beating on the subject – particularly behind the closed doors of the President's Hyde Park residence – had probably gone some way to ensuring Britain did not starve; but happiness, as he had pointed out in all his novels to date, depended on much more than that, and he and Sir John were of one mind in so far as the 'pint of beer' and the 'greasy fish and chips' were concerned.

Before leaving England, Knight had one final piece of business to undertake. Aunt Emily had lived in Leeds since her husband Edwin's death in 1932. Uncle Percy too had died, in 1940, but Aunt Sarah was still in Wellington Street South, Halifax, taking in theatrical lodgers. Wartime measures meant that she was also obliged to take in an apprentice from the nearby munitions factory. Joe Hutchinson, a lad from the Yorkshire town of Pocklington, and too young for military service, was finishing his Saturday lunch when Knight arrived at his former home. Many decades later, Joe remembered the visit very well:

'I have never met anybody in my life who made such an impression on me. He was very smartly dressed, like a Hollywood star, his personality filled the room. He was a man with great intelligence but was willing to talk to a green youth who knew nothing much about life or anything outside Yorkshire.'

It was Joe's practice to leave his lodgings on Saturday afternoons and catch a bus home for the remainder of the weekend, but the memory of his only meeting with Eric Knight still stands out in his mind as the most inspiring of his life:

'I had all afternoon and evening to catch my bus, but I couldn't drag myself away from this magnetic individual. When I looked at the clock I realized I had ten minutes to catch the ten-fifteen departure when I should have been on the one that left at one-fifteen in the afternoon. Sixty-odd years later I still have no idea where those nine hours went. We talked about war and America and things I'd never talked about with anybody else, he just seemed to know how a lad's mind worked. I shall never forget Eric Knight, never.'

With his business in Yorkshire completed, Eric and Jere joined an Atlantic convoy headed for Canada where he was to make a further radio broadcast. Knight was by now well known for his Sam Small stories, and *This Above All* had revealed him as a writer of serious intent, but he still felt it necessary in his introduction to impress upon listeners that what they were about to hear was no fiction:

'There is only one thing worth speaking over the radio, in any land, at any time, and that is truth. But truth is not a positive thing. It is not absolute. Each man brings his own truth, colored by his own life, his own prejudices, his own prides, his own loves and hates. Tonight I try to bring you my truth. That you should like it or not is a secondary matter. Only believe it is a truth as I see it.'

He goes on, however, to drive home his message with a story-teller's expertise and all the colour of a soap-box orator in full flow:

'When a trapped soldier dies in a Malayan swamp, that is your own grown-up son. When a Polish civilian, treated like a slave, emaciated by hunger, falls finally into a mass grave, that is you, you who listen now in your fine comfortable house with your good fatty Canadian dinner under your belt.

Do not be fooled by this war, Canada. Do not be deluded by goose-headed thinking! When the Nazi chiefs howl of *Lebensraum*, do not think they are talking of Britain! No, there's no living room in Britain, that tiny island is overcrowded by its forty-four million people! When the paranoiacs scream about colonies, do you think they are talking about some strip of banana land, or some unholy spot in the malaria-ridden jungle?

Let us not be idiotic. When the thief smashes a plate glass window with a brick, he doesn't take a dollar watch. He grabs the diamond crown in the center.

Germany and Japan don't want swamps and jungles. They want you – great rich sprawling Canada, rich with her endless wheat-bearing acres where a *Herrenvolk* could lord it over a slave population; Canada with its great and untold wealth of unexploited raw material. Those are the goals of the Nazi war: Canada, Brazil, Russia, the United States.'

The address continued in similar vein, and such was the response to it that the accompanying pamphlets, sold at a dollar each, raised $350,000 in two weeks, the exercise being hailed a triumph by all concerned. The broadcast was followed by what Knight called a 'Victory Loan shindig' where, he told Rotha, he had pressed home his message:

'Told them off – wealth, butter, cars, lights – too much of everything. Bombs are needed badly here. Russia works and is led; Britain works and isn't led; America is led and isn't working. I guess I am still too near to the reality of the way you live there to fall back on the lush life here without qualms. One hates having too much sugar, reaching for too much butter, buying cartons of cigarettes, seeing matches still given away with each pack. One resents too much food and seeing evening dress and seeing women laughing in low-cut gowns in New York. It is not equality of sacrifice and effort.'

His frustration, however, was not just with the American attitude to a war in which they were now inexorably involved, but with the idiosyncratic nature of public opinion. Oddly, Knight concludes his next letter to Rotha with disparaging words about the man he had seen as the next champion of Britain's cause, Winston Churchill:

'I think Churchill must go. His personality endeared him here. His policy and spirit have fortified a feeling of defence and never yet inspired to attack – and that is the policy that will let us lose the war and that will split us as allies. Make no doubt of it – to win this war Churchill must go.'

In *The New York Times Book Review* of April 5th, the 'attack' theme is present in the article 'An Interview With Mr. Eric Knight': 'Things are fine in England. London is a proud city and they'll never give in. They're still thinking of holding out – not attacking. You can't blame them. When your homes are being bombed away, and you just stay there and stick it, you hold onto one thought: 'I'm going to hold on and not give in or run away.' You think and feel that so intensely that it becomes part of you, and you don't shed it quickly. London has had to think so hard about taking it; it will be hard to change over to thinking about dishing it out.'

So 'sticking it out as best you may' was now, in Knight's view, no longer an option; attack was now the best form of defence. *Quill and Quire* magazine's April issue also included an interview with Knight, but this one steers him away from the war towards writing technique:

'I don't believe in reading. It's the same as an artist spending his time looking at pictures. He'd soon get only a reproduction of a reproduction of what someone else thought of life. He's got to go out and look at people and fields and sunlight, and think about it and feel about it – and spend ten times as much time as that looking at his own canvas. The thing is, I can't find in modern British literature anything that has any relation to what I am feeling and thinking and getting all steamed up about. The trouble with wonderful writing – and many modern writers do write wonderfully – is that wonderful writing shuts me out instead of letting me in. I know many Britishers who started out and looked like really fine writers, but soon they began writing marvellous English and got 'style' and beautiful perfection in prose and they too were ruined and never got anywhere.'

That he never read while he was engaged in writing is true; he did not want his style to mimic that of any other writer. That he had his own style is also true; there is no hint that he was ever influenced by any other author. There is an element of distraction in this and other interviews conducted at a time when his literary success meant he was much in demand by magazines and newspapers keen to exploit his fame and fill column inches with interesting copy. And the reason for that distraction, though he mentioned nothing of it at the time, was Frank Capra, the movie director.

In his 1972 autobiography, *The Name above The Title*, Capra claims to have met Knight for the first time in May 1942. He was a month out. He actually sent a telegram to Knight on 15th April, instructing him to go immediately to Washington D.C. Over lunch at the Carlton Hotel, Capra handed Knight a set of scripts he had commissioned for the Army Information films he was due to direct. Knight returned to Pleasant Valley after the meeting to go through them. Two days later, he wrote to Rotha:

'Frank Capra wired me from Washington and said: 'We need you, we need your capabilities. You can write like stinko, and you've been in on the British film end. I want you to do something for me'. I was never so grateful, because you know how I'd feel about Capra, as counter to about 50,000 other Hollywood bastards.'

Knight was referring to the fact that the highly acclaimed director of *It Happened One Night, Mr. Deeds Goes To Town* and the 1938 hit *Lost Horizon*, had been brave enough to leave Hollywood and set up his own production company – but had now abandoned it for the top job at the US Army's Film Production Unit. Knight tells Rotha, 'So I do a script for him about Britain – what the people are like, the land, the habits – take 'em apart. It's for Army use, and they have a grand, sane plan for documentary use in Army movies.' There is no evidence to support this statement and it is not mentioned in Knight's letters to Capra. That is not to say, though, that the idea of a documentary about Britain was not discussed, and it must be remembered that Capra knew of Knight's Hollywood reputation and perhaps offered the potential of a solo project as a device to persuade a man, known to loathe working on other writer's scripts, to do just that.

If indeed that was Capra's plan, it backfired. The idea served to crystallise Knight's thoughts on how American soldiers might view Britain and the British and how they might react on arriving there ignorant of a vastly different way of life. An idea occurred to Knight, which would be immediately and enthusiastically accepted. *The US Forces Handbook* was the outcome. It may be described as a work to which Knight was suited above all others, for it called for a mind equally at home in either country, one familiar with army routine and the conduct of soldiers abroad. He left his readers in no doubt as to what was expected of them – especially those who had never seen a female Army Officer:

'If you see a woman officer with a lot of gold braid on her cap, damn well treat her with respect; she is an officer and she didn't get where she is by knitting more socks than anybody else in Norwich.'

In his introduction to the booklet, Knight uses 'we' in his references to Americans, not the British, and goes on to offer practical advice to ordinary soldiers – most of whom had not travelled outside their own state, or even their own county – which had to be simple enough for the least educated to understand, while speaking to officers too:

'The important thing to remember is that within an apparently old-fashioned framework the British enjoy a practical, working twentieth century democracy which is in some ways even more flexible and sensitive to the will of the people than our own.

The British have seen a good many Americans and they like Americans. They will like your frankness as long as it is friendly. They will expect you to be generous. They are not given to back-slapping and they are shy about showing their affections. But once they get to know you they make the best friends in the world.'

The handbook covers the love the British have for sport, in particular fishing and shooting, their passion for spectator sports like football, 'which is nothing like American football and takes two forms, soccer and rugger', the basic rules of which are then explained. 'Cricket,' he informs his readers, 'may strike you as slow when compared to American baseball, but it isn't easy to play well'. Knight explains that crowds at sporting fixtures 'may be more polite than those at home. If a fielder misses a catch at cricket, the crowd is more likely to be sympathetic. They will shout 'good try' even if it looks like a fumble.'

Some language differences are noted and attention is drawn to regional dialect variations, but the matter is not treated in any great depth. He has more to say on that great British institution, the pub:

'You will be welcome in the British pubs as long as you remember one thing. The pub is 'the poor man's club,' the neighbourhood or village gathering place, where the men have come to see their friends, not strangers. If you want to join in a darts game, let them ask you first (as they probably will). And if you are beaten it is the custom to stand aside and let someone else play.'

The British make much of Sunday. All the shops are closed, most of the restaurants are closed, and in the small towns there is not much to do. You had better follow the example of the British and spend the afternoon in the country.

The American soldier was left in no doubt either as to his role in British society in time of war:

'You can rub a Britisher the wrong way by telling him 'we came over and won the last one.' Each nation did its share. But Britain remembers that nearly a million of her best men died in the last war. America lost 60,000.'

This note on the First World War sits among others on everyday life where even seemingly insignificant matters are explored:

'British automobiles are little and low-powered. That's because all their gasoline has to be imported over thousands of miles of ocean.

British taxicabs have comic-looking front wheel structures. Watch them turn round in a 12-foot street and you'll understand why.'

The map of Great Britain Knight chose to include in the handbook shows land picked out in white against a black sea. The impact is immediate, and more so because the coast of France is clearly drawn with the distance between the enemy in Calais and the home port of Dover being no more than that separating Bristol and Bath in the south west. If they didn't know it before, American soldiers were in no doubt now that *This Above All* had not exaggerated the proximity of the guns and the enemy firing them. The British, he concluded, 'will welcome you as friends and allies. But remember that crossing the ocean doesn't automatically make you heroes. There are housewives in aprons and youngsters in knee pants who have lived through more high explosives in air raids than many soldiers saw in first-class barrages in the last war.'

The final two pages are dedicated to *Some Do's And Don'ts:*

'BE FRIENDLY – but don't intrude anywhere it seems you are not wanted.

You are higher paid than the British 'Tommy.' Don't rub it in. Play fair with him. He can be a pal in need.

Don't show off or brag or bluster – 'swank' as the British say.

If somebody looks in your direction and says, 'He's chucking his weight about,' you can be pretty sure you're off base. That's the time to pull in your ears.

If you are invited to eat with a family, don't eat too much. Otherwise you might eat up the weekly rations.

Don't make fun of British speech or accents. You sound just as funny to them but they will be too polite to show it.

NEVER criticize the King or Queen.

It is always impolite to criticize your hosts:

It is militarily stupid to criticize your allies.'

Knight closes with a glossary of terms, from *aisle (gangway)* to *windshield (windscreen)*. His authorship is not credited anywhere on the document, a copy of which was given to every soldier, sailor and airman, regardless of rank, coming to Britain. Some of them might in due course carry with them a copy of *Lassie Come-Home*, quite unaware that the two were authored by the same hand.

Knight admired Capra not just for leaving Hollywood but also for giving up his career for his country. Coincidentally the men discovered that they were born less than six weeks apart and had both grown up in poverty.

Capra had also enlisted in the Army late in World War I, but unlike his new friend had not seen active service. Both men had raw talent. Capra had received little formal education – and perhaps that is why Knight refrained from treating him to the 'I was at Yale, you know' introduction.

Knight's trawl through Capra's draft *Why We Fight* scripts was comprehensive, his comments polite but scathing. Whoever had been responsible for writing them clearly did not share Knight's ideas on documentary making. They couldn't. His ideas were based upon the work of the greatest documentary-makers of their time coupled with his own experiences as a serving soldier engaged in battle. Capra saw Knight as an original thinker and wanted him as his script-writer. They would not work alone, however, and would recruit a team which included Capra's 'Hollywood knights' John Huston, William Wyler and Anatole Litvak.

Knight's documentary hero Robert Flaherty would also lend his weight to the cause. Others drawn into the circle as Capra's aspirations for war documentaries and propaganda films progressed would include Knight's old friends Paul Horgan and Peter Hurd, as well as the financier Bernard Baruch, an advisor to FDR known to Knight from the Hyde Park meetings. Capra's remit, he told Knight, was to produce a film or series of films that would give the serving soldier in every theatre a sound idea of their particular war's causes and its likely consequences. That the work should also carry the Capra trademark of the triumph of the humble man over adversity was essential. But Knight, in keeping with his usual method, was more interested in talking to the soldier in soldier's terms and in language he would understand, without the usual Hollywood gloss.

There would be nothing idealistic or triumphalist about Knight's interpretation of what was needed to boost morale and prove to those in the front line that what they were fighting for was justified. Luckily, with people like Flaherty and Litvak on board, his ideas would not take much selling. He started by telling Capra in a letter that, being one of their number, he understood the mind of the ordinary American, and since he knew that Capra considered himself to be of that same breed, he could spell out his message in no uncertain terms.

He placed himself in the mind of a soldier and asked himself why he should go to a foreign country to fight and perhaps die in a war, the outcome of which could not affect America. The Americans had, after all, heard German propaganda on the radio which clearly stated that the Nazis were not interested in their country, or Canada, but the attack on Pearl Harbor and the events following it meant America was in the war whether they liked it or not. What still concerned Knight was that drafted men, while full of anger towards the Japanese, might not be so keenly motivated about taking on the Germans. The ordinary American draftee might see President Roosevelt as a man who thought that victory in a European war would secure his place in history. The same man might surrender rather than fight on in a war he wanted no part of and whose outcome, as far as he knew, could not affect him.

This was the scenario placed before Capra, the man charged with convincing American soldiers that the fight was just. If minds could be trained to follow army orders and obey commands, Knight argued, they could be equally receptive to a positive message if presented in words and terms they could understand and appreciate. 'And if that message cannot be put across,' Knight said, 'America has no business being in the war.'

His main concern was the method to be employed, and though he had not yet told Capra of his deepest fears they were clear in his mind, as he outlined to Rotha:

'I shall not be lost among the Hollywood ideas, for Hollywood ideas shrivel quickly when out of Southern California climate, and my battle is to make the big Hollywood directors understand that we are never going to get out films if we stage and shoot everything – that we must cut, cut, cut from acres of existing film of actuality, and maybe shoot three maps and animated charts in one finished film.'

What Knight was advocating was the use of news footage, and a minimum of dramatic improvisation. The process ought to be fast; any unnecessary delay could cost lives. However, this new challenge was not the only focus of Knight's attention at this time. Back home he still had the farm to worry about, and he was busy on articles that would be published in various magazines later in the year. *They Don't Want Swamps and Jungles* was about to win him the Northern Hemisphere Radio Conference Award for Best Speech and Dignity of Subject, and his short story, *The Marne*, received the coveted *O. Henry Memorial Prize* for Best Short Story. In June, *Lassie Come-Home* won The American Librarians' Award for Best Children's' Book.

CHAPTER FIFTEEN

Eric barely had time to absorb the good news about the new book when he received, in June, the letter he had been expecting for almost two years:

June 11th 1942
War Department, Washington D. C.

Captain Eric Mowbray Knight AUS
Springhouse Farm, Pleasant Valley, Pennsylvania.

1. By direction of the President you are temporarily appointed and commissioned in the Army of the United States, effective this date, in the grade and section shown in the address above.

2. This commission will continue in force during the pleasure of the President of the United States for the time being, and for the duration of the present emergency and six months thereafter unless sooner terminated.

3. There is enclosed forthwith a form for oath of office which you are requested to execute and return promptly to the agency from which it was received by you. The execution and return of the required oath of office constitutes an acceptance of your appointment. No other evidence of acceptance is required.

4. This letter should be retained by you as evidence of your appointment as no commissions will be issued during the war.

5. Waiver is granted for the physical defects, evidence of intestinal hemorrhage, 1941 (probably colitis); nasal polyposis; hernia, inguinal, incomplete, indirect, left; for appointment for limited service only.

By order of the Secretary of War.

A Western Union telegram arrived the same day:

'You will proceed on June eighteenth to Washington DC reporting to the commanding general services of supply with special services branch stop.'

Eric Knight was assigned to Special Service Operations and would soon be wearing the insignia of a Captain in the US Army, claiming allegiance only to the Film Unit which, though boasting some of the biggest names in Hollywood, was hopelessly ill-equipped for the task at hand. Knight admitted that the Unit would have to 'learn as it went along' and he told Rotha:

'We haven't your documentary background or skill, nor your many production units whose abilities and styles are recorded and known. We must build our own units and it seems almost like fate that you called me in in London and put my mind to scripting the food film. Having seen your work there I am that much ahead. It isn't much to work on but it's something. I cry for films, now – let's get films out even if not perfect, but let's get them streaming out. A man's reputation is less than getting things said forcibly.'

Objections had been raised to the depiction of the living conditions of the masses and the deeply searching nature of Rotha and Knight's method of commentary. What was required, they said, was a film 'restricted to showing food use in Britain at this time'. Knight insisted that any editing would lead to 'a total destruction of form and the grand principles of strategy and propaganda'. He committed his arguments to what he saw as 'censorship' to paper:

' 1). How the hell did we get the world in this bloody mess of war?

2). How the hell are we going to win our way through out of it?

3). How the hell are we going to see that we use intelligent plans to forestall any other world holocaust by bloody aggressive forces and nations?'

Knight was concerned the film editing and production facilities that Hollywood directors and producers were used to were not available to Capra's team. There was a severe shortage of editors, and the process of training directors to produce work quickly, when they had grown accustomed to what Knight called Hollywood's 'slow magnificence', was faltering. There was, however, a light on the horizon. Richard Griffiths had been Rotha's assistant at the Museum of Modern Art Film Library during his 1937/38 visit to New York. He now edited the US Army-Navy Screen Magazine and would go on to become Director of the National Board of Review. He had been destined for regular military service but the Army Film Unit had managed at the eleventh hour to secure his services, and he immediately endeared himself to Knight, who said of him, 'The youngster is more valuable than ten Hollywood directors.'

One of the first official duties of the Film Unit was to screen some early rushes of the *Why We Fight* footage in the presence of Commanding Officers General Frederic Osborne and Colonel E. Lyman Munson. The General was not impressed. Criticism from this burly bull of a man with a parade-ground voice struck terror into the Hollywood men. Knight, far from taking offence, remarked, 'That's what I want the boss of my department to be like.' And he weighed in with his own broadside:

'There is a constant feeling that you have to pull every punch, lest somebody's feelings get hurt. Hell, this is war, and a real one, and a goddam big bunch of people are going to get hurt before it's through – and I want it to be Jerry that gets hurt rather than us. We have to get tough – tougher than the Nazis. We're going to lose a hell of a lot of lives, and we might as well get mad about it now.'

The team had met several times prior to the screening, with new members being introduced as they were recruited. One such meeting had taken place at Col. Munson's home in Alexandria, Virginia, to which Capra had been unexpectedly invited when apparently depressed by the Unit's slow progress. Over drinks, Munson's Second-in-Command, Lt Colonel John Stanley, arrived with his wife. 'With them,' Capra wrote later, 'surprise – a moustached American Captain with a British accent; a Yorkshireman whose shock of unruly dark red hair seemed as full of mischief as his deep, ferret-like eyes. He was Eric Knight.' This is, of course, another rather startling example of Capra's confused chronology as he recalled past events. The two were by this time well acquainted, but he goes on to give a vivid impression of the impact Knight had made on him:

'For me it was love at first sight with Eric Knight. He had all the qualities that could be compressed into a single writer: wit, composition, sensitiveness, an intriguing style, and a great, great love for human beings. He had Keats' 'mighty idea of beauty in all things.' But this above all – Eric was a rollicking good companion; one of the three most charming men I ever met in the service; the other two being his good friends Paul Horgan and Peter Hurd.'

All further Film Unit meetings took place in Room 308 at the Carlton Hotel in Washington where as many as a dozen men would cram themselves in to drink, smoke, discuss, and, more often than not, be entertained at the end of each evening by Peter Hurd playing guitar as Knight and Horgan sang folk songs. A great deal of hard work was also taking place, of course. Translators drafted in by Griffiths' Museum of Modern Art colleague, Iris Barry, and by Army Intelligence, worked on German and Japanese propaganda films that would be used in the Unit's productions. Editors and writers also squeezed in as the process of compiling seven fifty-minute films unfolded.

Capra would claim responsibility for the scripts and credit Huston's associate Anthony Veiller with almost equal input. These two, having shaped the outline of the script content, then handed it to Knight and his new recruit, James Hilton. Screen writers Alan Rivkin and Leonard Spiegelgass, and journalists Bill Henry and William Shires completed the team. It has been said that Knight was less than satisfied with having his words overseen by men he felt unqualified to carry out that task. All he said to Rotha was, 'It isn't worth telling you what I'm working on – after the war we'll yarn.'

The work of cutting and writing voice-overs for foreign-made footage involved collaboration with John Ford. John Grierson, now the head of the National Film Board of Canada, had been in on the project from the start and was advising on how best to secure the right equipment for the job in hand. There was a price to pay for bringing in these big names. 'If only our Hollywood lads could leave behind their sentimentality and find true sentiment; and find out about American hard, swift cleanliness of character,' Knight wrote. Otherwise he was full of praise for those involved in a project that was about to send him back to a place to which he had vowed never to return.

The Film Unit was moving out to California where Darryl Zanuck, now a Lieutenant-Colonel, had offered the use of premises at Western Avenue. 'It has taken a war,' Knight wrote, 'and the orders of a General, to get me back on a train to Hollywood', but he was returning in a very different frame of mind – for he was going to be working with his old friend Walt Disney, in whose studios the graphics and animations for the Unit's films were to be created. Knight's mood was further buoyed by the war news. He was fully aware of the Germans' bitter struggle against the Russians, who were now resisting fiercely on the eastern front, and felt 'a turning point might come.' He was still certain that American servicemen would 'take their fair share of a beating' but he was equally sure that the films in production would strengthen their resolve and save at least some lives. Even MGM's latest offering, *Mrs. Miniver*, it seemed, was doing something for morale, not that he thought much of it:

'Jere saw Mrs. Miniver. It stinks. It's tremendous. It's hogwash. It makes people cheer. My wife says it's a picture she's glad she saw, because now she thinks even This Above All wasn't really so putrid.'

Back in Hollywood, Knight found that his documentary expertise and knowledge of British propaganda made him the most overworked of the Unit's officers. But, he wrote, 'I like it. I like it especially in a town where I once did nothing so boringly for so long'. The Disney set-up was quite different from any Hollywood regime he remembered. It was informal, only first names were used, and even the most minor artist, if he or she had an idea, was encouraged to voice it. If the team thought it feasible it would be acted upon. What he called 'this oasis in the golden arid waste' suited Knight's personality and he worked seven days a week from the day of his arrival, often putting in a fourteen-hour shift.

Growing tired of what he called 'that bloody la-di-dah hotel' which had been his first billet, Knight moved out to stay with 'Tola' – Major Anatole Litvak – close to the 'shack' on the beach near the white rock on Pacific Palisades. He and Jere exchanged letters, but they were often so hurried that he had no time to date them, making it hard to place his activities chronologically. They discussed selling the farm. Neither could truly face giving it up, and Knight left the decision to his wife.

The work of Knight the writer was continuing, despite the huge workload. In the midst of the film work, he embarked on his most serious journalistic undertaking to date – an interview for the *Saturday Evening Post* with Poland's General Wladyslaw Sikorski, Prime Minister of the Polish Government in exile. The commission had arrived on Knight's desk during June, and he had tabled several questions while awaiting a meeting. Sikorski's aides had rejected several of them, but when Knight argued that they were 'vital to the war' the General agreed. He would attempt answers, but if he fell silent Knight was to move on to the next topic. The resulting article, *Will Peace Bring a United States of Eastern Europe?* represented something of a coup for the newspaper and for Knight, who got along very well with the General, describing him as 'everything a General should be – even in popular imagination. He is handsome enough to play his own part in a motion picture. He is an idealist, yet a ruthless realist as a statesman; he is a liberal, and a general with a record of victory. His record is flawless.' Just a few weeks later, in July, Sikorski was killed when his plane crashed off the coast of Gibraltar in mysterious circumstances.

Despite telling Rotha he had 'no time for anything but work just now', Knight was anxious to tell his friend that their joint project *World of Plenty* had finally been passed by the censors, as to its content, for US distribution. It wasn't quite as either of its makers had planned but, 'Apart from that,' he said, 'I feel wanted and am enjoying hugely the Disney studio experience.' His request that he receive no accreditation for work produced by the Film Unit had been agreed to, and he now did the same with articles submitted to newspapers, contributing to the *Saturday Evening Post* thereafter under the by-line 0-477891 of the Army of the U.S.

So many big names were now involved in the Film Unit that the old and inevitable Hollywood arguments had begun to creep in. At first Knight took on more responsibilities than he could cope with but soon realised he was overstretching his resources and becoming restless, frustrated and argumentative. Regular officers were still not wholly sympathetic, either to Britain's plight or that of any of the other European country. Many had not seen active service and, in his opinion, lacked the urgency necessary for the production of films aimed at saving lives.

As he always did in times of stress, Knight retreated into his favourite character, Sam Small, who had by then 'made himself up' another story. On discovering that he and Rudolph Hess are identical twins, the bluff Yorkshireman finds himself in a variety of world-saving situations. Sam had found a new audience in the American troops who, he claimed, had 'turned oop i' Polkingthorpe Brigg'. Sam Small rescued many a desperate situation but his greatest achievement was always in raising his creator's spirits. And now Knight's other creation was racing to his rescue.

MGM had optioned *Lassie Come-Home* and were busy shooting the film in Culver City. Knight went there on a five-day break from Hollywood in early September. He arrived on set in civilian clothes where he posed for photographs with Pal, the stunt dog brought in to play *Lassie* in the action scenes. Knight reported his visit to Rotha:

'Lassie is becoming a super-dooper-dooper dog at MGM, with the shooting dragging on and on, and the budget going up and up – so what was a nice little dog story maybe will be summat, lad. I can't tell. I saw the exteriors done in Technicolor – the rushes – and they begged me to say that the shore of the State of Washington looked like Scotland. I say they were exactly the same, all except the points where they had pelicans on the rocks in the background.'

Studio executives took some convincing that there were no pelicans in Scotland but at length agreed to cut them out. There was, of course, the problem that *Lassie*, like Tootsie, was a she, whereas Pal wasn't.

'The dog is the most magnificent collie I've ever seen – in conformation, colour, and brilliant sense. Oh gladly do I call him a movie star. I coveted him more than I ever did la Fontaine, la Lamour and all the other pretty stars. (They couldn't get a bitch for the part that looked right, so he's a female impersonator – and thank God he's got a long coat that covers his manhood.)'

MGM had, to his astonishment, asked Knight for suggestions regarding the casting of *Lassie Come-Home* and 'because you always have to base it on something they know,' he said, 'I put forward the idea that the film should be based roughly on the format of 'How Green Was My Valley.' Following his advice, the studio cast Roddy McDowall, Donald Crisp and Elizabeth Taylor in the major roles. As production costs soared, Louis B. Mayer upgraded *Lassie Come-Home* from a B movie to an A but wisely turned down Knight's tongue-in-cheek alternative title suggestion: *How Technicolor Was My Lassie Come To My Valley Home*.

For all its star actors, it was Pal who shone for Eric Knight – thanks to Rudd Weatherwax's expert training. Weatherwax and his family would impart identical skills to countless other canine stars but Pal was the one genuine element of *Lassie Come-Home*, a movie which took cinema-goers by storm, despite being called everything from 'a potboiler' to 'a bit of boggery-doggery'.

Far from cashing in on the movie's success, however, Knight realised he had shot himself in the foot. Despite Hemingway's urging to 'go for the money', he had accepted his agent's advice – that there was no future in a shaggy dog story – and sold the rights for $10,000. This wasn't the only time he let rights go cheaply, it is worth noting. In 1937, he had accepted $750 for the film and radio rights to Sam Small from Earl Carroll, a movie director who later optioned them to RKO, his agent having also signed away the author's rights to resell them.

After the visit to Culver City and a star-studded birthday party at Litvak's beach home, it was back to a Film Unit mired in complex production issues. The relationship with Capra had become more strained and Knight was beginning to realise that his old Yorkshire inclination toward desk-thumping and evangelising was returning, only now men's lives and not just a movie were at stake. He was contemplating how best he might extricate himself from a project he loved when Colonel Munson came to his rescue with a new job offer.

Knight had always confided in Jere, and as the Film Unit descended into chaos she tried to bolster his flagging spirits: 'You're a Yorkshireman, you can take it,' she wrote. Now he was able to send her good news:

'Four years ago Hitler started war. Today Knight starts war. And don't breathe a word or I may be horsed out of here so damn fast no-one will know it - not even me. I sense things and talked to Lyman [Munson] today, and he asked me how I'd like to work with Horgan on the training camp film - and I said 'would I!'

So in all probability I'll be shifting out of this mess that I hate so much, and see you in a few weeks. I am convinced I can't get any film sense knocked into their heads here. Call me a bastard or what you will, but it's no use kicking myself. I want to get out, I could do far more good out of the army than here. And I want to be in and I want to work with Lyman, so by god I think I'm coming east again.'

It was a timely move. Jere was herself a gifted writer and was now selling her work. Her article *Britain's Petticoat Army*, on the subject of women in the armed services, had appeared in the *Saturday Evening Post*. Eric now told her, 'I sometimes wish you would take the job in Washington.' He was referring to an opening that had been offered her, a trial period as speech-writer for WAAC founder and director, Oveta Culp Hobby, and on August 3rd she did just that, travelling to the capital to meet her new boss.

Hobby, just a year younger than Jere, was a law graduate who had been Assistant City Attorney in Houston, Texas, where she had married the state Governor, William P. Hobby. For an honorarium of $1 a year, she took the post as Head of the War Department's Women's Interests Section, and the rank of Colonel in the WAAC. To say Colonel Hobby was impressed with her new assistant would be something of an understatement, and the feeling was clearly mutual. On August 27th, Jere made the journey to Des Moines, Iowa, where, with the minimum of ceremony, she became a WAAC Lieutenant. Post-war, Colonel Hobby would become the first American woman to enter the Senate, as Secretary for Health, Education and Welfare under President Eisenhower. Jere would progress to the rank of Major. She would win a Bronze Star and several citations for her work as a much-respected member of Eisenhower's SHAFE staff responsible for the management of all European operations following the D-Day landings.

In October, Capra took the first of the *Why We Fight* series, *Prelude to War,* to the White House for its screening before the President and the highest-ranking military officers in the US Army. The film was months behind schedule. As it began rolling, a man Capra described as 'wraith-like' slipped into the seat beside him:

"Frank Capra,' he whispered, 'I'm Harry Hopkins. Welcome.' I shook the soft hand and looked into the soft doe eyes of FDR's lean, lanky, hatchet man whose ulcers had become international items.'

Hopkins was based in Washington and, thanks to Munson, Eric Knight was about to be shipped there to work on film projects with Paul Horgan, now Pentagon Information Division Officer, and Peter Hurd, Air Force artist. There was, however, a small problem on the horizon. Captain Eric Knight, of the US Army was not an American. To be more precise, he once had been, but no longer was. He had arrived in America in 1912 while still a minor. His mother had married an American citizen, so her son became an American by default. When he joined the Princess Patricia's Canadian Light Infantry he automatically reverted to British citizenship. After the war, a newly-passed US law reinstated US Citizenship to any Allied soldier whose nationality had been lost due to military service. When he wanted to return to Britain on vacation, however, so many complications arose over his dual background that he reverted to British citizenship in order to obtain a passport, whereupon he became a resident alien in the US. Never sure that he wanted to be an American, and not certain he wanted to remain British – yet convinced that none of that mattered because he would always be a Yorkshireman – he now had to swear allegiance to the United States, which he did on October 26th.

The Washington workload was lighter. He put the finishing touches to his *World of Plenty* script while discussing a second *Lassie* movie, writing propaganda material, broadcasting for war bonds and discussing all manner of post-war projects with Horgan, Hurd, Rotha, and anybody else who might be interested. The 'training camp' films on which Knight and his most trusted friends were working appear to have occupied little of their time. Peter Hurd had just returned from England where he had been collaborating with Rotha, also on *World of Plenty*, but claimed that his only contribution was to advocate slower cutting, thereby leaving more time for the viewer to study the images. 'So much for your Americans-won't-understand-a-slow-shot-and-leisurely-pace,' he told Rotha. Back east, Knight was able to see more of his old friend Cummings – with whom the coded correspondence had never ceased – and immediately fell under the spell of his friend's surreal humour.

As we have seen, Knight and Cummings were two men on one wavelength, perfectly tuned to their own vibrant, alternative world – one far removed from that occupied by the rest of humanity and shared with nobody else. Knight was closer to Rotha idealistically and artistically, but there was never with him the mutual eccentricity Knight allowed full rein when he was with Cummings. And it was the idiosyncratic style of their correspondence that would later reveal a vital clue as to the nature of Knight's wartime endeavours.

GREG CHRISTIE

CHAPTER SIXTEEN

We have seen Eric Knight re-invent himself as an American, and as an author of some renown. And the facts surrounding that narrative have been relatively easy to come by. But we have now arrived at the passage in his life when he moves into the shadows, his work furtive, his movements not always faithfully recorded, and his actions fudged by the few records he left behind. Perhaps this is the moment for his biographer to step into the light and talk about the material we are now to deal with, not for any dramatic purpose, but rather to allow for a frank discussion of the sources uncovered. It was while I was conducting my researches in the Beinecke Library at Yale that I started to find a number of threads that led slowly but unerringly from the upper echelons of government into the world of secret intelligence. My researches led me to read in the records and memoirs of many of the leading players in U.S. and British intelligence at this time. It is from these accounts – and the gaps in them - that I have pieced together a narrative of events that swirled around Knight during this time. Beyond the facts, however, and the written records, are Eric's own accounting for his activities, and it is in this area that I realised I had, after fifteen years of research, become so familiar with his voice, his method, his very character, that I could sometimes read between the lines and find answers where none were, on the face of it, apparent.

So let us make one thing clear: I am presenting here information I have uncovered in the Knight archive – much of it on scattered sheets of note-paper rather than in the bound volumes of any journal. Pieces of a jigsaw, you might say. I am offering material gleaned from my reading in biographies, memoirs and archives of the many participants in this new phase of Knight's life. I am offering too, information drawn from interviews with people who knew the man. And I stress at the outset that the world of secret intelligence is, by its nature, secret. Information that might shed light on events is withheld. Misinformation is disseminated. False trails are laid, deliberately. Meetings are often furtive, and unrecorded. And so, here and there, I have deduced, from the movements known to have taken place, that certain parties are likely to have met, or must have done so. And I have offered suggestions as to the purpose of those meetings, and the subjects discussed. But while I put forward my own interpretation, based on twenty years of research, I am aware that I am opening up a box full of questions that will surely stimulate further investigation.

During his visit to Britain in 1938, Eric Knight had offered his services to the British Army, in the event of war. This much we know. Being too old for active service, he was turned down, and that is where the matter would end, officially. Unofficially, Knight had been directed to Dolphin Square, London, to the office of his namesake, Charles Maxwell Knight. Jere passed on that information to her son, from her second marriage, and he passed it to me when I met him at Spring House Farm. Bizarre as it may seem today, this other Knight was both a Military Intelligence operative *and* Director of Intelligence with Rotha Linton-Orman's British Fascisti, in which he had special responsibilities for the supervision and organisation of Fascist operations within Trades Unions.

Eric Knight was greeted cordially and with some curiosity by 'Captain King', one of his namesake's several aliases. Charles Maxwell Knight – a man possessed of extreme-right views from an early age – had served in the Royal Navy and worked for the Economic League, an organisation founded in 1919 by MP William Reginald Hall and a group of prominent industrialists who worked to expose subversive elements operating against free enterprise. It was as a result of this association that he was recruited to the Security Services in 1924 by the then Director of the Secret Service Bureau, Major General Sir Vernon Kell. His responsibility was to recruit agents dedicated to countering the espionage and sabotage activities of subversives. His department was otherwise known as MI5.

By the early 1930s Maxwell Knight was running B5(b), a department charged with monitoring the activities of both left and right-wing organisations. That he was a member of the British Fascisti (BF) seems to have been of little concern to MI5. Whatever threat the infant organisation posed was offset by his willingness to inform on those who joined the ranks of such movements as cover for their Communist sympathies and activities. In any case, the Fascisti were soon to be eclipsed by Oswald Moseley's rapidly growing British Union of Fascists.

Some historians have claimed that Maxwell Knight was in fact as vehement in his loathing of Fascism as he was of Communism and that he joined the BF when already an MI5 operative for the specific purpose of spying on the organisation. It seems a perfectly reasonable assumption. He had been instrumental in defeating the General Strike of 1926 by identifying several subversives, and through the work of one of his double-agents identified three Communist Party members who had infiltrated the Woolwich Arsenal, all of whom were jailed as a result. Perhaps his most famous MI5 recruit was *Sunday Worker* columnist and party headquarters worker during the General Strike, Tom Driberg, more widely known as William Hickey, gossip columnist for the *Daily Express*. Oxford-educated Driberg had joined the Communist Party at the age of fifteen, only to be expelled in 1941 when he was exposed as an MI5 informer. At this point Maxwell Knight became aware that MI5 had been infiltrated by the KGB, but it would take three decades to unmask Anthony Blunt – by then Surveyor of the Queen's Pictures – as the Russian agent responsible for exposing Driberg, a future Member of Parliament and Chairman of the Labour Party's National Executive.

In May 1940, Maxwell Knight uncovered a more immediate threat in Anna Wolkoff and Tyler Kent, a U.S. Embassy cipher clerk. The pair were activists with links to Sir Oswald Mosley. Kent was alleged to have copied transmissions between Churchill and Roosevelt with the aim of exposing the latter's intention of entering the war on the side of the Allies when, in public, he was opposing involvement. Kent, Wolkoff, and several others involved in the plot, would subsequently be jailed under the Official Secrets Act. Maxwell Knight reported that American Ambassador to London, Joseph Kennedy, had 'panicked' at the thought of American participation in the war and Roosevelt's alleged negotiating to that end. Heightened vigilance would therefore be required to ensure that none of what Kent knew slipped into the wrong hands. Maxwell Knight stepped in, assuring the Ambassador and those around him that their President was not negotiating with Churchill, while at the same time impressing upon him the belief that American intervention would secure victory for the Allies.

It was during Knight's later visit to London towards the end of 1941 – the trip on which he was accompanied by Jere - that Maxwell Knight acquainted him with the Kent-Wolkoff case. He stressed that there were still those close to the President who believed he opposed participation, and those who were beginning to see through the façade, all of which rendered Eric Knight's role highly sensitive, he being one of a handful of men in America in the President's confidence.

Maxwell Knight enjoyed many triumphs in his work but there was one notable failure. It was he who recruited to the ranks of BF's Communist and Nazi infiltrators William Joyce, later executed for his collaboration with the Nazis through his infamous role as radio propagandist Lord Haw-Haw. But it is important to remember that in his dealings with minor agents Maxwell Knight used numerous code names, thus obscuring his own identity – and, by default, putting his namesake Eric into the picture painted by post-war researchers. Add the fact that Maxwell Knight was also a man with multiple musical skills, a published author with two crime novels and some half dozen works on natural history, and a radio broadcaster. When he went into television in the 1950s he was again occasionally confused with the author, but did little to clarify matters. Indeed, during his earliest appearances on British TV it was often said that it was he and not Eric Knight who had been responsible for *Lassie Come-Home*. Many historians have confused the roles of Eric, Maxwell, and a third player, Ridgway Knight of the Office of Strategic Services (O.S.S.); and that is hardly surprising since each of the latter two would perpetuate the story that 'the man who wrote *Lassie* was a spy, you know', thereby blurring any view of their own involvement in secret intelligence operations.

So Charles Maxwell Knight's name is rarely mentioned as a high-ranking secret service operative. It lives on obliquely, however, in the work of his most famous recruit, Ian Fleming, whose character 'M' in the James Bond books is partly based on him. Another to be entangled in the web of secrecy was the *Sunday Graphic* journalist, thriller writer, and Maxwell Knight's closest friend, Denis Wheatley. With an unrivalled knowledge of the occult, and best known perhaps for *The Devil Rides Out* and *Total War*, Wheatley would enjoy a long and distinguished career resulting in the publication of almost eighty books. He and Eric Knight were almost exactly the same age, and though Wheatley was born into a middle-class family, he gained Eric Knight's respect as a First World War veteran who had served as a 2nd Lieutenant at Passchendaele, where he was gassed.

Following his Dolphin Square meetings, and with a letter of introduction from Rotha, Eric Knight had called on the person he considered 'the only man fit to run Britain', Richard Stafford Cripps. A Christian Socialist and a pacifist, Cripps had qualified as a research chemist but had practised law since 1913. He had served with the Red Cross in France during World War One I before returning to a highly successful career as a barrister. Elected to the House of Commons in 1931 after winning the East Bristol by-election, Cripps was appointed Solicitor-General by Prime Minister Ramsay MacDonald the following year and subsequently knighted. He had converted to Marxism in the mid-1930s and by the time he met Eric Knight was one of Britain's most prominent left-wing figures. Cripps was bitterly opposed to Fascism. He supported a Popular Front embracing all of Europe's left-wing groups against the spread of Fascist doctrines. So although Cripps supported a stance of non-aggression, the two found common ground in their loathing of the Nazi regime. A year after their meeting, Cripps would be expelled from the Labour Party. Despite this, he would still represent the main opposition to the wartime Coalition Government, and in time Churchill would feel it necessary to remove him as a threat to his own leadership by appointing him Lord Privy Seal and member of the War Cabinet. Cripps would hold that position until 1942, when his continued resistance to Churchill's strategy led to his removal to the post of Minister of Aircraft Production.

Cripps and Eric Knight would, after numerous meetings, enter into a considerable body of correspondence, no record of which Knight chose to keep or even mention – which is surprising, considering that he fastidiously retained letters of a far less critical nature. Cripps' name does, however, pop up in a letter to Rotha, when Knight was trying to spread the word about the mood in America: 'When you see Cripps, pass on to him whatever of my letter you feel may do him good.'

oOo

It was Maxwell Knight who had first suggested that, as a high-profile author, Eric Knight might be a useful recruit to the cause – and issued an invitation to attend a meeting at the President's New York Hyde Park residence. Maxwell Knight's brief, as is made clear in Henry Hemmings' biography of him, was to advance ideas on the need for American support. From that moment on he would be doing everything in his power to influence the President's opinion in favour of Britain while at the same time ensuring that British propaganda chiefs, through Rotha, learned of both Roosevelt's own mindset and the popular opinion of the American people. Knight was uniquely qualified for this job: at this early stage he had no connection with the armed forces, and a plausible reason for international travel. Meetings with high-ranking politicians and officials could legitimately take place under the pretence that he was conducting literary research, or doing voluntary war work. He was British enough to be outspoken on matters of war and American enough to be seen by Americans as 'one of us'. He was a man with both US and British affiliations, he was well known enough to carry public opinion but not so famous that he couldn't walk down the street without being mobbed. He was too old for active service, had no political axe to grind, and was associated with no recognised political party. His Quaker leanings were known to only a few, and, had they been known, would have led to an assumption that he was a pacifist. Here was an honest, transparent individual, one perfect for a job requiring the ability to hide his true self behind an utterly plausible other self. In short, a man capable of absolute duality.

Until the Hyde Park meetings, Eric Knight's opinion of Churchill had fluctuated, Eden being his preferred choice for British leader. He had told Rotha, however, that 'public sentiment' had 'swung swung wildly in favour of Britain,' and that 'Churchill is acceptable in every way to the American mind'. More importantly, Churchill's fitness for leadership had been impressed upon Eric Knight by a man whose presence at the meetings can

179

mean only one thing: that Knight and fellow attendee Harry Hopkins were to be informed of a highly significant development that would effectively seal the outcome of the war. Knight does not mention the man by name, but a photograph, immaculately preserved in the Knight archive of the Beinecke Library at Yale, reveals that he, Hopkins and this third man, photographed together at Hyde Park, were the closest of associates. The man in the picture is William 'Wild Bill' Donovan, a millionaire Wall Street lawyer who had opposed the New Deal but who shared with FDR and Hopkins a detestation of Nazi Germany.

It is well known that the President had personally recruited Donovan in 1940 to undertake covert fact-finding assignments in Germany and throughout Europe. As an American, he was of course still free to travel in Europe at that time. Through the contacts he made, Donovan would set up a network of spies and informants extending to 15,000 operatives, most of them acting behind enemy lines.

Shortly after the Hyde Park meetings with Knight and Hopkins, Donovan became Coordinator of Information, and a year later, as a Major General in the US Army, Head of the Office of Strategic Services, the O.S.S., to which Eric Knight was recruited within days of Donovan taking up his post.

On Donovan's European tour of June 1940, he arrived in London only days after the Kent-Wolkoff arrests and began learning the British intelligence and counter-intelligence techniques he would employ as the model for the OSS. The visit had been suggested by William Stephenson and organised by MI6 chief, Stewart Menzies, with whom Stephenson liaised in his capacity as the chief of the FBI's Secret Intelligence Services (S.I.S.). This much we have from William Stevenson's biography of Stephenson, *A Man Called Intrepid*. He met with Churchill and other high-ranking British officials, was briefed on Britain's powerful new weapon, radar, and familiarised with the subtleties of propaganda.

Donovan often found himself accused of being unreasonably pro-British, but his interests were not simply in saving Britain from her enemies. He wanted to help her save the rest of Europe, and he naturally allied himself to any Englishman possessed of that same mindset.

In the period when Knight was most active in beating the drum for American intervention, there is a gap in one of the principal sources for this story. That is the flow of correspondence between Knight and Rotha. From June 1940 to June 1941 Rotha, had received no communication from his friend. The fact is that several letters he wrote had gone astray and Knight, having received no replies to his own letters, stopped writing in the belief that they were being intercepted.

What can be pieced together, however, is that in late March 1941, the Knights had spent some time in New Mexico. From there, they had returned to Pleasant Valley, from where Eric travelled to New York City for the launch of *This Above All.* According to independent reports, on May 24th he was back in New York City, ostensibly conducting meetings with his publishers, Harpers. His real purpose, however, was a clandestine meeting with two men engaged in high-level intelligence operations.

Commander Ian Fleming arrived at La Guardia Field on May 25th and journeyed by taxi to the Rockefeller Centre in Manhattan to meet with director of British Naval Intelligence, Admiral John H. Godfrey. Fleming would later claim that while there he had dispatched, James Bond style, a Japanese secret agent whose office in the building acted as a front for covert activities such as the interception of US ciphers, which were then decoded and forwarded to Tokyo. The spy had indeed been eliminated, although it was not Fleming who pulled the trigger. He was in the city to assist Godfrey in reporting on US intelligence organisations and co-ordinate them with those of their British counterparts, the idea being to centralise operations under a single commanding officer.

Fleming worked closely on the project with William Stephenson, also cited as one of the models for James Bond's 'M', and later associated with Donovan. Stephenson was a Canadian millionaire and former world boxing champion of Scots descent. As revealed in the biography mentioned earlier, he was responsible for recruiting hundreds of agents among whom the names of stars like Greta Garbo, Noël Coward, Leslie Howard and David Niven have been widely mentioned.

Stephenson's official post of Passport Control Officer masked the duties of the most important and trusted spymaster of World War II – one whom Churchill held in the highest possible regard. It is said that, among his other well documented exploits, Stephenson recruited Mafia bosses to rid New York's docklands of Nazi agents, but his main task in the city was to persuade the American government to create a formal spy network and secret service of their own, rather than relying upon the activities of several disparate groups. He saw America's secret activities as vulnerable to infiltration and exposure. While the FBI, Military and Naval Intelligence organisations were in active operation, the three were, in his opinion, not properly co-ordinated and in some cases even working against one another. This topic had been discussed at a specially convened Hyde Park meeting chaired by the President, when the Chiefs of Staff had been told that such matters were overseen more effectively in Britain by one man, referred to only as 'Mr. X'.

Many of these Hyde Park meetings took place on Sundays, and, to ward off any press interest in the comings and goings, were passed off as social gatherings. The President would refer to 'Intrepid' on these occasions as 'just a friend of Eleanor's', a title he also bestowed upon Eric Knight who was often referred to as being 'here to play tennis'.

Once Stephenson had persuaded Roosevelt that one man should take on a role similar to Britain's 'Mr. X', it fell to Fleming to identify a suitably qualified individual. He found him on the 44th floor of the International Building posing as the director of a law practice, which was in fact the headquarters of the FBI's Special Intelligence Service. Thirty-five-year old Percy Foxworth – known also as Bud or Sam – was a man of high intelligence, outstanding organisational and investigative skills, whose work during the 1932 Lindbergh kidnapping had propelled him to the post of second-in-command to the FBI Director, J. Edgar Hoover.

It is unlikely that Knight and Foxworth were introduced at this time as Fleming would not yet have finalised his vetting of Foxworth. They met subsequently, however, through Harry Hopkins, who had been in England in January 1941, at which time Foxworth, in his role as Roosevelt's Lease-Lend emissary, met with Churchill and other high-ranking officials as a dinner guest of the King.

The future creator of James Bond was eleven years younger than Knight. He was nine when he lost his father, Valentine, whose *Times* obituary was written by Winston Churchill. Fleming had attended Sandhurst but did not graduate, becoming instead a *Reuters* correspondent before accepting a *Times* assignment to cover a trade mission to Russia, at which point it is generally accepted that he began spying for both Maxwell Knight and friends at the Foreign Office. From there he was recruited into Naval Intelligence and quickly became second-in-command to Godfrey.

Given Knight's association with Donovan and others involved in covert operations, it seems no accident that when his U.S. Army application was finally accepted he found himself closely associated with the OSS, where we now know there was a great deal more to his duties than scripting Army information films. And clearly, when Capra moved the outfit to Hollywood, it became essential to return him to Washington and the company of his most trusted friends, Horgan and Hurd. There he was introduced to a man whose name, when he heard it, must have made him smile quietly.

oOo

Some thirty-five years previously young Eric had wandered through bluebell woods on private land, dreaming his dreams of the 'Nava-Nava-Navajo'. The man who owned those woods was one Edward Frederic Lindley Wood, Lord Halifax, and now Britain's Ambassador to Washington. Sixteen years Eric Knight's senior, he had served in World War I despite having been born with no left hand. When Britain's beleaguered Prime Minister Neville Chamberlain resigned, a meeting at 10 Downing Street was called to decide upon his successor. There were two candidates. One was Winston Churchill, the other Halifax, incumbent

Foreign Secretary and former Viceroy of India. The latter had the backing of King George VI, the House of Lords, the financial institutions, much of the popular press and the public. He was even preferred to Churchill by Cripps and Bevan. The only men, it may be said, who did not want him to take highest office were Churchill and Halifax himself, and in an act of unrivalled political selflessness, Halifax recommended Churchill. Some historians even say that on the afternoon of the meeting Halifax left to attend an appointment with his dentist. Only months later he was appointed Ambassador to the United States, at which point he took on the role of persuading President Roosevelt through official channels that Britain was sorely in need of America's help.

Halifax was eminently qualified for his new job. He may not have been the dynamic individual that Churchill was, and there were those who looked upon the post of U.S. Ambassador as a kind of banishment, but Halifax was a diligent and reliable man, ideal for the job. He would not have been aware of Eric's association with Maxwell Knight, nor how deeply he was involved in intelligence operations; he was not a man interested in the covert. Indeed, it is unlikely he knew about the coded messages that had been passing between Churchill and Roosevelt since 1939. What he did know was that Eric Knight was a trusted friend of high Government officials, that he had an encyclopaedic knowledge of the air raids taking place over Britain – carefully culled from newspapers – and that he was close to the U.S. President. It is therefore safe to assume that their discussions centred on initiatives that might encourage greater American participation in Britain's war.

During his first six months in Washington, Halifax saw Roosevelt fewer than half a dozen times. A diplomat rather than a salesman, he followed diplomatic rules. The attack on Pearl Harbor in December 1941, however, and the subsequent declaration of war by Germany, changed everything. Halifax became much closer to the President. After the Japanese attack, of course, Knight was no longer required as a lobbyist for U.S. action on Britain's behalf. Once he was in the Army and stationed in Washington, however, the pair met on numerous occasions. There was a new and even more important role he could play. It would mean further meetings with Fleming, probably Wheatley, even Churchill, and continued contact with Lord Halifax.

Now in uniform, he was closer in all respects to the seat of power. For an accomplished documentary filmmaker and respected broadcaster, the offer of a posting to run a Forces Radio Broadcasting Station in North Africa appeared entirely appropriate. The final charade had begun.

CHAPTER SEVENTEEN

There now enters another key figure into the narrative. Charles E. Bedaux was a time-and-motion man in the tradition of F. W. Taylor, intimately familiar with American and British engineering techniques. He had in fact emigrated to the States in the mid-1930s and taken U.S. citizenship. His unique style of management had revolutionized industrial output. He had devised a universal measure for all manual tasks, which was named after him, and become a multi-millionaire. He returned to France in 1937 and would soon embark upon a new career – as a German collaborator.

Bedaux had plans for the more efficient running of Germany's munitions factories, their railway system and general industrial infrastructure, all of which impressed his new masters greatly. He feigned sympathy with his homeland while becoming a close friend of Franz Medicus, the German general who would be largely responsible for seizing Jewish-owned property in France. His grand scheme for a network of international oil pipelines hinged on North Africa in general and Algeria in particular; it was, in broad terms, his intention to extract enough oil from all over the African continent to power Germany's industries worldwide, and to supply fresh water to irrigate even the most inhospitable desert in order to feed what he believed would be a global German nation. German High Command may not have been admitting to any plans for the invasion of the USA, Canada or South America, but Bedaux was in no doubt that the continent would in time fall to the Nazis.

His work began in earnest in 1942 when the Germans granted him a visa to enter Algiers, but his plans were soon disrupted by the Allied invasion of North Africa. Initially, he assumed that the attack would be repelled. When it became clear that the invading forces were not to be beaten back, he went on the run. His liberty was short-lived. It has been said that he was arrested by the French as a collaborator – and the French may well have been responsible for his detention – but the orders had come straight from General Eisenhower. The Allied C-in-C wanted to know what American and British manufacturing secrets had been passed to the Germans, and more importantly, what his captive could be persuaded to divulge about German armaments manufacture.

Bedaux would eventually be brought to trial in the US as a traitor, and would end his own life on February 18th 1944 with an overdose of sleeping pills. Under arrest in Algiers in late 1942, however, he was to be interrogated by a master of that art, the FBI's Assistant Director Percy Foxworth and his associate, 31-year old FBI Special Agent Harold Dennis Haberfeld. According to the FBI, Foxworth and Haberfeld were to travel to North Africa 'at the specific request of General Dwight D. Eisenhower to perform a secret mission of critical importance'. They would have a notable travelling companion.

Christmas was approaching, and Knight had been given three days' leave, which he spent at Springhouse Farm. Back in D.C., on January 1st, he had a studio photograph taken which he mailed to Jere. On January 8th he was promoted to the rank of Major and received orders in a letter from the Director, Special Services Operations, marked 'SECRET'.

'Orders:
To: Officers Involved.

1.   The Secretary of War directs that each of the following named officers proceed on or about January 10th, 1943 from Washington, D.C. to New York and/or Miami, Florida, thence via the South Atlantic route to the British Gold Coast; Anglo-Egyptian Sudan; thence to Cairo, Egypt, reporting upon arrival to the Commanding General, for temporary duty. Upon completion of this temporary duty you will return to Washington, D.C.

Lt. Col. John B. Stanley, 0-19549
Major Eric M. Knight, 0-477891'

The dispatch goes on to mention a baggage allowance and reminds those being posted that the time difference between the two continents would need to be remembered in any transmissions. It is signed by the Adjutant General. Ostensibly, it was the need for a US Forces radio station that had prompted Knight's posting to Cairo, and his promotion to Major.

The manifest of the aircraft in which Knight flew, however, makes no mention of any radio transmitting equipment. The passenger list further shows that Knight was unaccompanied by any army personnel with relevant technical or broadcasting experience. Leaving aside Foxworth and

Haberfeld, the others travelling included a number of junior officers en route to India, a number of Army civilian employees, a clerk to the Consular General in Algiers and some oil company employees.

FBI files reveal that subversives were known to be operating in and around U.S. military and civilian airfields, so there was a real concern that they might have learned of the impending Casablanca Conference to be attended by Roosevelt, Churchill and French leader-in-exile Charles de Gaulle. No American President had ever left his country in time of war, but this conference was of huge significance. It was here, notwithstanding Stalin's absence, that the Allied leaders would agree upon the conditions for Germany's total surrender when the war was finally won. The meeting was scheduled for January 14th. The American public would only learn that it had taken place when their President was safely back on U.S. soil.

Knight now travelled in an Army jeep driven by a Lieutenant John Doe, presumably not his real name but the one traditionally applied by Americans to any unidentified male. His destination was New York – a distance of 225 miles. There he collected secret orders, in person, from William 'Intrepid' Stephenson, before returning to Bolling Airfield, Washington. This is quite extraordinary and of great significance. If Knight were merely going to Africa to set up a radio station he would surely have no business with Churchill's spymaster, who worked under cover and would have been extremely wary about contact with personnel not directly involved in clandestine affairs. And if secret documents were to be sent over the ocean, would they not have been entrusted, in normal circumstances, to serving intelligence officers such as Foxworth and Haberfeld, Knight's travelling companions? It seems clear that Knight had business with Stephenson – a shadowy figure whose work was unknown to most people, even at the highest level – and equally clear that that business was top secret.

With the documents secured in a special satchel, Knight boarded a Douglas C-54 Skymaster under contract to the Air Transport Command but manned by a TWA crew. The plane set off towards Miami, Florida, the same destination as the President was making for by train, and touched down in the early hours of January 11th.

When Roosevelt arrived in Florida he was driven to the Pan American Airways base at Dinner Key where two C-54s stood prepared for him. However, at the last moment, according to Boeing records, he boarded a Pan American 314 Clipper. The flying-boat, named *The Dixie Clipper*, was piloted by Howard M. Cone, a Pan American pilot and reserve Lieutenant in the US Navy. A second 314, *The Atlantic Clipper*, carried Secret Service and other support staff. The two seaplanes took off shortly after 6 a.m., with Roosevelt travelling under the name of Jones.

Knight, Foxworth, Haberfeld and their fellow-passengers, meanwhile, were seated in a third plane. As they awaited departure their pilot, Captain Benjamin Hart Dally, reported that he had a problem with the radio and that the passengers would have to disembark. This was no brief delay. It would in fact be close to three days before the party finally set off for Africa on a C-54.

It would have been during this hiatus that Knight received further orders from the War Department. In a letter dated January 12th, he was appointed Officer Courier 'for the purpose of carrying official United States Army Mail, exempt from censorship from Washington D.C. to Cairo and return. The said mail,' it continued, 'involves one package No. 1001 from the Director, Special Service Division, Services of Supply, to Lt Col John B Stanley, Officer in Charge, Special Service Detachment, Cairo, Egypt.'

This seems odd, seeing that Stanley was travelling in the same plane and under the same instructions as Knight. Did Stanley have a companion package addressed to Knight, and was this therefore a belt-and-braces measure to ensure that one package got through? As to the content of the package, it has been suggested that it might have been money or a money order, for use in North Africa. The fact that the letter was signed by one Karl W Marks raises another question: was that his true identity, or someone's idea of a joke?

Crossing the Atlantic by aircraft was not a journey to be lightly undertaken in 1943. Charles Lindbergh had made the first flight over the ocean as recently as 1927, making the 3,500-mile journey from Long Island to Paris. During wartime, however, it was considered that the less time spent over submarine-infested waters the better. So there were two options: north via Greenland, or south via 950 miles of the South American coastline and an even shorter crossing over open sea to the west coast of Africa. Neither was a joy-ride: aircraft taking this southerly course were frequently shot at by enemy submarines; the weather was unpredictable, and attempts to sabotage aircraft had been made. Some had been misled by radio signals transmitted from German U-boats. Navigators had therefore been advised to ignore all signals and plot their course by the stars and dead reckoning.

Thirty-five-year old Captain Dally was an ex-Army Air Corps pilot with eleven years' experience and 8,000 flying hours behind him, including fifty on the C-54, which had come into service only a few months previously. His aircraft, though fresh from the production line, now developed a problem with number four engine and put down in Trinidad, where Flight Engineer Clyde E. Quisenberry worked on it while the passengers rested at a nearby hotel.

With the repair completed, Captain Dally undertook his pre-flight inspection. He noticed an open inspection hatch at the rear of the plane and found a screwdriver inside, close to the IFF (Interrogation Friend or Foe) box. This was a piece of hardware designed to emit signals to friendly aircraft patrolling the skies, identifying the sender as non-hostile. Dally had also received a warning that a bomb might have been planted, but after he and his eight crew members had made a thorough search and found nothing, the C-54 left Waller Field, Trinidad, at 0426 GMT (that is, around half past midnight local time) on January 15th.

At around 0300hrs the plane crossed the coastline of Dutch Guiana, now Surinam. It was 25 miles north-east of Paramaribo, flying over a patchwork of mudflats, dense undergrowth and stretches of shallow water. Knight, seated in one of the lightweight canvas seats with which the aircraft had been fitted, may have been dozing. He may have been enjoying a cigarette. Or mulling over the mission that lay ahead – a mission whose true nature remains a mystery to this day. Whether he would have had the chance to express his concern to a fellow passenger about the plane losing height, about the 180-degree turn the pilot executed as the troublesome number four engine coughed and stuttered, we can never know. The one thing of which we can be certain is that his life was terminated with awful suddenness as the plane exploded in mid-air, scattering its fragmented frame, its baggage, and the 35 passengers and crew over the landscape below. The richly textured life of a Yorkshire mill lad made good came to an abrupt and violent end as he died in circumstances laden with an irony that might have been written into a Hollywood movie: while he was flying, with no *Lassie*, and no Sam Small to come to the rescue.

News of the crash took some time to emerge from the remote outpost of the Dutch colonial empire. The nature of the location – and the fact that the crash took place at dead of night – would have impeded access to the site, and the scattering of debris and human remains would have added to the task of ascertaining what had happened. An FBI memo, dated 16 February 1943 and signed by Edward A. Tamm, states that the aircraft disintegrated in mid-air, one wing hitting the ground 'considerably before the rest of the wreckage, which was strewn over a mile and a half. He makes the significant point that it was common for planes to lose radio contact with their port of departure and that, despite not hearing from the captain for many hours, the people at Waller assumed he had got to his destination safely. It was not until the morning of the third day after departure that the plane was reported missing. Had an immediate search been mounted, and the wreck located, Tamm believes that several of the people on board might have been saved. A number of passengers, he says, were later found in light rafts, and some of those had been dead but a few hours. This does not tally with local reports, as we shall see.

The story didn't make the American papers until the morning editions of Friday 22 January, a full week after the crash. In Britain, which is five hours ahead of New York time, it made the BBC's nine o'clock news on the evening of Thursday January 21st 1943. A baldly factual bulletin, read by John Snagge, stated:

'An American Army Transport plane has crashed in Dutch Guiana. Among the thirty-five dead was Eric Knight, author of This Above All.'

There was no eulogy to the dead author, although in the American papers he was granted quite a few column inches. Reports in other outlets added a few scattered details, emanating from varied sources. According to De West, a Surinam regional newspaper, the aircraft was 'taking part in a secret mission' – although where that came from we cannot be sure. The report added that a great deal of cash in dollar bills was recovered from the crash site. A report from the local police chief relayed through Commewijne District Commissioner, Mr. J.V. Patten, stated that 'Military personnel returned from the crash site with heavy boxes full of coded documents for the British Supreme Commander in North Africa, General Harold Alexander.

The fact that Alexander was to be a key figure at the Casablanca conference suggests that the aircraft, or at least its occupants, was in fact making for the Moroccan city, rather than Foxworth and Haberfeld's supposed destination, Algiers. Official records, however, make no mention of any personnel or paperwork being absent from the conference. The presence of a large amount of cash on the plane could have many explanations, the most likely being that it was to pay Allied agents working in Casablanca.

For many years after the fatal crash, little was said or written about it. However, in the mid-1990s Eric Knight's grand-daughter, Betsy Mewborn Cowan, started badgering reluctant officialdom before finally opening a few doors by invoking the United States' Freedom of Information Act, which came into effect in 1967. So we have further sources to draw on.

Among the documents recovered by Betsy Cowan is an official crash report, which she finally tracked down in 1998. It had been in the hands of a private collector who told her he had found it 'misfiled' by the Army with a collection of documents dated 1942. This could well be the result of a clerical accident of the kind so often made in January: putting the previous year's date instead of the new one. Or it might have been deliberate. Among a file of papers still bearing the marks of peripheral burning, and stained by water, was a note on U S Army headed paper stating that other 'sensitive material' had been removed. Material that has not, to my knowledge, come to light.

The report that Betsy Cowan tracked down raises questions about statements that emerged directly after the crash. It states that the wings and engines 'could not be examined', which is at odds with what local residents said – that they found almost all of the aircraft parts, albeit scattered, with the wing-tips half a mile distant. The earliest report, dated January 19th, was written by one A E G Brown, Headmaster of nearby Reyndorp School. His rather hesitant tone suggests that he was simply relaying a version he had been fed, opening with the comment, 'I have been informed by participants of the American expedition, who returned yesterday, of the following.' He suggests that the causes were as yet a mystery, stating rather quaintly, 'it is a problem to anyone how the plane could be met with an accident.' He goes on to say that, 'Parts of the bodies of the occupants were found at great distances from each other and buried there. None of the dead bodies could be recognised or were whole.' He continues, 'You would probably be able to learn more about this aeroplane accident in town.' He further reported that: 'Some bodies or parts of bodies had been buried by natives near the crash site where they had also erected a wooden cross. Some were buried at Constantia on January 18th.'

A later report, dated February 13th and written by a Captain in the U.S. Medical Corps, states that, 'Only fragments of bodies were found, which were badly deteriorated. There were many bodies and parts of bodies never found. No parts or fragments of bodies were identified as that of any specific individual except one fragmented torso which had attached a part of the trousers containing the identification card of Major Eric Knight.'

The description surely points to a mid-air explosion, rather than simple mechanical failure, a view corroborated by a local resident, Olav Klosteren, who lived on the west bank of the Mata Pica Canal. Sightings of aircraft would have been rare at that time and in particular in that locale, and, given that this plane droned across the skies over his house around three in the morning, one can readily imagine him stepping outside to see what was happening. He must have been transfixed by what he witnessed. 'I saw a burning aeroplane coming down slowly,' he said. 'It disappeared behind some bushes on the coast, then there was an explosion'. Another, unnamed eye-witness said, 'I saw the plane's red light; it was headed east; four minutes later it came back when I heard a series of loud noises, some louder than others – then I saw a bright flare.'

Here and elsewhere, eyewitness and local post-crash reports are at odds with the official version. Clearly, something had exploded – which raises the question, why was Jere Knight told only that 'pilot error or mechanical breakdown' was to blame for the crash? Or is it the case that the explosion was caused on impact with the ground?

Local witnesses reported having seen aircraft parts being removed from the crash site by military personnel. Leaving aside the details as to the damage inflicted, the question remains, what caused the crash? Was crew fatigue a factor? An Air Force Historical Research Agency report draws attention to a general shortage of personnel at the time, which meant that an aircraft often had to be guarded, around the clock, by crew-members. So fatigue and pilot error might be factors. But tiredness played no part in the loss of this C-54. The crew had been well rested and prepared for a long flight, and, according to the report, the aircraft had been guarded by trained men since the moment it left the factory. Greater than usual vigilance had in fact been the case; it was, after all, on the tarmac with four other planes at the President's disposal and therefore the subject of high security.

What then of the crash victims' remains? According to Johan De Greve, manager of the bauxite plant in Paramaribo in the immediate post-war period, 'all the bodies' were exhumed in 1947 and re-buried at the Graves Registration Cemetery at Fort Read, Trinidad. Later, a solitary coffin was buried at Jefferson Barracks National Cemetery, St. Louis, Missouri. It supposedly contained the remains of Eric Knight.

Information about the crash has been hard to find, and questions remain unanswered to this day. Certain US Government departments are still reluctant to talk about it. There was one passenger on board who held 'multiple identities' – a fact noted in documents held by Knight's grand-daughter. Several other relatives of the victims have made their own attempts at research over the decades but though they found the FBI and CIA unfailingly courteous and respectful, none have been entirely satisfied with the outcome. I was told more than once in response to an enquiry: 'That information is classified, sir.' So did Dally really change planes at Dinner Key due to a faulty radio system, or was there some other reason? Where did the bomb threat that he reported come from? These were not rare but were almost always without foundation. Why did a new C-54 – of which only three of over 250 built were lost to mechanical failure – suddenly dive out of the sky when it was capable of flying on any one of its four engines? Most importantly, we must question why A E G Brown talks of multiple burials when the FBI's own Hall of Honor clearly states:

'Although 35 people were on board the aircraft, search teams were only able to locate sufficient remains to be placed in a single casket.'

As to the sabotage theory, seven distinct Fascist or subversive groups subsequently claimed to have planted a bomb on board the plane. But there was little new in this. Such groups would claim responsibility for anything that might further their cause, despite the fact that they were mostly ineffective in their operations.

It is clear that a searching enquiry was undertaken after the crash. Foxworth and Haberfeld, after all, were only the second and third FBI agents to die on active service, so their deaths were never going to be dismissed with a shrug. They were on a hugely important mission, to interrogate Bedaux. It is interesting to note that barely a month after the crash, in February 1943, a new Liberty Ship was launched, and named the SS *P.E. Foxworth* – so this was a loss keenly felt.

While the FBI Hall of Honor states only that 'the cause of the crash has never been ascertained', someone surely had suspicions, or at least deeply grounded fears. Within hours of the crash taking place, Foxworth's wife and family were removed from their New York home, permanently, with all their belongings. Even their garbage cans were taken away. If we assume that the C-54 was sabotaged we have to assume that Foxworth was the target.

But if there was a deliberate act of sabotage, how was it effected? When Dally and his crew searched the C-54 following the alleged bomb threat, they found nothing. On the other hand, passengers re-boarding the aircraft were not searched, according to Boeing records. In such circumstances today we would instantly think of a suicide bomber. These were effectively unheard of in those days. The 'loud noises' and the 'flare' reported by an eyewitness may point to a bomb, but may equally well be unconnected. If engine number four *was* faulty it could have backfired, and Dally, having made for open water, might well have elected to return to dry land, which would explain the plane's U-turn.

Among the theories put forward to explain the crash is a build-up of fuel vapour around a faulty engine. Had that occurred, and had the fuel ignited, would the resulting explosion not have caused more damage to the wings than was the actual case? Would it have ripped the plane to shreds? And then we have the bodies of the victims. It is an established fact that they were 'blown apart' – apparently by an explosion within the plane rather than by the impact of a crash-landing. Eric Knight, as we have seen, was identifiable only by the contents of the wallet in his hip pocket, there being no upper-body remains. There was no all-engulfing fire. The wings, though damaged, were removed from the crash area more or less intact but minus their tips.

And so we speculate. But the most telling evidence that this was not simply the unfortunate accident it has been portrayed as over the decades is that there are still elements of it which are classified and about which U.S. Government departments will say nothing. Further, we know that the first U.S. team to arrive on the scene was pre-occupied with a search for a special satchel containing secret documents.

Naturally, as with so many unexplained incidents, ignorance of the facts has led to the spread of falsehoods. For years there was a myth abroad that the actor Leslie Howard, whose aircraft was shot down over the Bay of Biscay in June 1943, had been 'killed with Eric Knight'. It prevailed for some years until the truth about his death was revealed in a British television documentary based on the life of Churchill's bodyguard, Walter H. Thompson. Howard – one of Stephenson's agents – was sacrificed, we finally learned, in order that the Germans would not learn of the Allies' most zealously guarded secret. Thanks to the now celebrated achievements of the 'boffins' at Bletchley Park and the development of the Enigma code-breaking machine, the Allies were reading the Germans' cyber-traffic as if written in plain. Churchill was due to fly home from a Lisbon conference on the day Howard was making the same journey from Algiers and in the same type of aircraft. Thompson, the documentary reports, disabled Churchill's aircraft by the removal of a simple engine part, which prevented its take-off and postponed the flight until the following day, thereby removing the possibility of it being confused with Howard's plane which, through the interception of coded messages, the British knew was to be attacked. Had Howard's flight been cancelled it would have raised suspicions amongst Luftwaffe chiefs that their messages were being read by the Allies. That would have seriously damaged future Enigma operations and, ultimately, the outcome of the war.

So was Knight's plane sacrificed to save Roosevelt? The President was, after all, flying the same route at the same time and only changed planes at the last moment. That notion overlooks the fact that Foxworth was on board – and his business in Africa was of huge importance to the Allied cause. It is surely beyond the bounds of probability that such a sacrifice would have been sanctioned.

The outcome of a research project such as this investigation into the life of Eric Knight can hinge on a number of factors. Diligence can certainly increase your chances of success, as can persistence – as Betsy Cowan has shown. But there is also the fact that, in going over and over a person's correspondence, one learns not only to recognise his or her voice but also to decode an aside here, an offhand remark there. On reading the extensive collection of letters that Knight exchanged with Cummings, the poet, which we have mentioned several times, I was fortunate to notice an item that might easily have passed by a reader unfamiliar with these individuals' style, their way of engaging with each other, laid down a decade earlier in Knight's Hollywood days.

In February 1942, while he was in London, Knight wrote to this friend, with whom he had corresponded in code for ten years. The letter contains no discussion of the war itself and concentrates instead on reminiscences, on bland talk of the weather, of London in the blackout. The casual reader would be correct in assuming that the various 'spelling errors' were part of the two men's private language, but to one familiar with their correspondence, with the workings of Knight's mind, his wartime activities and links with MI5, a single line stands out: 'I am in London and proud to be in Enigma.'

Cummings, who died long before Bletchley's wartime decoding secrets were divulged, probably assumed that the word stood for 'England'. But doesn't it now seem more likely that Eric Knight was telling him that he had been initiated into that shadowy coven of men and women who knew about the most crucial wartime secret of all – the de-coding machine that had come out of Bletchley Park?

Hitler consistently refuted any claim that the Allies were able to decipher messages transmitted by his system. Like his beloved Reich, which he believed would last a thousand years, his coding system was, he insisted, infallible. The dictator died ignorant of the truth. Indeed, even on the Allied side only a handful of men knew what was going on. The two men who later become best-selling authors – Ian Fleming and Denis Wheatley – were among them. The creator of James Bond was second-in-command at decoding headquarters; the master of the occult was his 'fortress bunker' emissary. Maxwell Knight's greatest successes were linked to information that he could only have acquired through Enigma, and Donovan, as we have seen, had been at Bletchley in 1940 learning the secret. 'Intrepid', of course, was the final arbiter on who should be trusted and Knight's meeting with him in New York, just before he flew to Miami, surely points to his being in the spymaster's confidence.

In view of the fact that Knight actually uttered the word 'Enigma' in his letter to Cummings, we must ask the question, was Stephenson's trust in him misplaced? No, he was merely telling Cummings that if he, Knight, died in suspicious circumstances and if, when the war ended, the Enigma secret came out, it might ring a bell in his mind and he might seek out that letter, recall their chess-playing days and say to himself, 'Well, poor Captive Knight, locked in by a secret he could not tell.'

There is, however, a double irony of which Eric Knight would have been proud. Firstly, there was Percy Foxworth, who despite his secret service training in London could not know the Enigma secret because, as Stephenson's second-in-command in Secret Intelligence Services, he might have fallen into enemy hands and given away both it and therefore 'Intrepid's' identity. Secondly, is it not possible that Eric Knight was only on board the same plane because, had he travelled with Hopkins and the President and been shot down, there would have been nobody at Casablanca in possession of the Enigma secret, for it is likely that only five men in America knew of it: the President, Hopkins, Donovan, Stephenson, and Eric Knight.

The entire Enigma operation was handled with great care and attention to detail. Secrets uncovered by the code-breakers – word of planned military operations, for example, or assaults on specific convoys or cities – were not always acted upon. They couldn't be. Intercept a succession of air-raids, for example, and German suspicions would have been aroused. And when there was information it could not be passed on by radio, for fear of interception. Word of mouth was by far the safest means of communication. And what better conduit – or, let us say, courier – than a wordsmith going to Egypt to set up a radio station? We come back to the secret documents Knight was handed, and which the search team were so anxious to find and remove from the crash site. Did these include some message for FDR? And was that another reason why he could not fly on the same plane?

There is one other clue that seems to link Knight with Enigma. In a letter to Jere he reminds her of their trip to England in late '42. 'I took you on that Atlantic convoy, didn't I?' he asks her. He must have been pretty certain that they would be safe, that they were part of a convoy that was not under threat and would most likely arrive safely. Had that not been the case, his superiors would surely have placed him on another ship.

Clockwise from the top left:

1. 1941 Boulder, Colorado, with Harry Hopkins, for launch of 'This Above All'.

2. Book signing, Boulder 1941.

3. Eric Knight sketch for circus story.

4. Eric Knight, 'Lassie' and Fred Wilcox (director) examine script for 'Lassie, Come Home'.

5. Eric sharing a drink with Anatole Litvak (right) – director of 'This Above All'.

Above: On the steps of US President's New York house, Hyde Park. From left, two journalists who had been detained in North Africa but released, Harry Hopkins, Jere Knight talking with 'Wild Bill' Donovan – O.S.S. chief, Eric Knight talking to an unidentified, but extraordinarily tall man, who many believe to be Roald Dahl.

Left: Eric Knight and Eleanor Roosevelt, his tennis partner.

Above: Seven men in uniform. Eric Knight on far right, General Geo. Marshall (of the Marshall Plan) in centre; also present Lyman Munson and John Stanley (who died in the plane with Eric Knight).

Left: Eric Knight in the centre, along with two witnesses to his US citizenship signing, 1942 – (left) unknown, (right) Paul Horgan.

*Above: Eric Knight
with two
unidentified
servicewomen –
publicity shot.*

*Left: Eric on the set
of 'Lassie, Come
Home', Washington
State (on leave from
Army).*

CHAPTER EIGHTEEN

In October 1942, shortly before he left for England with Jere, Eric Knight had been notionally posted to Fort George G. Meade in Maryland, home of the Special Services Unit and any number of Army entertainers, including names such as Glenn Miller. He may have visited the Fort, but there is no evidence to suggest he was ever actually stationed there. There is, however, a gap in his activities that cannot be explained and which may have been contrived to synchronise with the activities of his OSS namesake.

Ridgway Knight had arrived in North Africa some time that same month, October '42, and on the 22nd – after clearing a beach of mines using only his bayonet as a probe – greeted General Mark Clark, commander of the U.S. Fifth Army, whose submarine *Seraph* had surfaced at 2100 hours. Knight guided him to the headquarters of General Alphonse Juin, commander of French troops in Algeria. It was Clark's job to gauge the strength of the resistance his troops might expect during the British and American invasion of French North Africa, codenamed TORCH, to convince the French commander that the mission was actually going to take place – and to persuade him that his forces, at that time allied to the Germans and Italians, should link up with the invaders when they arrived, on November 8th.

Eric and Ridgway Knight were intended to meet at some prearranged point during the progress of the invasion. That rendezvous would not now take place, although Ridgway would remain in North Africa for some time. It is interesting to note that the actual time and place of Eric Knight's death would later be contested, with some historians claiming that he had been active in North Africa in the early months of 1943. They were confusing him with Ridgway Knight, who operated so deeply under cover as to be virtually invisible.

At the crash site in Surinam the search party did eventually find Eric

Knight's satchel, and immediately removed it. It contained sodden copies of a film shooting schedule headed 'Africa Film', one of Knight's handbooks, or 'Pocket Guides', and an expenses sheet filled out by his driver Lieutenant John Doe. There was also a copy of an article on the progress of the war in the desert, roughly torn from a newspaper, and $150 in cash. With the exception of the money, all these artefacts are still intact, though water-marked and burned at their edges. With them is a note on Army headed paper saying that other 'sensitive material' was removed after recovery. Whatever this was, it has either disappeared or has been kept under wraps. It was surely the secret documentation entrusted to Knight and in all probability destined for Roosevelt's eyes.

So we are left, finally, to speculate, to hope that further researches prove fruitful, and to wonder what will emerge when the secret documents are finally released for the public at large. But we started out to record the life of an author, and to uncover the mystery of his effacement from the history of twentieth century literature. Perhaps this, then, is the moment to ask why the life and work of a man so close to the President and so widely known in America, so celebrated as an author and speaker, so highly placed in Army intelligence, has remained hidden for so long. His literary identity has been almost totally erased by the giant shadow cast by his most celebrated creation, *Lassie*. And of course he was to some degree responsible for his own disappearance, the misinformation on his life, which he regularly disseminated, leading other would-be biographers up blind alleys – exactly as he intended. Let us not forget his friend Barnie Winkelman, who had produced a biography of Rockefeller, asking Eric why he didn't get someone to write his life – and Eric's answer: 'No-one could write it but me because no-one knows anything about me. Ninety percent of what's been written is half-true, which is worse than a total lie because it sounds more credible.'

Over seventy-five years after his death Eric Knight is, it must be said, more widely known in the USA than in Britain. His name is more regularly recognised, but it is always for *Lassie*, never for his literary works. If he is spoken of in Britain, it is often as an American writer. Knight's obscurity has also been engineered in the cause of national security. Those who, like Fleming, stood to benefit from the publication of their wartime exploits have mentioned in their work such fellow operatives as Wheatley and Driberg, high-profile writers or politicians who could help build their reputations. Others, like Maxwell Knight, chose to forget what they knew and move on with their lives while doing nothing to clarify matters best served by confusion.

When other members of those covert clubs finished their intelligence work, they were sensitive enough to realise that divulging the identities of their fellow-conspirators served no purpose. Hopkins did not mention his friend Eric Knight's intelligence work, simply because he would have had to give away more of himself than he desired, and more than he would have been allowed under the law. If Eric Knight had survived it is unlikely he would have admitted to having been anything but a serving soldier.

The biographer of William 'Intrepid' Stephenson does not mention Eric Knight, but neither does he mention the spymaster's closest undercover associate, Percy Foxworth; and though the trained eye might find him hiding in the identity of another, the details of his death are absent. Ian Fleming features extensively in Stevenson's book *A Man Called Intrepid*, as does Ridgway Knight, but Maxwell Knight does not.

William 'Wild Bill' Donovan is absent from Anthony Masters' *The Man Who Was M – The Life of Maxwell Knight*. Neither does he get a mention in the best-selling *Most Secret War* from 1978. One of the most important chronicles of World War II, it tells the story of British scientific intelligence and the development of radar. The author of the work was Professor R.V. Jones who, as Assistant Director of Intelligence (Science) must have been aware of the visits to his top secret establishment by the Chiefs of O.S.S. and the British Secret Intelligence Service, later MI6; yet they are not mentioned. Andrew Roberts' *The Holy Fox: The Life of Lord Halifax* (1991), could hardly have avoided mention of Harry Hopkins, but once again Donovan, Stephenson, and the Knights are absent.

F. W. 'Fred' Winterbotham, the MI6 agent known as 'Ultra', who masterminded Enigma operations, mentions Ian Fleming briefly in his 1989 autobiography *The Ultra Spy*, but Driberg, Donovan, Wheatley, and Maxwell Knight are only mentioned obliquely, under other names. Stewart Menzies features, but only as 'SIS Army Section' when in other works he appears as the Head or Chief or Director of MI6. That the involvement of certain individuals in intelligence work or covert operations is not mentioned does not mean they were not involved in such activities, merely that their cover was so deep that even those in the highest positions were unaware they existed.

Had he survived, it is likely that Eric Knight would have 'forgotten' his wartime experiences and exorcised them through his 'fiction' or films. That was, generally, how he worked. His life, and his achievements as a writer, on the other hand, would likely have been paid as much attention as that of his contemporaries: Orwell, Hemingway, Cummings, and Wodehouse. Sam Small might now be as familiar to us today as Bertie Wooster and *This Above All* as *Animal Farm*.

In an enviable career, Eric Knight won high critical praise for his eight published novels. He produced four international bestsellers with *Sam Small The Flying Yorkshireman, Sam Small Flies Again, This Above All* and *Lassie Come-Home*. He won the O. Henry Memorial Prize for *The Marne*, Best Short Story Award (British) for *Mary Ann And The Duke*, the Book Society of

America and British Book of the Month Club recommendations for *The Flying Yorkshireman*, and the American Librarians' Award for Best Children's Book for *Lassie Come-Home*. His contribution to *World of Plenty* may still be seen and heard, for the documentary is preserved by the British Film Institute. His voice, however, is present only in the first half, the actor Miles Malleson taking up the remainder of the commentary, which was incomplete at the time of Knight's death.

As a boy roaming in Lord Halifax's Middleton Wood and on the eve of his eleventh birthday, Eric Knight had dreamed of the 'Nava-Nava-Navajo' and later, while living with Pueblo Indians in New Mexico, he had dreamed of the bluebell wood, all of which would come together in the story he had long insisted 'needs telling'. He did not have the satisfaction of seeing *My Navajo And The Bluebells Of Yorkshire* in print, but readers of the *Saturday Evening Post* in April 1943 were able to enjoy a remarkable piece, written with a freedom of narrative style not seen in his other works. It is discursive, sentimental, and utterly revealing of his thoughts as an innocent boy pondering his forthcoming manhood. In the story, which begins with the line 'Oh damn foolish world', Eric Knight admits that he was truly torn, not between two countries – Yorkshire was always far more important to him – but between two very specific places where he felt most at peace:

'I shall not go to Middleton Wood to lie in the bracken nor to smell the wild hyacinths.

For I am wise – how wise.

I know that if I did, my heart would cry out and my senses would be sick again for the scent of hibiscus – or almendros or eucalyptus – or the smell of piñon-wood smoke from far fires. And my ears would be straining to hear drums on the desert.'

We may see the story as prophetic; it was certainly written at a time when its author had cause to reflect upon his life in the face of an uncertain future. We might also say that in it he told all of his truth, and if it were all that was left of him it would stand as a fitting epitaph.

So Knight was not to be fêted as a dead genius in the years after the war. Kind words did come in, however, in dribs and drabs. Early in February, a few short weeks after Eric's death, Jere Knight received a letter from an anonymous well-wisher:

'On Sunday January 31st, Springfield Township dedicated its Service Flag at the township High School in Pleasant Valley, PA. There were some 85 stars on the flag. One of them was a gold star for Major Eric Knight.'

But perhaps we should end where we began, in Halifax, West Yorkshire. In 1943, Albert Simpson's family still lived just three doors away from Eric's Aunt Sarah and her boarding house. Albert's father, George, was the same age as Eric and had served in the Royal Navy towards the end of World War I, losing a leg when his ship went down. George worked as a theatre electrician and was therefore very familiar with the stream of actors lodging at number 30. In 1919, it was George who loaned Eric the bicycle he could no longer ride, so that his visitor from across the Atlantic could cycle over the hills and into Lancashire. He'd seen Eric again on his last visit home when they'd enjoyed a pint of ale, and shared memories of their boyhoods in the mills. They even rode out together, George now using a modified machine with one rotating pedal for motive power and one fixed 'peg' for his rigid artificial limb.

At the time of Eric's death, George's son Albert, too young for active service, was working as a Post Office telegram boy. He had delivered many messages bringing untold grief to wives and mothers around town. On this cold, wet morning he had three to deliver. And so he had stood on the doorstep of Mr. and Mrs Whitfield's home as they read that their sergeant son, Leslie, had been posted 'missing in action'. A little further along his round, Mrs. Anderson had bravely borne the news that her son David had been killed in action in Africa. But knowing his neighbour as he did, George found the task of delivering a telegram to Mrs. Creasser much, much harder.

'Dear God, not Eric,' she said as she reached into her apron pocket for a handkerchief and quietly closed the door through which her nephew had bounced as a lad of thirteen, full of enquiry and adventure. Albert nodded respectfully and coaxed his bicycle up the steep gradient of Wellington Street South and into the cold, stinging, Yorkshire rain. As he passed the Halifax Picture Theatre he stopped to read the poster displaying the name of the film showing that evening. It was *This Above All*.

RESEARCH CREDITS

This book started out as a simple narrative account of a life that was more or less unrecorded. As I followed the serpentine paths down which my research led me I found myself in fields alien to my experience: particularly in the area of military intelligence and the secret services.

Eric Knight was careful about what he revealed of himself and his activities, at times wilfully misleading even his closest friends. The story I tell is, however, based in scholarly research, as acknowledged in the credits (below). At times, however, I have had to piece together a narrative that makes sense of fragmented information gleaned from private correspondence, public papers, interview notes and other snippets. In places I have felt obliged to reach conclusions that make sense, not only of my researches but also of my reading of Knight the man: unreliable in his own account of himself – playful, inventive, dutiful in serving his country's need for secrecy.

Over twenty years I consulted with a small army of scholars, historians, archivists, librarians and other experts in various fields. There are, as the saying goes, too many to mention. All of them gave of their time and skill generously.

I am also grateful to the many people – family, friends, colleagues, and those keepers of special memories like Joe Freeh who actually knew Eric and Jere, and whose lives were touched by that special couple. Betsy Cowan has been wholeheartedly supportive of the project from the very beginning, accommodating me when I visited California and freely sharing information about the grandfather she never knew.

In sum, I owe a huge debt to these people. They helped me untangle a seemingly endless thread that started with a note on the fly-leaf of *The Flying Yorkshireman* and took me on a twenty-year journey through the labyrinth of dark byways that is the previously hidden life of Eric Knight.

I would like to thank the following. Their assistance has been and remains invaluable.

UK

The Winston Churchill Memorial Trust
Mr. Alan Wilkinson
Mrs. Vera Gravil
The Doctors O'Brien
Mr. Jack H. Kell
Mr. Geoffrey Storr
Mr. Joe Hutchinson.
Mr. Ian McMillan
Mr. John Noakes
Andrew Gordon, Roger Clark,
Prof. Judy Giles, York St. John University
Mr. Michael Green (*The Boy Who Shot Down an Airship*-1989 Bantam Books, London

207

ISBN 0-553-17607-2)
John (Jo) Owen Smith (*Liphook, Bramshott and the Canadians*. Published by the Bramshott & Liphook Preservation Society)
Mr. Graham Rimmer (RAF retd.)
Mr. Raymond Briggs
Dr. Mark Dawson
Capt. Robert B. Dixon-Carter
The University of Leeds
Office of the Registrar, Leeds, West Yorkshire.
The Halifax Courier
Annette Wright, Wharfedale & Airedale Observer.
The Yorkshire Post
BBC Radio Leeds
BBC Radio York
BBC Sound Archives
BBC Written Archives
Viv Beeby, Sally Heaven, Allison Crawford, BBC Radio Four
Jo Scott at the Bramshott & Liphook Preservation Society.
Isle of Man Archives Office
Menston Parish Church
Menston Parish Records
Menston Primary School
Oakham School
Yorkshire Education Authority
The British Film Archive
The National Film Archive
The Yorkshire Film Archive
Imperial War Museum
National Census Records

Libraries

Altrincham Public Library, Manchester
The British Library
Nigel Bewley, The British Library Sound Archives
Driffield Public Library
East Ham Public Library, London Borough of Newham
Halifax Public Library
Harrogate Local Studies Library
Ilkley Public Library
Pat Egan, Leeds Municipal Library
Suzanne Grahame, Leeds Local Studies Librarian
Susan Stepan LEODIS
Malton & Norton Public Libraries
Melton Mowbray Public Library
Menston Public Library
Skircoat Green Public Library
Stratford Local Studies Library

USA

Betsy & Gordon Cowan
Winifred Knight Mewborn
Allan Dash, Philadelphia
Prof. Mark Davidson, New Haven, Connecticut
Mr. Joseph F. Freeh
Mr. Geoff Gehman
Donald E. Green, Professor Emeritus of American History,
University of Central Oklahoma.
Jeff and Barbara Lindtner, Springhouse Farm, Pleasant Valley, Bucks County,
Pennsylvania.
Elise Sasso, Ed and Natalie Rotkof & Croton-on-Hudson Historical Society.
Allison Rhodes, Cherry House, Finney Farm, Croton-on-Hudson
William A. Studer, Esq.
The Cambridge Latin School
New York Artists League
Patrick Schilling, Libertyville, Illinois

US Libraries and Archives

American Battle Monuments Commission
The Beinecke Rare Book and Manuscript Library, Yale University, New Haven,
Connecticut
Croton-on-Hudson, New York State, Public Library
Echo Park Historical Society
Bill Miller, The Ferguson Library, Stamford, Connecticut
Hellertown, Pennsylvania, Public Library
The National Archives and Records Administration, National Archives at College
Park, Maryland.
New Haven, Connecticut Public Library
Charles Oellig, Pennsylvania National Guard Military Museum
Penn University Archives, University of Pennsylvania
San Fernando Valley Historical Society, 10940 Sepulveda Blvd, Northridge,
(Zelzah), Mission Hills, LA, Cal. 91346
The Smithsonian Institute
The Statue of Liberty Ellis Island Foundation Inc.
The Sterling Library, Yale University
UCLA 20th Century Fox & MGM Archive
The Walt Disney Organisation
20th Century Fox
Paramount Pictures
The Lassie Network
Pennsylvania Light Infantry Regimental Archives
Pleasant Valley High School
Fort Sill
The FBI
The CIA

<u>Russia</u>

Dr. Zakhar Ishov

<u>Canada</u>

Princess Patricia's Canadian Light Infantry Archives
Kath Williams (Creasser family historian)

<u>New Zealand</u>

Ms Laurie Knight

ABOUT THE AUTHOR

Greg Christie is a Yorkshireman, born and raised in the village of Rillington, to the east of York. While he enjoyed a happy childhood, he was never in love with formal education – especially after his primary school teacher told his parents that he was 'backward' and would never amount to anything. He had always loved reading, and always nurtured dreams of being a writer, so it seemed natural that he should take it up after a back injury forced him to quit a successful career as a car salesman. As he lay on his back for eighteen months his wife plied him with books, including a copy of *The Flying Yorkshireman*. Fascinated to learn that the author had also penned the '*Lassie*' stories he had seen on TV, Greg determined to write Eric Knight's life story. He set about it methodically, taking a degree in English, followed by an M.A.

His researches led him to the Knight archive at Yale, where he spent three months as a Winston Churchill Travelling Fellow, then further west to New Mexico and California, where he met Eric's grand-daughter Betsy. As he progressed with the book he wrote a number of articles and a BBC Radio documentary based on his findings. But in 2008 tragedy struck: his wife of forty years died, and Greg's eyesight began to fail. By 2014, he was completely blind, reliant on his guide-dog, and ready to accept defeat. However, with the collaboration of a friend and fellow writer, and after a break of eight years, he finally managed to complete what now amounted to a twenty-year project.

Always happier before a live audience, Greg undertakes tours on a regular basis, lecturing on Eric's life and the remarkable story of his own researches.

OTHER PUBLICATIONS
FROM OUEN PRESS

Other biography...

THE SOHO DON *by Michael Connor* is a biographical narrative about a London gangster whose unique power was strongest in the 25 years after World War II - a very powerful read. The Krays said he feared no-one, and was the one man they truly respected. Likened to Graham Greene's period thriller *Brighton Rock*, and the style of Truman Capote's *In Cold Blood*.

Crime thrillers...

IMAGINE GHOSTS TELLING TALES IN FRONT OF SMOKY MIRRORS *by S.L.Masunda* – is a fictional memoir exploring a writer's quest for literary recognition. The atrocities he commits in the name of ambition become increasingly gruesome, but we are drawn back in time to reveal pivotal moments in the writer's life that challenge the reader to seek out redemption for our hero turned killer.

MAY ALL YOUR NAMES BE FORGOTTEN *by Michael Connor* – a fast moving crime thriller set in south London, containing as many pointers for budding telesales staff, prepared to break the rules, as it does for the ordinary citizen seeking to avoid being hustled.

Other rites of passage...

CODY, THE MEDICINE MAN AND ME *by Alan Wilkinson* – a trip across the USA transforms into the ultimate voyage of personal discovery. Attempting to establish the truth of his baffling ancestry, Ray West struggles to prepare himself for a reunion with his estranged twin brother – old rivalries quickly resurface. **A showdown brews – but ultimately only one of the brothers can ride off into the sunset**.

THE CLEANSING *by Michael Connor* – weaves a powerful plot, full of vivid encounters and fascinating characters. It depicts the harsh reality that still faces many, particularly the women, in Africa today.

More..

LAST CALL & OTHER SHORT STORIES *including Ouen Press Short Story Competition Winners 2015* – a variety of fictitious working-dogs portrayed in many different circumstances as their 'jobs' dictate or their conditions demand; a collection of compelling tales that reflect that vast, often unfathomable melting-pot of human emotions and intention.

JOURNEY THROUGH UNCERTAINTY & OTHER SHORT STORIES *including Ouen Press Short Story Competition Winners 2016* – featuring physical and emotional journeys, endured and enjoyed, with humour and courage – each one a testimony to a place, or an event, or a sentiment.

All books available in paperback & ebook from Amazon

www.ouenpress.com

Printed in Poland
by Amazon Fulfillment
Poland Sp. z o.o., Wrocław

59024801R00125